Divorce Lawyers and Their Clients

DIVORCE LAWYERS AND THEIR CLIENTS

Power and Meaning in the Legal Process

AUSTIN SARAT
WILLIAM L. F. FELSTINER

OXFORD UNIVERSITY PRESS
New York   Oxford

Oxford University Press

Oxford   New York
Athens   Auckland Bangkok Bogota Bombay Buenos Aires
Calcutta Cape Town Dar es Salaam Delhi Florence Hong Kong
Istanbul Karachi Kuala Lumpur Madras Madrid Melbourne
Mexico City Nairobi Paris Singapore Taipei Tokyo Toronto

and associated companies in
Berlin   Ibadan

Copyright © 1995 by Oxford University Press, Inc.

First published in 1995 by Oxford University Press, Inc.
198 Madison Avenue, New York, New York 10016

First issued as an Oxford University Press paperback, 1997

Oxford is a registered trademark of Oxford University Press

Library of Congress Cataloging-in-Publication Data
Sarat, Austin.
Divorce lawyers and their clients: power and meaning in the legal process /
Austin Sarat, William L.F. Felstiner
    p.   cm.
Includes bibliographical references and index.
ISBN 0-19-506387-2
ISBN 0-19-511799-9 (pbk.)
1. Divorce suits—United States.   2. Attorney and client—United States.
I. Felstiner, William L. F.   II. Title.
KF535.S24   1995
346.7301'66—dc20
[347.306166]   94-24538

9 8 7 6 5 4 3 2 1

Printed in the United States of America
on acid-free paper

To two of my teachers, Joel B. Grossman and Stanton Wheeler, and to my daughters, Lauren and Emily
A. S.

To my wife, Gray, and my friends, Dave and Bill
W.L.F.F.

Preface

This book tries to live in two worlds, the world of legal theory and interpretive legal scholarship and the "real world" lives of the people whose difficult and painful stories it tries to tell. Its subject—the exercise of power and construction of meaning in lawyer-client interaction—speaks most immediately to theoretical issues and debates in the academic communities in which we work. However, its description of what goes on in divorce lawyers' offices also speaks to the concerns of people caught up in the legal process of dissolving marriage.

Where other scholars focus on the tangible results of the interaction of lawyers and clients, we are interested in its cultural effects. We call the meanings produced in that interaction "elusive" because they are seldom fully shared and are often at war with one another. Yet we see in law's contradictory narratives a source of strength rather than weakness. For us, the importance of the mutually constitutive effects of law's meanings and the everyday world that we observed is not best expressed in the language of cultural domination. In the lawyer's office, law's power is "fragile" because it is contested in ingenious and unpredictable ways.

Where others see power in lawyer-client interactions as a tool wielded by either lawyer or client, we see power as unstable and evanescent, as existing beyond anyone's immediate control. Where others trace the interaction between lawyers and clients by inquiring about it in surveys, we believe that the meaning-making power of law, as well as the elusiveness of the meanings that are made, are best understood through direct observation in the multiple sites—the lawyer's office, the traffic court, the Internal Revenue Service audit, and the welfare office—where legal officials and professionals interact with ordinary citizens.

In choosing to study lawyers and clients in divorce, we have chosen to examine an area where law is touched by, and touches, real pain in the lives of real people. The stories told in the following pages are of people rearranging their lives through a procedure mandated by law. They are stories of people who, in addition to coping with all the complications that accompany the end of marriage, must cope with the strange world of law. The manner in which they do so, the ways that they invent, avoid, and resist the prescribed paths, may say as much about their resilience as about their mistrust and suspicion of the lawyers whom they retained to help them deal with adversity.

What follows is also a story of the men and women who practice divorce law and of their own struggles to use power responsibly. Divorce is one of the most difficult and least appreciated areas of legal practice. What divorce lawyers do and how they do it are widely misunderstood. Having attended carefully to what goes on in their offices, we hope that this book can diminish that misunderstanding.

While this book does not advance policy proposals, a reform agenda, or "how-to" advice, we hope that those whose stories this book tells and those whose theoretical projects it seeks to engage will recognize themselves and their contributions to it.

Amherst, Massachusetts   A. S.
Santa Barbara, California   W.L.F.F.
January 1995

Acknowledgments

We are most grateful to the people, divorce lawyers and their clients, whose stories are told in this book. They generously opened their lives and work to us. In their lives and in their work we have found much to admire, much to identify with, and much we hope will change.

This book is the result of a collaboration begun more than fifteen years ago. For each of us it has been the best of both friendship and scholarship. We have learned from each other, pushed each other, and had an irreplaceable intellectual companionship. If there is any sadness in its completion, it is in the end of our official collaboration.

We are grateful for the financial support provided by the Law and Social Sciences Program of the National Science Foundation, the American Bar Foundation, and Amherst College, which has made this project possible.

Over the years we have been the fortunate recipients of penetrating and constructive criticism. Many colleagues have generously read portions of this book as articles or papers presented in numerous academic venues. We are grateful to all of them, but especially to David Trubek, who provided essential encouragement at the start of our work. For Austin, the contributions of the Amherst Seminar are especially worthy of note as is the sustaining loyalty and friendship of Susan Silbey. For Bill, the patience of Bryant Garth, Director of the American Bar Foundation, is deeply appreciated.

We gratefully acknowledge the journals that have granted us permission to draw on the following articles in this volume: Austin Sarat and William Felstiner, "Law and Strategy in the Divorce Lawyer's Office," *Law and Society Review* (1986) 20: 93–134; Austin Sarat and William Felstiner, "Law and Social Relations: Vocabularies of Motive in Lawyer/Client Interaction," *Law and Society Review* (1988) 22:737–770; Austin Sarat and William Felstiner, "Lawyers and Legal Consciousness: Law Talk in the Divorce Lawyer's Office," *Yale Law Journal* (1989) 98:1663–1688; William Felstiner and Austin Sarat, "Enactments of Power: Negotiating Reality and Responsibility in Lawyer-Client Interaction," *Cornell Law Review* (1992) 77:1447–1498.

As we approached the completion of this project several friends and colleagues took the time to read the entire manuscript. We express our appreciation to Mavis Maclean, Alison Anderson, Thomas Dumm, and Lawrence Douglas. Special thanks go to Barbara Yngvesson and Hazel Genn for unusually insightful critiques and for pushing us in opposite, but equally helpful, directions.

For their distinctive contributions to the data organization and analysis we are grateful to Kathleen Hall, Mindy Lazarus-Black, Wendy Espeland, and Jennifer Friedman, all now accomplished academics in their own right. We would like to thank Aaron Schuster and Lurlene Dowell for their excellent effort in preparing the manuscript for publication, and Valerie Aubrey and Helen McInnis, our editors at Oxford University Press, for their patience and support of our work.

Any project in which so much has been invested is likely to assume various nicknames. In one of our households, this work was appropriately called the "albatross." That name conjures the great sea bird who was the bane of the _Rime of the Ancient Mariner,_ but the dictionary calls it a cause of persistent concern and anxiety, and something that greatly hinders accomplishment. For their invaluable help in alleviating the anxiety and overcoming the barriers to accomplishment, we are grateful most of all to Stephanie Sandler, Lauren and Emily Sarat (A. S.), and Gray, Ben, and Paul Felstiner (W.L.F.F.).

Contents

Divorce Lawyers and Their Clients

1

Introduction

Every year more than 2 million Americans get divorced.[1] The divorce rate is not just a significant component of the demographics of American family life; it is also important for what it tells us about the way many Americans are introduced to the legal system. Many parties to a divorce have never before been involved in litigation, used a lawyer, or been inside a courtroom. For them, the divorce is their first serious involvement with the legal process. It is both the end of a marriage and the beginning of an education in law.

That education starts with the selection of a lawyer. Once in place, divorce lawyers play critical roles in introducing and explaining the legal process, as well as doing the formal legal work necessary to secure the divorce (Herrman et al., 1979). Although lawyers do not think in these terms, an inescapable attribute of their practice is the construction of legal ideology. On the surface, this ideological production takes place within the framework of a cooperative relationship in which lawyers work to realize their clients' goals. Yet it is widely recognized that divorce practice is as messy a business for most lawyers as getting a divorce is distressing for most clients (O'Gorman, 1963; Kressel et al., 1978; Turner, 1980). Practicing divorce law often requires lawyers to deal with clients in emotional turmoil who may be very difficult to manage and to satisfy (Kressel et al., 1978; McEwen et al., 1994: 163). Divorce lawyers provide a useful and important professional service, but divorce work is frequently frustrating, unpleasant, tedious, tense, and financially unrewarding. And, if that were not enough, it brings little professional prestige (see Heinz and Laumann, 1982). As a result, few lawyers enthusiastically plunge into the business of helping people dissolve intimate relations, divide the consequential and inconsequential property accumulated during married life, and resolve the painful questions that frequently arise in making child custody decisions (see Kressel et al., 1983).

The practice of divorce law has neither the high-toned polish of Wall Street corporate law nor the pace and cachet of *L.A. Law*. Divorce lawyers regularly deal with clients who are angry and embittered by feelings of disappointment and betrayal (see Griffiths, 1986). These clients are often in a state of crisis brought on by the need to face unresolved emotional issues and, at the same time, to figure out how to make income(s) that formerly maintained one household accommodate the demands of two (Goode, 1956; Levinger, 1979; Turner, 1980: 704). Divorce lawyers have the difficult job of understanding, even responding to, these crises while avoiding becoming caught up in their central dramas (Doane and Cowen, 1981; McEwen et al., 1994: 169). Based on their expertise and experience, divorce lawyers seek to control the terms on which they provide service, define the strategies and tactics to be employed in pursuit of their clients' objectives, and socialize clients into modes of behavior appropriate to the legal process of divorce (Reed, 1969). As a result, divorce work is taxing and difficult for anyone, including those few who are specially trained in the complex interconnections of psychology and law that are necessarily part of divorce practice.

While the classic sociological texts on divorce practice (O'Gorman, 1963; Kressel et al., 1978) document these difficulties, they represent the perspectives and experiences of clients only derivatively, if at all. In contrast, the research reported in this book focuses on both parties in the lawyer-client relationship, gives voice to each, and examines their interactions. We find that dealing with the legal divorce and with divorce lawyers is no easier for clients than is the practice of divorce law for their lawyers (Sabalis and Ayers, 1977). Getting a divorce means having to enter the foreign world of law and participate in procedures and rituals designed to deal in an abstract and distanced way with issues that seem all too concrete and immediate to the divorcing spouses. While clients have formal power over the lawyers who, at least technically, are their agents, they often are both frustrated in their efforts to define the objectives their lawyers will pursue and unable effectively to control the provision of services (see Alfieri, 1991a). Dealing with a divorce lawyer means having to expose the most intimate details of one's personal and financial life to a stranger. It means having to trust the lawyer's commitment and loyalty at a time when a far stronger set of commitments and loyalties have proven untrustworthy.[2] It is not surprising then that clients are often wary or suspicious of their own lawyers (Huebner, 1977), and that they are ready and able to resist what may seem to outside observers to be the most benign direction those lawyers seek to provide.

While the legal world is arcane and ritualized in ways that make it difficult for the uninitiated to comprehend, the world of the client is itself one to which the lawyer has access in only a limited, highly mediated way. The reality of the client's social experience can be grasped by the lawyer only through the fragments of her life that the client chooses to reveal (Cunningham, 1992). Client resistance complicates the work

of the lawyer when it takes the form of a refusal to provide information or a refusal to cooperate in the lawyer's efforts to understand the client's social world (White, 1990, 1992: 1504).

When lawyer and client interact, they each face, in the world that the other represents, something new and opaque, and yet still something of indisputable relevance for their relationship. Lawyers and clients confront the fact that making landfall in the treacherous waters of each other's world can be a threatening experience for both of them. In the world of the law, the client faces unknown rules, alien processes, and forbidding surroundings, all manipulated by strangers who have the ability to influence or decide matters of great moment—child custody, the rights of a noncustodial parent, the disposition of the family home, and the division of property and income. In the social world of the client, the lawyer's professional skills may be severely tested by the consequences of the client's guilt about marriage failure, by unresolved feelings for the spouse, by continuing and often irritating interactions over children and money, or by a new relationship whose salience to the divorce may or may not be acknowledged (Riessman, 1990; McEwen et al., 1994). Even when the lawyer tries to keep it at bay, the social world of the client is continuously present (Griffiths, 1986).

For both lawyer and client the stakes are high as each determines what to reveal in their interactions. While the client must rely on the lawyer's legal experience, the lawyer is largely dependent on the client's interpretations of her social world (McEwen et al., 1994: 169). But motives and goals as well as data may be suppressed by plan or inadvertence (Goffman, 1956; Scott, 1990). Both lawyer and client may consciously adopt a narrative style and rules of relevance that limit what the other can assimilate (White, 1990; see also Cunningham, 1989). Each may say both more and less than they intend as they explain what they want the other to know.

Although lawyers and clients are thus highly dependent on each other, the stories they tell about their interactions are full of suspicion and doubt. Clients are suspicious about the depth of commitment their lawyers bring to their cases and about their own ability to control the content and timing of their lawyers' actions. They worry about lawyers who seem too busy to attend fully to the idiosyncracies of their cases, and about divided loyalties, limited competence, erratic judgment, and personality conflict. Lawyers, on the other hand, are concerned because they have to deal with, and depend on, people who often are emotionally agitated, in the midst of a profound personal crisis, ambivalent about divorce, determined to hurt their spouse, and misguided about what they can reasonably expect from the divorce process.

These concerns lead to responses that produce another layer of problems. Lawyers worried about the emotional instability of their clients, and therefore about distortions introduced into client accounts,

seek ways of testing client stories without expressing overt skepticism. As
a result, these lawyers often appear hyper-rational, detached, disloyal,
and callous in response to the emotional intensity of their clients' situations (Griffiths, 1986: 148–49). Clients, put off and alienated by such
suspicions and distance, appear even more unstable and unpredictable
to their lawyers. Such second-order effects and the mutual suspicions
from which they arise contribute to what we will describe as the fragility
of power in lawyer-client interactions.

Nonetheless, the social world of the client and the legal world of
the lawyer do not exist separately and in isolation. While both client
and lawyer may experience them as separate and distinct, these worlds
are, in fact, highly interactive and interdependent (see Harrington and
Yngvesson, 1990: 140–41). Law exists and takes on meaning in and
through the everyday world of social relations, while everyday life is, in
turn, constructed and made meaningful by legal ideas and practices.
What seem to the participants like independent domains on a collision
course are inseparable and mutually constitutive. As David Engel (1993:
125–26) argues,

> Law, despite its apparent claim to "self-totalization," is dependent on
> everyday life to give meaning to its central concepts . . . [and] to root
> its abstract rules and principles in human understanding . . . . Every-
> day life is not opposed to law, nor does it exist merely by insinuating
> itself into the interstices of law. Everyday life constitutes law and is con-
> stituted by it.

The experience of the separation of the social and legal worlds
that marks lawyer–client interaction in divorce is, in fact, one that legal
practices and ideology help to produce. Those practices and ideology
construct "a peculiar kind of world, specifically, a liberal-legal world
constituted as separate spheres of 'law' and 'community' . . ." (Harrington and Yngvesson, 1990: 140).[3] As we will see in subsequent chapters,
conversations in the divorce lawyer's office often focus precisely on
constructing an "ideology of separate spheres" by defining what is
inside and what is outside law, and what is relevant and what is irrelevant to law's concerns. Lawyers attempt to draw rigid boundaries
demarcating the legal as the domain of reason and instrumental logic,
and the social as the domain of emotion and intuition.

Attempting to distinguish the legal from the social excludes much
that is of concern to clients. Rhetorically marking law's boundaries also
helps constitute an idea of profession and professionalism, an idea of
what lawyers can claim to know and to deal with. When clients contest
those boundaries, they are contesting both the nature of law and of professionalism presented in the lawyer's office. The lawyer's office thus
becomes an arena in which law and professionalism are given meaning
in "exchanges . . . about the meaning of the words, and actions that

bring people [to lawyers]. In these exchanges and in the collective practices that develop around them 'cases' . . . are constructed . . . ." (Yngvesson, 1993: 11).

The meaning given to law and to professionalism in the course of divorce cases does not emphasize rules, technical expertise, disinterested service, or fairness and a commitment to justice. Instead, the meanings constructed emphasize the local and informal nature of the legal process, the relevance of individual character and personality in the way cases are handled and issues decided, and the pervasiveness of adversariness and the search for advantage. This emphasis runs up against the expectations and images of law that inexperienced clients often bring to the lawyer's office. It constructs a meaning of law far different from celebratory civics book and Fourth-of-July rhetoric of constitutionalism and the rule of law. It involves a substitution of knowledge of the ropes for knowledge of the rules as a constituent element of the meaning of professionalism. As lawyers describe the legal process itself, a process in which personal idiosyncracy is as important as rules and reason, in which confusion and disorder are as prevalent as clarity and order, in which the search for advantage overcomes the impulse toward fairness, the factors claimed by the ideology of separate spheres to be outside the law seem quite vividly alive on the inside. It is the presence of these divergent messages that helps account for what we will call the "elusiveness" of meaning as it is constructed in lawyer-client interaction in divorce.

In this book we examine one site—divorce lawyers' offices—where meanings are produced, deployed and contested.[4] In those offices the legal world, for which the lawyer speaks and to which the lawyer provides access, and the social world of the client, a world beset with urgent emotional demands, complex and changing relationships, and unmet financial needs, are both made meaningful.[5] In those offices ideologies of the legal and the social are articulated in, rather than abstracted from, the social relations of professionals and their clients.

Three aspects of those ideologies stand out. First, the meanings produced, though contested, transitory, and elusive, are *independently* significant as signs of law's power and are, as such, worthy of study in and of themselves. Second, the production of meanings is inextricably bound up with the strategies and tactical efforts of both lawyer and client to "control" and direct their interaction. Third, power, as revealed in the process of contested meaning making, is as fragile as the production of meaning is elusive.

In the chapters that follow we examine the way lawyer-client interactions "produce legal and moral frameworks that justify a decision to handle a case in a particular way" (Yngvesson, 1988: 410). While lawyers appear to play the dominant role, using their knowledge of the law to validate some interpretations and brand others irrelevant,[6] clients are rarely simply acquiescent. They bring their own ideas of relevance and their own interpretations of events to the lawyer's office and maneuver, more or less overtly, to get those ideas and interpretations heard and accepted. They contest the ideological productions of their lawyers. Thus lawyer-client interactions always involve the play of, and contests about, power in a relationship in which both parties have, at least in theory, a common agenda and shared goals.

FIELDWORK

This book is based on our in-person observations of lawyer-client interactions in actual divorce cases as they were occurring.[7] Those cases took place in the mid-1980s in two sites, one in California and the other in Massachusetts. As observers, we were present when lawyers and clients confronted the full range of issues that occurs during a divorce, from disputes about money and property to allegations of sexual infidelity. As observers, we had an unusual vantage point, one virtually unprecedented in our field (see Danet et al., 1980), from which to see how the meaning of law and professionalism is constructed and communicated in the process of delivering professional services, and how, in spite of an ideology of separate spheres, law and society come together in the acts and practices of both lawyers and clients.

Over a period of thirty-three months we studied one side of forty divorce cases, ideally from the first lawyer-client interview until the divorce was final. We followed these cases by observing and tape-recording lawyer-client sessions, attending court and mediation hearings and trials, and interviewing both lawyers and clients about those events. One hundred and fifteen lawyer-client conferences were tape-recorded, and 130 interviews were conducted.

One of the research sites was a medium-sized city in which the local university was an economic force and a major employer. The other was smaller, though higher education also played an important role in its cultural and economic life. The California site was generally more affluent, while the Massachusetts community still showed remnants of the transition from an old industrial to a service economy. In both sites, however, the lawyers we observed practiced by themselves or in small firms. They included some whose practice was dominated by divorce work, and some who considered themselves trial lawyers for whom divorce made up but one part of their work.

The offices in which we conducted our observations ran the gamut of professional accommodations, though most tended to be near the local courthouse. At one end were offices so small and cluttered that there was barely enough room to accommodate lawyer, client, and observer. In these offices, there were few of the usual accoutrements of professional status beyond the degree hung, in an obligatory fashion, on the wall. Instead of neatly shelved law books, files and papers were piled here and there, and clients invited to sit among the piles. Some of the lawyers in our study did not have secretaries or any other support services; they truly practiced alone. At the other end of the spectrum were large, comfortable, tastefully furnished offices with dignified waiting areas. In those offices there were more visible displays of professional status in rows of file cabinets, bound case reports, the latest high-tech equipment, and a staff of secretaries and paralegals.

The interviews with lawyers and clients that supplemented our observations of their meetings were generally conducted with lawyers in their offices and with clients in their homes, although we also interviewed lawyers over lunch and in courthouse hallways and clients in restaurants, laundromats, supermarkets, and doctors' waiting rooms where the boundary between ordinary conversation and interview was quite fluid.

Neither the lawyers nor the clients that we studied were randomly selected, nor could they have been, given the acknowledged difficulties in securing access to lawyer-client conferences (see Danet et al., 1980). We began the process of securing lawyer participation by asking judges, mediators, and lawyers to name the lawyers in each community who did a substantial amount of divorce work. In each instance, the list eventually contained about forty names. We stopped trying to add names to the list when additional inquiries did not provide new names. We asked all lawyers on each list to cooperate in the research. Most agreed, but only slightly more than one-quarter in each site actually produced one or more clients willing to participate in the research. We left the choice of clients to the lawyers, except that we did ask them to focus on cases that promised to involve several lawyer-client meetings.

The lawyer samples have two obvious biases. In both sites they involve a higher proportion of women than exists either in the bar or among divorce lawyers generally. Nevertheless, the samples contain more men than women lawyers. More important, the samples appear not to include many lawyers high in income, experience, or status. We have come to this conclusion first because of the general clientele of our lawyers; very few doctors, lawyers, businessmen, and others with substantial income and assets are represented. Second, our lawyers are not generally talked about in these communities as the most prominent divorce practitioners. And third, the lawyers in our samples generally attended less prestigious law schools than did those usually considered to be at the top of local divorce practice. As a result, the findings of this project should not be considered representative of all divorce lawyers. However, other than their relative status within the local bar and the higher proportion of women, we know of no other relevant trait on which these lawyers differ from the rest of the divorce bar, and consider it fair to say that our findings are based on samples that are characteristic of the lawyers that most people with ordinary financial resources are likely to consult.[8]

In all instances we asked participating lawyers about the grounds on which they had selected the clients who eventually became part of the study. Frequently these clients were simply those who had come to the lawyer's attention immediately or soon after we had persuaded the lawyer to participate in the research. From time to time we were told that clients had been selected because they appeared to be more interested in research or less emotionally upset than many others. We were also on occasion told that lawyers had tried to avoid choosing clients who were "crazy." However, the clients in the samples did not differ in crucial respects from the clients of these lawyers generally.

POWER AND MEANING IN LAW AND LEGAL INSTITUTIONS

Recently legal scholars have begun to examine the operation of law, and of various legal institutions and actors, in the generation and reproduction of structures of meaning, or what Clifford Geertz calls "webs of signification" (1983; see also Harrington and Yngvesson, 1990; Trubek, 1984). For these scholars, law is "part of a distinctive manner of imagining the real" (Geertz, 1983: 184); it is "a mode of giving particular sense to particular things in particular places (things that happen, that fail to, things that might) . . . ." (Geertz, 1983: 232; see also Trubek and Esser, 1989). Following Geertz, legal scholars have deployed "interpretive" methods to study a range of legal phenomena. As David Trubek (1984: 604) argues, interpretivists

> understand the world in terms of . . . structures of meaning. . . .
> [A]n interpretivist does not split action into a soft and arbitrary core
> of individual volition and a hard shell of external constraint. Rather,
> he sees action as the result of socially constructed systems of meaning
> which constitute the individual, providing the grounds for behavior
> and defining the channels of conduct.[9]

Meaning is the key word in the vocabulary of those who speak about law in interpretivist terms. "Our gaze focuses on meaning, on the ways . . . [people] make sense of what they do—practically, morally, expressively, . . . juridically—by setting it within larger frames of signification, and how they keep those larger frames in place or try to, by organizing what they do in terms of them" (Geertz, 1983: 232). So conceived, law is inseparable from the interests, goals, and understandings that shape or comprise social life. Law is part of the everyday world, contributing powerfully to the apparently stable, taken-for-granted quality of that world and to the generally shared sense that as things *are,* so *must* they be.[10]

Thinking about legal processes in terms of the meanings generated and conveyed by them requires that the scholar who adopts the interpretivist perspective attend to the links between law and society at the level of networks of legal practices, on the one hand, and clusters of beliefs, on the other.[11] It requires recognition that meaning is found and invented in the variety of locations and practices that comprise the legal world and that those locations and practices do not exist outside the webs of signification that, in turn, make them meaningful. Meanings are advanced and resisted strategically, though neither the meanings advanced nor the goals purportedly served in advancing those meanings exist independent of one another. Power is seen in the effort to negotiate shared understandings, and in the evasions, resistances, and inventions that inevitably accompany such negotiations. To acknowledge that law has meaning-making power, then, is to acknowledge that social practices are not logically separable from the laws that shape them and that social practices are unintelligible apart from the legal norms that give rise to them. Interpretivists believe that law permeates social life and that its influence is not adequately grasped by treating law as a type of external, normative influence on independent, ongoing activities.

In non-interpretivist scholarship, law and lawyers are treated as "tools" whose power lies in their ability to realize certain goals and advance the interests of certain people or groups.[12] In this view, rules and legal processes are used or avoided in the everyday world to facilitate the accomplishment of various ends, goals, or purposes whose origins tend to be treated as substantially independent of law itself.[13] In this sense, law and the lawyering process become, in James Boyd White's (1985: 686) words, "reducible to two features: policy choices and techniques of their implementation. Our questions are 'What do we want?' and 'How do we get it?' In this way the conception of law as a set of rules merges with the conception of law as a set of institutions and processes. The overriding metaphor is that of a machine."

In the conception of law that White describes, law is understood entirely in terms of the material results it produces, or in terms of the distributional consequences of legality, of Harold Lasswell's (1936) famous "who gets what, when and how,"[14] or "as a clever device to keep people from tearing one another limb from limb, advance the interests of the dominant classes, defend the rights of the weak against the predations of the strong, or render social life a bit more predictable at its fuzzy edges" (Geertz, 1983: 232). Research in this tradition typically ignores law's ideological dimension or its importance as a site for the negotiation and contestation of meanings. Where ideology or meaning is noticed, it is treated as distinct from the behavior in which it is revealed or to which it is attached.

In the context of divorce, the overriding concern of non-interpretivist scholars is to explain matters such as the economic consequences of divorce (Weitzman, 1985) or the consequences of the allocation of child custody (Wallerstein and Kelly, 1980). While this work is of real practical significance, it ignores or underplays the significance of law as ideology and contributes to the construction of the "distinction between ideas and experience . . . and between subjective and objective 'realities'" (Harrington and Yngvesson, 1990: 140).[15] Centrally interested in law's first-order effectiveness (roughly, in the extent to which law has intended or unintended consequences, is followed or violated, used or ignored), this scholarship is not concerned with law's consequences more broadly conceived, with the manner in which law is involved in constructing the very foundations of social life (see Ackerman, 1984; Sarat and Silbey, 1988).[16]

On the other hand, interpretivists insist that law is not only more ubiquitous than the law-as-tool model would suggest, but that it is already an integral part of that which it regulates,[17] and thus has effects that, because they are hard to detect, are often overlooked entirely (see Engel, 1993). In this view, legal thought and legal relations influence self-understanding and understanding of one's relations to others. We are not merely pushed and pulled by laws that exert power over us from the "outside." Rather, we come, in uncertain and contingent ways, to see ourselves as law sees us; we participate in the construction of law's "meanings" and its representations of us even as we internalize them, so much so that our own purposes and understandings can no longer be extricated from them. We are not merely the inert recipients of law's external pressures, but law's "demands" tend to seem natural and necessary, hardly like demands at all.[18] As Trubek (1984: 604) writes:

> [S]ocial order depends in a nontrivial way on a society's shared "world view." Those world views are basic notions about human and social relations that give meaning to the lives of society's members. Ideals about the law—what it is, what it does, why it exists—are part of the world view of any complex society . . . . Law, like other aspects of belief systems, helps to define the role of an individual in society and the relations with others that make sense. At the same time that law is a system of belief, it is also a basis of organization, a part of the structure in which action is embedded.[19]

The interpretive turn in legal scholarship is, at present, best developed in Critical Legal Studies (CLS) (Trubek, 1984). Critical scholars have examined many areas of legal doctrine to decode the meanings about social life that they convey (see, e.g., Kennedy, 1976; Klare, 1978; Gabel, 1980). CLS suggests that in each of those areas (1) law reifies social life, conveying the message that prevailing social relations are natural, normal, inevitable, and just; and (2) that the meanings contained in legal doctrine are rigorously indeterminant and contradictory (see Kelman, 1987).

Critical legal scholars analyze the constitutive effect of law and its power to manufacture necessity as well as assist in the creation of consciousness (Gordon, 1982: 289); they believe that social knowledge should explicate "the deep structures of law and demonstrate the relationship between these structures *and action* . . . in society" (Trubek, 1984: 601). These scholars generally endorse the claim that at a global level law, like other pervasive social institutions such as religion, education, and the family, shapes how individuals conceive of themselves and their relations with others. The underlying proposition is that social institutions are actualized through a set of assumptions, categories, concepts, values, and vocabularies that we have internalized so that we are not consciously aware of how they have affected our ideas and behavior. The result is that we tend to think and act as we do in these spheres as if no alternatives were available. The constitutive nature of social institutions is not limited to the pillars of social life such as law, the family, religion and education. As Pierre Bourdieu has pointed out, there is "the gentle invisible form of violence which is never recognized as such, and is not so much undergone as chosen, the violence of credit, confidence, obligation, personal loyalty, hospitality, gifts, gratitude, piety" (1977: 192).[20]

Yet CLS itself seems to reify law even as it calls attention to its constitutive power. It does so by treating the judicially produced doctrinal work of appellate courts as if it were coextensive with law, instead of examining the diverse sites in which the play of law's power and the constitution of its meanings occur. In addition, CLS fails to attend to the interactive, dynamic, and strategic quality of meaning making in law and legal institutions. Law is not only constitutive in shaping our understandings of institutions like property, the family, and the state, as well as the nature of individuals and the relationships between them (Gordon, 1984), but law is also involved in the constitution of its own meaning, in creating and sustaining the meaning of its own operations.

Legal meanings are not simply invented and communicated in a unidirectional process. Because they are produced in concrete and particular social relations, meaning and the materiality of law are inseparable. Litigants, clients, and others bring their own understandings to bear; they deploy and use meanings strategically to advance interests and goals. They press their understandings in and on law, and, in so doing, invite adaptation and change in the practices of judges, lawyers, and other legal officials (Yngvesson, 1989). Law thus exists as "moving hegemony" (Williams, 1977: 114). This concept, as Barbara Yngvesson (1993: 121) explains, allows us to recognize the "coexistence of discipline and struggle, of subjection and subversion and directs attention toward a dynamic analysis of what it means to be caught up in power."

Interpretive approaches that take into account the dispersion and interactive nature of law's meaning making have emerged, particularly in empirical scholarship on courts and communities (see, for example, Greenhouse, Yngvesson, and Engel, 1994). That scholarship looks at courts as crucial cultural institutions as well as institutions to resolve disputes and allocate tangible resources. It characterizes litigation as a process of contesting meanings, and adjudication as the choice and imposition of one structure of meaning over another (Merry, 1985). Contests over meaning in courts or communities thus become occasions for observing the play of power. Meanings that seem natural, or taken for granted, are described as hegemonic, but because the construction of meaning through law is, in fact, typically contested, scholars show the many ways in which resistance occurs (see Williams, 1977; Comaroff, 1985). The exercise of power in the construction of meaning is thus conflictual and dynamic, and the meanings that are constructed are contradictory, but no less powerful for being so.

The move to interpretation can be viewed as a transfer of attention from the investigation of specific problems to broader inquiries that are concerned with questions about the power of law as it is exercised through language. This move emphasizes the independent significance of the meaning-making activity of legal institutions; at the same time, it regards examination of the production of meaning as a valuable way of studying the operations of power in legal institutions. The move to interpretation can be illustrated by contrasting Marc Galanter's (1974) famous argument about adjudication and Stewart Macaulay's (1979) well-known article about lawyers in consumer protection cases with two more recent studies, one by Sally Merry (1990) and the other by Barbara Yngvesson (1988).

Galanter's "Why the 'Haves' Come Out Ahead" (1974) describes the sociological advantages of powerful social groups and institutional aspects of adjudication that limit the role of courts as instruments of progressive social change. He suggests that "repeat players" have built-in advantages in the litigation process, and that, as a result, they are able to structure rules that favor their long-term interests and raise the costs of litigation in ways that deter or punish weaker "one-shot" court users. Galanter (1974: 98–101) argues that repeat players do better in litigation than one-shot players because they have superior information, more specialized assistance, closer relationships to power centers, better bargaining reputations, and stakes commensurate with superior strategies. In so doing they limit the capacity of courts to alter existing social arrangements. For Galanter, power is made visible in the outcomes of contests over the tangible allocation of legally imposed benefits and burdens. In the scholarship of the 1970s there was no concern for law as a system of meanings or with the courts as sites for ideological production whose hegemonic power creates, as it is created by, the social relations that researchers then sought to understand.

Macaulay's "Lawyers and Consumer Protection Laws" (1979) describes the role played by lawyers in enforcing consumer protection laws in Wisconsin. These lawyers do not, for the most part, depend on the strategic use of money and power, or the lack of it, to motivate their clients in the intended direction. Rather, these lawyers adopt the role of "therapist or knowledgeable friend" (1979: 124). They cool out their clients by letting them express their frustration and "then lead the client to redefine the situation so that he or she can accept it . . . . By helping the client see the case in a new light, the lawyer may be indulging in a kind of therapy" (1979: 124–25). "The lawyer's task . . . is to persuade the client to see the problem as an adjustment between competing claims and interests, rather than as one warranting a fight for principle" (1979: 128).[21]

However, Macaulay should not be thought to have abandoned a focus on material outcomes simply because he adopted an enlarged view of the kinds of resources that legal actors mobilize to secure the objectives they seek.[22] Macaulay is just as concerned with those outcomes, and the apparent failure of legal interventions to achieve legal goals, as is Galanter. The avowed purpose of Macaulay's article (1979: 118) was to figure out whether the Magnuson-Moss Warranty Act, a consumer protection statute, was effective in redressing problems arising from consumer purchases. For Macaulay, as for Galanter, the measure of law's power was to be understood in terms of its effectiveness in changing the material conditions of social life.[23] His interpretation of the behavior of legal actors looks at the techniques they adopt to reinforce the distribution of power in society, but does not reflect any interest in the independent significance of the meanings generated in lawyer-client interaction, or in their significance in explaining how law helps to maintain and reproduce existing social arrangements.

In contrast, Merry (1990) begins her study of the management of interpersonal disputes in criminal, juvenile, and small-claims courts in eastern Massachusetts by echoing Geertz: "Law," Merry argues, "consists of a complex repertoire of meanings and categories understood differently by people depending on their experience with and knowledge of the law" (1990: 5). Unlike Galanter, she sees the litigation process as one in which litigants quarrel

> over interpretations of social relationships and events. Parties raise competing pictures of the way things are as each strives to establish his or her own portrayal of the situation as authoritative and binding. Third parties also struggle to control the meaning—and hence consequences—of events through their distinctive forms of authority. Law represents an important set of symbolic meanings for this contest. (1990: 6)

Merry summarizes her work by calling it a study of "processes of cultural domination" exercised over people who bring their personal problems to court, in which language is the key medium and in which the focus is on what officials and litigants say to each other.[24]

Like Merry, Yngvesson focuses her description of show cause or complaint hearings in the district courts of two Massachusetts communities on "the negotiation of meaning in neighbor and family conflicts" (1988: 409). Analyzing exchanges between complainants and the clerks who handle their complaints, Yngvesson found that "the clerk plays a dominant role by controlling the language in which issues are framed . . . . He silences some interpretations and privileges others, constructing the official definition of what constitutes order and disorder in the lives of local citizens" (1988: 410).

According to Yngvesson, "law creates the social world by 'naming' it; legal professionals are empowered by their capacity to reveal rights and define wrongs, to construct the meanings of everyday events (as just or unjust, as crime or normal trouble, as private nuisance or public grievance) and thus to shape cultural understandings of fairness, of justice, and of morality" (1989: 1691). Like Merry, she argues that the way law names the world and the way legal professionals construct meanings is hegemonic, but, unlike Merry, she insists that hegemony

> assumes plurality: "[I]t does not just passively exist as a form of dominance. It has continually to be renewed, recreated, defended, and modified. It is also continually resisted, limited, altered, challenged by pressures not at all its own." . . . The interpretation of key symbols . . . is contested, while the dominance of a particular structure of differences in society is left unquestioned. (1989: 1693)

Plurality, resistance, contestation suggest the fragility of the power that Yngvesson somewhat surprisingly labels "dominant." Indeed, although Yngvesson does not provide any indication in her study of complaint hearings that the clerk's views are accepted by those complainants who enter with opposing views,[25] she nevertheless alleges that "the hearings thus become arenas where particular notions of order and rights are articulated *and reinforced*" (1988: 444).[26] Similarly, Merry suggests that examination of contests over meanings provides an important site for the examination of power. For her, power is exercised at the level of culture and consciousness. Courts are powerful in that they convey hegemonic ideologies. She argues that courts work

> not just by the imposition of rules and punishments but also by the capacity to construct authoritative images of social relationships and actions, images that are symbolically powerful. Law provides a set of categories and frameworks through which the world is interpreted. Legal words and practices are cultural constructs which carry powerful meanings not just to those trained in law . . . but to the ordinary person as well (1990: 8–9).

To Merry, law influences the way that ordinary people imagine life;

where legal categories speak to interpersonal affairs, they are decisive. The social world is understood according to the legal order that circumscribes its potential and limitations. But in Merry's own study, law is "polyvocal"; it speaks in three different discourses, which she labels "legal," "moral," and "therapeutic" (see Merry, 1990: 111–12). These discourses "weave in and out of the discussions of particular problems" in the courts she studied. This polyvocality suggests, against Merry's own argument, that the meanings that are constructed in legal institutions may be contradictory and elusive, that law's words may be an amalgam of discourses that do not sit easily together.

Merry's and Yngvesson's studies of community courts draw our attention to meaning-making that is "locally" constitutive. Law and legal processes are said to play important roles in creating or reinforcing the way in which the local world where they are situated is understood or interpreted. Legal activity is part of the process of creating, substantiating, spreading, or protecting specific views about social life that, by virtue of officials' behavior, come to be *shared by the people subject to legal action* (see Merry, 1990: 209).[27] Locally constitutive meanings are case specific; they evolve in the context of a specific legal matter and, unreported and unpublished, they reach only the participants in that matter.

POWER AND MEANING IN LAWYER-CLIENT RELATIONS

It is the kind of interest in meaning and power that Merry and Yngvesson have applied to the study of interactions between citizens and officials in local courts that we bring to the study of the legal profession and of the interactions between lawyers and clients in divorce. In the lawyer-client interactions that we observed, the separate and partially hidden worlds that the lawyer and the client represent and embody become known mostly by the accounts that each provides (Scott and Lyman, 1968). This means that lawyer-client interaction is a process of story telling (see Scheppele, 1989; Bennett and Feldman, 1981) and interrogation in which lawyer and client seek to produce for each other a satisfying rendition of their distinctive worlds. In this book we treat the stories that lawyers and clients construct as a process of negotiation of ends, means, and meanings, a process in which lawyers bring the allegedly distinct interpretive lens of law to bear on a human and social process, and in which clients bring a lay perspective, though one already saturated with taken-for-granted legal meanings, to the legal process. What is accepted, however fleetingly, as "real" and what provides the basis of action in lawyer-client interactions is negotiated, implicitly as often as explicitly, and frequently is transformed over the course of those interactions (Felstiner, Abel, and Sarat, 1980–81; Mather and Yngvesson, 1980–81). The meanings that emerge are often elusive because they are constructed out of contradictory discourses and messages, the elements of which may tell different and divergent stories.

It is in this process of negotiation and meaning making that power exists. Power, in Michel Foucault's words (Bernauer and Rasmussen, 1988: 3), becomes "domination" when one's account or understanding of events or phenomena in the social and legal worlds is accepted as "real" and becomes authoritative,[28] when one "legislates" the meaning of those events or phenomena that provide the basis for action.[29] But, as we shall see, the negotiation of meanings and values in lawyer-client interactions is more fluid, and less final, than suggested by Foucault's concept of domination.

Negotiation and Power

The view that social relations are constructed and power exists in complex processes of negotiation is now widely shared (see, e.g., Scheff, 1968; Lyman and Scott, 1975; Berger and Luckmann, 1966). While the dynamics of power and negotiation are always uncertain and difficult to chart, contemporary theorists no longer assert either that "society is . . . an association of self-determining individuals" (Wolff, 1965) or that social action is epiphenomenal and determined by underlying structural realities (see Lévi-Strauss, 1967; Rossit, 1974). They realize that power is always "involved institutionally in processes of interaction" (Giddens, 1979: 88). In the past, the effort to understand power oscillated between the antinomies of structure and action (Giddens, 1979: 95); today, every variety of theory recognizes that "notions of structure and action *presuppose one another*" (Giddens, 1979: 53).

Social structure exists in the constraining patterns of behavior generated through negotiations and recreated in people's daily lives.[30] However it appears to those so constrained, social structure is produced and reproduced through human action. Thus neither social structure nor the power associated with it are external to, or abstracted from, the practices of everyday life. They are encoded in seemingly uneventful and routinized experiences. As Alfred Radcliffe-Brown noted, institutions are simply "standardized modes of behaviour" (1940: 70; see de Certeau, 1984).

Because they are present in every situation, structure and power are vulnerable to major changes of practice. As Foucault (see Bernauer and Rasmussen, 1988: 12) suggests, "[R]elationships of power are changeable relations, i.e., they can modify themselves, they are not given once and for all . . . . These relationships of power are then . . . reversible and unstable." While structure and power are created through self-conscious, strategic action, past practice does limit the "choices" that can be made. People work out the terms of their interactions daily, but they do not begin anew each day or in each situation; within any setting there are a limited number of available moves (Goffman, 1959).

Whatever the form of these interactions, the social phenomena that occur are negotiated, if not explicitly, then through more subtle deployments of power and attempts at resistance (Scott, 1990; Comaroff, 1985). Surprisingly, a review of the empirical literature on the lawyer-client relationship hardly suggests that lawyers and clients are involved in negotiated relationships, or that the structure and meaning of professionalism, as well as the nature of professional power, are enacted through such negotiations. That literature portrays professional practice as either dominated by the lawyer or by the client (Rosenthal, 1974; Cunningham, 1992; Alfieri, 1991b), depending on who has the superior status or resources (Heinz and Laumann, 1982), or as split into rigidly isolated spheres of influence, with clients autonomously defining goals and lawyers determining the means of achieving them (Kagan and Rosen, 1985).

Lawyer-client interactions in divorce fit with the great tide of social life rather than run counter to it, and power in those interactions is a complicated resource that, over time, is constructed and reconstructed so that its possession is neither necessarily obvious nor rigidly determined. Indeed, it is probably more accurate to say that power is not possessed at all. It is mobile and volatile, and it circulates such that both lawyer and client can be considered more or less powerful, even at the same time (see White, 1990, 1992; Lopez, 1992). Legal power, like all types of power, is relational (see Foucault in Bernauer and Rasmussen, 1988: 3)[31] and dynamic. It is "'not an impermeable "official culture" imposing its criteria on "popular culture," but cultural exchange, conducted inside the king's rules'" (Yngvesson, 1989: 1693). While in the ideology of professionalism, professionals maintain control over the production of professional services (Abbott, 1989), the cases we observed involved complex processes of negotiation between lawyer and client in which we saw resistance as well as acquiescence, contest as well as cooperation, suspicion as well as commitment.[32] These cases indicate that the services provided by lawyers to clients are contested and negotiated in the stream of interactions that constitute the professional relationship, and that the content and contours of the interaction vary considerably from case to case and from moment to moment within cases.[33]

Traditional Views of Power in Lawyer-Client Relations

The predominant image of the lawyer-client relationship is one of professional dominance and lay passivity (see Heinz, 1983: 892; Becker, 1970: 96–97; Johnson, 1972: 53; Bankowski and Mungham, 1976; Cunningham, 1989; Alfieri, 1991a). The lawyer governs the relationship, defines the terms of the interaction, and is responsible for the service provided. Even when lawyers seek to tell their clients' stories, they routinely silence and subordinate them (White, 1990; Alfieri, 1991a). The client is the consumer of a service whose quality is difficult to evaluate.[34] This image is bolstered by studies of a wide range of legal situations and types of legal practices. Thus, Robert Hunting and Gloria Neuwirth (1962), writing more than thirty years ago, found that the majority of litigants in automobile accident claims in New York City had no idea what their lawyers were doing in their cases and had no say in when to settle or how much to accept. Legal services lawyers of the kind studied by Carl Hosticka (1979: 604) rarely even ask their clients what they want them to do. Such lawyers habitually engage in maneuvers that "exploit and reinforce client dependency on the lawyer's specialized knowledge and technical skill" (Alfieri, 1991a: 2132).

Herbert Kritzer's review of a national survey of lawyers and clients in litigated cases finds low client involvement in case development and strategy (1990: 66). Both Abraham Blumberg (1967) and Stewart Macaulay (1979), writing about entirely different fields of practice, describe the ability of lawyers to control case development and strategy as unidirectional. Lawyers exercise power by manipulating their clients' definitions of the situation and of their role. The actions and reactions of clients, and the consequence of their presence, are barely visible. From these studies one might think that contemporary lawyers fulfill Bakunin's nineteenth-century prediction about scientific intelligence, namely, that it would produce an aristocratic, despotic, arrogant and elitist regime (Derber, Schwartz, and Magrass, 1990).

Indeed, even when clients are involved in the management of their own cases, that involvement often is limited. Thus Douglas Rosenthal's (1974) notion of a high level of client participation in personal injury litigation is confined in its interactive dimensions to expressing special concerns and making follow-up demands for attention. The few clients who take an active role in their cases are considered hostile and problematic rather than helpful and persistent (Hosticka, 1979: 607). In the conventional wisdom, people have "problems" and experts have "solutions" (Illich et al., 1978).

Some research emphasizes the context of legal practice as crucial in shaping lawyer-client interaction. Eve Spangler (1986: 166–67, 170), for example, reports that private practitioners and corporate counsel are less likely to dictate action for their clients than are legal services lawyers. John Heinz and Edward Laumann (1982: 108–9) recognize that there is considerable variation by area of law in the practice characteristic they term "freedom of action," a notion reflecting the lawyer's power to decide on strategy and to operate free of close supervision (Heinz and Laumann, 1982: 104).

While these scholars see variation in enactments of power by area of practice, others see variation on a case by case basis. Maureen Cain (1979) notes that the array of power between lawyer and client varies from client to client: the solicitors she observed adopted their clients' goals as the given agenda unless they had a conflict of interest or the clients exhibited unreal expectations.[35] In the same vein, A. E. Bottoms and J. D. McClean (1976) find that the extent of participation of criminal defendants in their cases varies by culture, personality, and ideology. Still other researchers find power to be differentially distributed between lawyer and client by task. Reminiscent of Terrance Johnson's (1972: 46–47) distinction between defining needs and the manner of fulfilling them, Robert Nelson's (1988: 264, 267) and Eve Spangler's (1986: 60–61, 64) work on large law firms indicates that even though corporations set goals and policy independent of lawyer influence, lawyers have a major say in tactical matters.[36]

Finally, other analysts suggest that power in the professional relationship directly reflects control over resources. Thus John Flood (1987: 386–90), having observed the life history of two lawsuits as part of his ethnographic study of a large Chicago law firm, suggests that allocation of power between lawyer and client depends on whether or not the clients are likely to produce repeat business or have the ability to pay fees that command attention.[37] Richard Abel is, perhaps, the strongest proponent of this view. He argues that corporate clients are typically the "dominant" actors in the relationship with their lawyers while solo and small-firm practitioners "dominate" their clients (1989: 204).

Observing the Microdynamics of Power

In the standard analysis of the professions, lawyers are presented either as agents moving tactically toward their clients' clearly expressed goals (Kagan and Rosen, 1985), as principals paternalistically operating in accordance with their sense of the clients' best interests (White, 1990; Alfieri, 1991a), or as opportunists using the client's case to work out their own agenda (see Blumberg, 1967; Casper, 1972: 194; Derber, Schwartz, and Magrass, 1990: 140).[38] Given these very different images of lawyers, it is natural to pose Rosenthal's (1974) well-known question, "Who's in Charge?" However, asking "Who's in Charge?" implies that a single, stable answer can be provided and that the possessor of power can be clearly identified.

While professionals and their clients in divorce typically occupy different and unequal positions and bring different and unequal resources to bear in their relationship, power in lawyer-client interactions is part of the "dynamic processes [that] characterize the interaction of law with the culture of common sense and the fluidity, negotiability and ever changing qualities of both law and everyday life" (Engel, 1993: 126). As a result of this fluidity, both lawyers and clients are sometimes frustrated by feelings of powerlessness in dealing with the other (White, 1990). Such feelings must be taken seriously. Often no one may be in charge: interactions between lawyers and clients involve as much drift and uncertainty as direction and clarity of purpose. It may be difficult, at any one moment, to determine who, if anyone, is defining objectives, determining strategy, or devising tactics.

As we see it, power in lawyer-client interactions is less stable, predictable, and clear-cut than the conventional view would have us believe. Power is not a "thing" that can be possessed; it is continuously enacted and re-enacted, constituted and reconstituted. As Lucie White (1992: 1501) puts it,

> [P]ower is not a tool. Rather, like an evanescent fluid, it takes unpredictable shapes as it flows into the most subtle spaces in our interpersonal world. In this picture, we no longer see distinct "persons" controlling power's flow. Indeed, we cannot really separate the agents of the movement from the movement itself. Sometimes we may think we see more or less familiar human actors, who seem to guide the fluid . . . . Yet at other moments, these familiar "persons" disappear, and we see only the patterns that linger as the bubbles dance.

Power in lawyer-client relationships would not be as ambiguous if it were just an attribute of position, or if it could be captured by attending simply to offices, roles, and forms. But whether in lawyer-client interactions or elsewhere, power does not exist outside of particular social interactions. It is always generated from the inside in a continuing series of situated assertions and rejoinders, by claims and responses to those claims, and by particular gestures and the resistances those gestures provoke (see de Certeau, 1984: xvii–xx). Power has many dimensions and is enacted in many domains. It is involved in interpreting the past, defining the present, and setting an agenda for the future. It is enacted in the domain of knowledge and understanding, in crafting definitions of situations and assigning meanings to them, as well as in the domain of action and behavior, of which knowledge and understanding are an indistinguishable part (see Foucault, 1979: 109). Power is not, however, like a tool sitting on a shelf waiting to be picked up and applied to the task at hand. It is seen in indirect moves and sleights of hand, in feints and unarticulated moves, in ruptures and ellipses, and in what is left unsaid and unacknowledged as well as in forceful, continuous, and overt assertion (see Scott, 1990: chap. 2).

Power is continuously produced in the regular, seemingly uneventful routines and practices that comprise most social interactions. It is conditioned by the cultural resources that particular lawyers and clients bring to their interaction. Thus even when it is apparently ferocious and irresistible, power may be fragile because it is contested (Williams, 1977: 112). Each of the social interactions in and through which power is constituted has its own distinctive history and its own particular future. In this sense power is always created anew and, as with any newborn, its progress and outcome are uncertain.

The malleability of power, however, does not mean that the respective positions of lawyer and client are decided by a coin toss or open to limitless development at the start of every session, or that the meanings constructed in lawyer-client interaction are not culturally significant. Lawyer-client interaction always occurs in the "space of law."[39] For the lawyer this means that interaction takes place in a familiar space and a space of privilege. The law books on the lawyer's shelves are books the lawyer has read or knows how to read; the language spoken is a language in which lawyers are trained and with which they are comfortable; the rituals performed give special place to the lawyer even as they are forbidding and unwelcoming to the uninitiated. Thus following Michel de Certeau's formulation, lawyers are able to act "strategically" in relation to their clients; that is, they act "in a place that can be circumscribed as proper and thus serve as the basis for generating relations with an exterior distinct from it" (de Certeau, 1984: xix). For the client, on the other hand, the space of law is unfamiliar and forbidding. In such a space the client's enactments of power are in de Certeau's sense "tactical."[40]

In lawyer-client interaction, as in each moment and location in society, there is a limited reservoir of possibility defined by history and habit. The possible enactments of power are situationally and organizationally circumscribed, and the ways in which they are circumscribed advantage some people or groups and disadvantage others (Yngvesson, 1988). To understand these limits fully, and the patterns of advantage and disadvantage with which they are associated, we must attend to the nature of professional projects and privileges and to their connections to legal institutions, as well as to the meaning of divorce in society and the prerogatives of class, race, and gender. Yet the lawyer is never solely in control of the production of ideology or legal services, and the client is never simply a timid consumer. Consumption of ideology or legal services is itself a domain of production.[41] As a result, the particular evolution of any lawyer-client interaction in divorce must be situated in the history and culture both parties draw on as they enact their particular plays of power (de Certeau, 1984). When that interaction involves ideological production—when reason is pitted against emotion, rules against insider knowledge, and equity against self-interest—entrenched positions in legal culture may be both hard for clients to overcome and, at the same time, available for them to exploit.

Overview of the Book

In the chapters that follow we illustrate the way power is enacted and meanings are both created and contested in lawyer-client interactions in divorce. We show that lawyers and clients have pressing differences about the way that the world is constituted. The most salient contests are over the nature of social relations in marriage and divorce, the "realism" of the client's posture in divorce, and the proper balance of reason and emotion in the legal process of divorce.

We begin, in Chapter 2, to examine those contests by describing the way lawyers and clients talk about the nature of marriage and the behavior of the divorcing spouses both in the marriage and in the divorce process itself. In these discussions, divorce lawyers and their clients construct what we call, following C. Wright Mills (1940: 904), "vocabularies of motives" as they together define, explain, and justify or critique the way people behave during marriage and during the processes through which marriages are dissolved.[42] Throughout the interactions between lawyers and clients there exists a relatively pervasive conversation about whether it is more reasonable to attribute human behavior to situational or personalistic factors. The situational orientation of lawyers becomes a powerful tool in their efforts to wean clients away from ego-centric views of social life toward what Jurgen Habermas (1970: 65) has called a "rational-purposive" perspective on motives and actions, in which technical endowments and a problem-solving orientation are more important than emotional reactions and justifications of self. In these efforts lawyers construct a picture of a world in which reason is separated from emotion and law is separated from society. They suggest that law can and should stand outside of, and against, a disorderly and conflictual social world, that law can and should be different, if not better, than the world it seeks to regulate.

In Chapter 3 we report how lawyers and clients negotiate a working definition of "reality." We consider, in particular, the strategies and tactics deployed as they identify and settle on the goals that will be their joint objectives in the legal process of divorce. In the effort to settle on goals and develop a mutually acceptable view of what is realistic, we see the construction of, and contestation over, the ideology of separate spheres. In addition, we describe strategic and tactical enactments of power as lawyers and clients negotiate responsibility and struggle about who is going to do what in the case and who is responsible for keeping it moving.

Chapters 4 and 5 discuss the negotiation of meaning in the domain of law itself. Both chapters show how that domain is infused with assumptions and meanings drawn from everyday life even as lawyers insist on its distinctiveness. Chapter 4 examines what we call "law talk," that is, the way in which lawyers and clients characterize the nature, operation, and efficiency of legal institutions and characterize the motivation and competence of legal actors. Such talk is deployed strategically and sets the context within which lawyers and clients make decisions about their cases. Chapter 5 takes up those decisions in the context of discussions of how to dispose of the divorce case, namely through settlement or contested litigation. Here the focus is on the meaning and value of adversariness as both a legal style and a mode of social interaction.

Chapters 4 and 5 focus attention on what we call the *internal* dimensions of meaning making, on the ways in which and the extent to which lawyers construct a picture of the legal system and its components that is very much at variance with the preconceptions and intuitions of lay people who have had limited exposure to the law. The discursive construction of the legal system in which we find lawyers engaged is comprehensive: it involves legal officials (judges, lawyers, mediators, bailiffs), legal resources (rules, dockets), and even the nature of justice and the law. Just as David Sudnow (1965), Abraham Blumberg (1967), Malcolm Feeley (1979), Kenneth Mann (1985), and others have revealed an "inner reality" to criminal defense work that had been hidden by unchallenged, conventional perspectives, our observations provide a new picture of law as lawyers unravel it for clients during the course of their interaction in divorce cases.[43] This picture suggests that law is, as Stanley Fish (1991: 203) argues, "a discourse continually telling two stories, one of which is denying that the other is being told," that in spite of its claims to distinctiveness, the picture presented by lawyers to their clients is replete with the very elements from which it claims to be distinct. It is in this capacity to tell two stories at once that one finds an important source of law's power, but also an important fissure that renders its power contestable, contingent, and fragile (Fish, 1991: 206).

Chapter 6 concludes this book by revisiting the theoretical connection between power and meaning. We ask how it could be that both lawyers and clients experience their interaction in divorce cases as unsatisfying, and we relate that experience to the contested, unstable nature of the negotiation of meaning and the fragility and transitory nature of power. We suggest that meaning constructed in lawyer-client interaction is elusive because it is contradictory, and power is fragile because it is so actively and ingeniously contested.

2

Reconstructing the Past, Imagining the Future: Defining the Domain of Relevance in Lawyer-Client Interaction

The negotiation of meaning and exercise of power between lawyers and clients occur within a framework of legal rules. While rules do not determine the nature of the meanings negotiated or the structure of the power exercised, they do provide a framework in which both take place. The rules define the realm of the legally relevant, and thus set an initial agenda for lawyer-client interaction (Gilkerson, 1992). The rules also provide a set of conventions that help to establish the nature of the legally persuasive story (Bennet and Feldman, 1981). As Gilkerson puts it (1992: 871–72), such stories

> assign characteristics and roles to people, constructing the positions from which they speak. [They] have the power to close off dialogue by locating certain substantive inquiries outside of the law. By restricting ways of framing questions and arguments, . . . the law thus constrains and limits possible stories a lawyer can tell. . . . [T]he law and its institutions establish form and substance requirements for stories that claim rights or express needs. Elements include a specified vocabulary for invoking claims, a paradigm of argumentation, formulae for proof, and narrative conventions for restricting individual and collective stories.

The negotiation of meaning and exercise of power in lawyer-client interactions are constrained by conventions generally well known to lawyers, but less well known to clients. This knowledge of conventions established by legal rules is the first, and perhaps most important, resource on which lawyers draw in their efforts to exercise power. But this resource can never in itself assure lawyer dominance because it operates solely in what Clark Cunningham calls "the domain of knowledge" (Cunningham, 1989: 2482) and, as a result, cannot change, and may not adequately capture or express, the client's experience. Because the client does not know the law and is unable to speak its language, she cannot know "her experience as a legal event" (White, 1990), and must be tutored about the dimensions of experience that are legally relevant.

In divorce, the rules that are most important in establishing the context for the negotiation of meaning and the exercise of power are those that concern dissolving the marriage, dividing property, custody, spousal and child support, and the legal steps that must be taken to bring the substantive matters to closure. In the past thirty years there has been a rather remarkable shift in such rules, especially those governing dissolution and child custody (Halem, 1980). The growth of no-fault divorce, for example, has embodied new conceptions of the reasons why marriages fail and how the legal system should react to these new visions. As Weitzman (1985: 23) puts it,

> There were two rationales for rejecting the traditional concept of fault: it was based on the artificial conception that one person was responsible for the marital breakup, and it was based on the assumption that the court could determine which person was. The reformers argued that even if the court could determine who deserved the greater blame . . . this question entailed an inappropriate invasion of marital privacy. The focus of the new law was to be on the present and the future (i.e., on fashioning an equitable settlement) rather than on the past (i.e., on trying to reconstruct who did what dreadful thing to whom). (See also Halem, 1980: chap. 8.)

No-fault rules were meant to prevent parties from using the legal process to tell stories of guilt and innocence; they were meant to alter the narratives that divorcing parties could construct as part of the divorce process.

In the area of child custody there has been an increase in statutes favoring joint custody. Joint custody rules try to shift the focus of contention from who would assume the primary, if not exclusive, role in parenting the children of divorce, to one of determining workable arrangements for continuing the meaningful involvement of both parents in the post-divorce lives of their children. Like no-fault, joint custody rules reduce the relevance of stories about flawed character, personal incompetence, or immoral conduct (Wallerstein and Kelly, 1980). Both are mobilized by lawyers to construct an ideology of separate spheres in which law's concerns are narrowed and cut off from the everyday world.

While these rule changes have contributed to the construction of the separate spheres ideology and "demoralizing" the divorce process, allegations of personal misconduct of many kinds come into the divorce process in the form of arguments about property, alimony, or child support. Even in the era of no-fault, divorcing parties come to lawyers with a story to tell, a story of who did what to whom, a story of right and wrong, a story of guilt and innocence.[1] They resist the rigid separation of law and the concerns of their everyday lives. As a result, "Divorce lawyers must repeatedly examine nonlegal issues at the same time that they work to frame problems in legal terms . . . . Thus, central to legal practice is a dimension that moves lawyers back and forth from dealing with technical issues to counseling clients about their problems of living" (McEwen et al., 1994: 169).

Even after no-fault, divorce clients consider marriage and marital conduct a highly moralized domain where judgments of right and wrong still seem both necessary and appropriate. Marriage is more than an economic union. The meaning of marriage remains tied to ideas of loyalty, commitment, and personal responsibility. As a result, lawyers and clients in divorce cases engage in conversations involving a reconstruction of the past in which descriptions of the behavior of the parties within the marriage play a large part.

In these reconstructions clients typically focus on the character and personality dispositions of their spouse and emphasize their spouse's most objectionable traits and personal defects. They frame these accounts in the language of rights, a language that "encompasses the belief that one should not be abused, mistreated, taken advantage of, harassed, insulted, or denied access to the means for securing life's necessities" (Gilkerson, 1992: 901). As Diane Vaughan observes, such accounts emerge early in the process of "uncoupling" and continue throughout it (Vaughan, 1986: 28–29). While some clients have little to say about what occurred during the marriage, most of those we observed devote considerable time to that activity,[2] generally on their own initiative and in the face of an unresponsive lawyer.[3] In so doing they stress personal and intentional explanations of their spouse's behavior (Coates and Penrod, 1980–81) and contest the boundaries and rules of relevance their lawyers seek to raise.

C. Wright Mills (1940: 910) noted long ago the centrality of what he called "motive mongering" in human interaction. By "motive mongering" Mills meant the frequency with which individuals impute motives in the effort to construct shared interpretations of action: "motives are the terms with which interpretation of conduct by social actors proceeds" (Mills, 1940: 904; see also Weber, 1947).[4] For Mills, the examination of what he labeled "vocabularies of motive" linked the study of linguistic behavior with social structure (see also Burke, 1950); it related the attribution of motives to the interests, patterns of power, and social positions that give rise to particular ways of talking about social relations and explaining human action (Mills, 1940: 904). Mills believed that a close study of the interpretation and understanding of action is important because such interpretations and understandings are "significant determinants of conduct" (Mills, 1940: 908).

Mills was particularly interested in the development of vocabularies of motive in different social situations. The creation of a vocabulary of motive was, in his view, a social act; thus "different situations have different vocabularies of motive appropriate to their respective behaviors" (Mills, 1940: 906). For Mills, an important part of the task of the sociologist is to investigate particular groups or situations to uncover the vocabulary of motives that a group makes available to its members or that particular situations seem to legitimate.[5]

Mills himself recognized that social conflict often revolved around questions of what would constitute a proper explanation or interpretation of action. Thus he noted (1940: 910),

> A labor leader says he performs a certain act because he wants to get higher standards of living for the workers. A businessman says that this is rationalization, or a lie; that it is really because he wants more money for himself from the workers. A radical says a college professor will not engage in radical movements because he is afraid for his job . . . . The college professor says it is because he just likes to find out how things work. What is reason for one man is rationalization for another. The variable is the accepted vocabulary of motives, the ultimates of discourse, of each man's . . . group.

Others, however, suggest that vocabularies of motive may be imposed without anything that could remotely be labeled a negotiation process (see Foucault, 1979), or that social interaction can proceed without agreement on interpretation, meaning, or vocabularies of motive (see, for example, Mishler, 1985). In this view, social interaction involves a series of continuing struggles between different ways of seeing the world, and interaction is more open and incomplete than is sometimes captured by images of a finally negotiated version of reality (see Yngvesson, 1985).

This chapter examines how lawyers and clients use vocabularies of motive in their interactions to construct meanings of marriage and marriage failure,[6] and how, in the discussion of motives and marriage, the ideology of separate spheres is asserted and contested. Through the construction of meaning in lawyers' offices ideas, beliefs, experiences, and interests are connected. As lawyers and clients define how people behave and explain why they behave as they do, as they try to make sense of life events, they give them shape and content. As Joseph Hopper (1993b: 811) suggests,

> [D]ivorce is one domain where the constructed, rhetorical, and hence contested nature of motives is unmistakably clear . . . . Meanings do not inhere in . . . behaviors or events themselves but are imposed onto them by social actors; and because in a divorcing situation a number of possible motives are out there to be discovered, having one vocabulary of motives accepted over another is always a matter of persuasion and negotiation.

Lawyer-client interactions provide one key arena for such negotiation and persuasion. What lawyers tell their clients about social relations, and how they respond to client questions concerning the behavior of other people, provides a professionalized understanding of the social world. At the same time, client interpretations and assessments of social relations channel the efforts of lawyers to carry out their professional tasks and control the instrumental aspects of their interaction with clients. Thus, maintaining their own interpretive scheme, or using a different vocabulary of motive, is one way clients resist the exercise of professional power and insure its fragility.

The exploration of marriage failure and of the divorcing couple's behavior occurs throughout the conversations between lawyers and clients. Generally such characterizations and interpretations have no clear narrative structure and rarely are they explicitly acknowledged by the listener. Moreover, they may have "no essential and necessary connection to antecedent events" (Hopper, 1993b: 810). While they sometimes emerge when lawyers ask clients to explain their own or their spouse's conduct, or when clients ask lawyers to speculate about why their spouse is acting as he or she is, more often such characterizations and interpretations are embedded in discussions of other subjects. They seem, for the most part, to emerge ad hoc, to be introduced out of context or to take the form of editorial commentary. Sometimes such commentary occurs in the context of wide-ranging discussions concerning the failure of the marriage, and sometimes it emerges from more focused discussions of particular events. Parts of these conversations arise from efforts by clients to explain their behavior, other parts from efforts to predict the spouse's behavior.

Lawyer and client sometimes negotiate agreed interpretations. However, agreement is more often reached when the discussion concerns behavior during the *divorce* than when the focus is on behavior during the *marriage*. In general, lawyers are more likely to secure "acceptance" of their interpretations than are clients. But often no agreement is reached; interpretations are advanced that elicit no response, or competing interpretations are put forward without any determined effort to reconcile them.

Clients focus much of their interpretive energy in efforts to construct an explanation of the past and of their marriage's failure (see Hopper, 1993a, 1993b). Lawyers avoid responding to these interpretations because they do not consider that who did what to whom in the marriage is relevant to the legal task of dissolving it. In this domain clients seem to talk past their lawyers (see Hosticka, 1979; Macaulay, 1979; Griffiths, 1986; Alfieri, 1991b),[7] and interpretive activity proceeds without the generation and ratification of a shared understanding of reality. In the face of such elusive meaning, however, lawyers are rarely derailed from their effort to focus on the business of securing the legal divorce and negotiating agreements about property and children.

The interaction changes when interpretive activity moves to the present and future and to behavior involved in the legal process; lawyers become more active in constructing vocabularies of motive when interpretive activity is linked to the rational-purposive goals of legal work. In this domain lawyers are able to mobilize their experience, expertise, and authority in support of their own interpretations and to use those interpretations, in turn, to reinforce their authority. Because decisions must be made that directly affect their lives, clients respond to lawyer interpretations even though they have little experience, expertise, or authority in the legal process. When closure is reached on an interpretation of behavior it usually embodies the lawyer's vocabulary of motive.[8] The rules of relevance that lawyers know and the experience that lawyers have give them a distinct advantage. Yet even here, the power that lawyers seem to exercise in the domain of meaning is fragile, and their advantage is often short-lived.

THE DOMAIN OF THE PAST: EXPLAINING THE FAILED MARRIAGE

Client narratives concerning the breakup of the marriage generally begin with a description of some disturbing spousal behavior and locate the source of that behavior *within* the allegedly offending actor. One such narrative was provided in a Massachusetts case involving a forty-year-old mother of four, Felica, who had been married, divorced, and subsequently remarried to a college professor, Ted, and who was, at the time of our research, seeking to end their second marriage. Both Felica and Ted were devout Mormons. For Felica, the divorce was a way of reclaiming her life from a man who had become both boring and overbearing. Ted, in turn, was infuriated by Felica's decision to divorce, which he attributed to her adulterous involvement with another man.

Despite the fact that Felica had taken the initiative in the divorce, her description of the breakup of her marriage focused on Ted and his "irrationality." She told us the following during an interview early in her case.[9]

> *Felica:* I went to work Friday afternoon and I should have suspected something was up because as I was leaving I asked if I could take the Toyota because when I come out of work late at night it is difficult to start up the van. He said "sure," and he gave me the key. This isn't normal. Usually it takes ten or fifteen minutes of fighting. And so I went off to work, came home, walked into the house. A lot of things were gone. He didn't tell me he was doing this. No indication whatsoever. He just took things. He didn't ask me what I needed or what I would like to hang onto. He just took whatever he wanted, strange things, curtains, bathmats, you name it.
>
> *Interviewer:* It wasn't like you had a fight with him that day?

Felica: Oh no. I guess that he had just decided he was going to move out. Ted's the type of person if he knew I wasn't here, that there was no one home, he would come by. I remember coming home from work one night and he was reading my diary that had been locked, and he forced the lock. And throughout our marriage he would go through my purse, find things, nothing I really wanted to keep secret from him, but that I hadn't told him about. He would say, "Why didn't you tell me about this?" And then it would become obvious that he could only have found that by going through the drawer or in my purse. He's always been that way. Ted comes across as very quiet, a peaceful person, but he is paranoid, and sometimes neurotic, psychotic. You name it, he has gone through the whole gamut. I have never been able to say that he would do this or do that. And for many years he made me feel that I was the one who was abnormal. And he actually almost had me believing that until I went into therapy.

At about the same time that Felica was saying these things to us, she was explaining to her lawyer, Robert (a third-year associate in a three-person firm), why her marriage had failed:

Felica: There was harassment and verbal degradation. No interest at all in my furthering my education. None whatsoever. Sexual harassment. If there was ever any time when I did not want or need sex, I was subject to these long verbal whiplashings. Then the Bible would be put out on the counter with passages underlined as to what a poor wife I was. Just constant harassment from him.

Robert: Mmn-uh.

Felica: Then he undertook to lecturing me, and I'd say, "I don't want to hear this. I don't have time right now." I could lock myself in the bathroom and he would break in. And I was just to listen, whether I wanted to or not. And he would lecture me for hours. Literally hours. There was no escaping him, short of getting in a car and driving away. But then he would stand outside in the driveway and yell, anyhow. The man was not well.

Robert: Okay. Now how about any courses you took?

Felica's narrative is one of blame and responsibility, guilt and innocence. Throughout their conversations, Robert's responses were evasive; he did not respond to her attributions of blame or characterizations of Ted, and he abruptly changed the subject. In so doing, he refused to negotiate a shared meaning of the marriage failure.

Yet Robert did have a version of why Felica's marriage had failed, one he was willing to share with us but not with her:

Felica is reaching a real difficult stage in her life. She is getting older, yet she wants to go out and have a good time. And she wants to get an education and start a career. Those are all difficult at the age bracket she's at now. And so she's caught between being a teenager and an adult. She's going back and forth between the two. Her husband, it's his second marriage to this woman that's not worked out. He's got to have a complete and utter sense of failure about this relationship. And I also think he may believe that he is losing his kids. I feel for the guy in a lot of respects. He's the sort of guy who is left out in the cold. I really feel bad for him, but he's not my client.

Divorce lawyers, like Robert, develop versions of events that often do not jibe with the stories told by their clients, but their responses to those stories are usually silence and evasion rather than joining and communication. As a result, while clients speak a language of guilt, blame, and responsibility that, to their lawyers, is at best irrelevant and at worst inaccurate, their characterizations are rarely directly challenged.

In another case, a male client explained the failure of his short and stormy marriage to a woman much younger than himself by focusing on the habitual untruthfulness of his spouse. In the midst of a discussion about the wife's previous testimony in court, the client said that he did not believe it and explained that the marriage ended:

Client: After she lied to me about the death of her parents in a car-train accident. And after she lied to me about where she went to school. And after she lied to me about the fact that she was an only child. She's lived a secretive life all this time.

Lawyer: Hmm.

Client: So everything she told me about her background was a lie. I can't believe anything she says. It would be news to me if she says anything truthful while I'm sitting there in the courtroom. I couldn't verify it for you. Because all this time I have been under the impression that she had no parents, no siblings, that she was a graduate of Radcliffe College. When you marry somebody, you don't check these things out. You don't call Radcliffe. She gave me an alias for her maiden name. Collins is the one that she said. She gave me an alias. She gave me a French name. She said her parents were French Canadian.

Lawyer: Hmm.

Client: We won't get any more information from her.

Lawyer: The only real way to find out anything would be to hire a private detective.

The lawyer in this case, like Robert in Felica's case, avoids commenting on the client's characterization of his spouse. He resists by remaining silent in the face of that characterization. When he does speak, he focuses only on the problem of how to get information about her present circumstances and finances.

Occasionally, however, lawyers participate openly in the construction of accounts about the failed marriage. In each instance when they did so, they reinforced rather than challenged the view that the failure of the marriage should not be blamed on their client. As one California lawyer put it when his client openly expressed some willingness to accept responsibility for the failure of the marriage:

> *Lawyer:* If there was a failure I just don't think it is fair to attribute it to anything you have done. You walked a country mile to try to make it work out well. You were married to a person who has any number of problems.
>
> *Client:* Confronting the alternatives as they presently exist—that's a very difficult thing. There seems much about this situation that I've got to do that I don't like to do. But I don't see any other way out. I guess this is when it gets tough.
>
> *Lawyer:* All right.

This lawyer, like the few others who play "blame the spouse," does so to support his client's decision to continue to seek a divorce in the face of her own growing ambivalence.

The strategic nature of lawyers' participation in such reconstructions of the past is further illustrated in the following exchange between a female lawyer and her fifty-year-old, poorly educated, female client.

> *Client:* He keeps saying he'd like to get it together.
>
> *Lawyer:* But Bob really hasn't changed his behavior. You see what you are telling me about the pattern of living is what you told me about the pattern of living during your marriage. He could probably live with this a great deal longer than you could. You have to own up to that. You made a decision when you came to me a while ago that that's not how you want it. I don't think you should keep saying to me that, if he wanted to get it together, you would. Because if I understand what you said to me way back then, that's not the way you want to live. And he could live like this indefinitely. I guarantee you that. I don't see any strain on him. The only strain that Bob is now enduring is the possibility that you are going to go through with this divorce. But his lifestyle hasn't changed. He's got you in the same position he had you in throughout the marriage. And that is not going to change unless we go through the divorce. The moment that you ever showed him a glimmer or a possibility that you were going to be a free woman, that's when he initiated a divorce. He just can't deal with that. You have to accept that. Your relationship is going to be the way your marriage always was or you're going to have to go through a divorce and have the kinds of things you want. And that's the bottom line.
>
> *Client:* I'm willing to sacrifice myself to live in hell, more or less, for the kids, but that's not right either.

The client's reference to living in "hell" suggests that she accepts the lawyer's characterization of her husband. Yet, as her case progressed, such exchanges of doubt and reassurance occurred frequently. When lawyers use the language of blame, it is to remind clients why the divorce is either desirable or inevitable and ought to be pursued, an end result in which the lawyer has an obvious interest.

When discussion turns to the client's conduct in or reasons for leaving the marriage, interpretations and styles of explanation change dramatically. In interpreting their own actions, clients shift from explanations based on personal dispositions and character traits and focus on circumstances and situations. They emphasize their own innocence, vulnerability, and injury, and suggest that any undesirable conduct on their part was the product of provocation or duress. The meanings they attach to their own behavior are consistent with their attempt to blame their spouses and to present their own actions as reasonable and justifiable responses to circumstances not of their making. Lawyers do not generally challenge their client's attempts at exculpation, nor do they validate them. Evasion is again the predominant response. One example of a client's self-portrait is provided in the following exchange:

> *Lawyer:* You know that she's really pushing to get this divorce going.
>
> *Client:* I know she doesn't want to have any connection to me. She hates to even have me there to say hello.
>
> *Lawyer:* That will calm down eventually.
>
> *Client:* What makes me mad is that I'm the injured party. She's acting like I am running out on her.
>
> *Lawyer:* She's hurting a little bit, and she thinks that if it gets into court the pain is going to stop.

This dialogue is unusual only in the directness with which the client asserts that he is "the injured party." Claims of this type are tacit in many cases even when the client initiates the divorce (Griffiths, 1986: 154).

Clients also portray themselves as victims to excuse their own marital misconduct. In Felica and Ted's case, for example, the following interaction occurred when Robert asked Felica to explain why she had physically assaulted her husband.

> *Felica:* They're going to bring up the time that I physically attacked him. Can we beat them to the punch and get that in so I can explain why I attacked him?
>
> *Robert:* Is that where you attacked him with the loaf of bread?
>
> *Felica:* No. Remember that day when I had the tubal ligation?
>
> *Robert:* Give me that whole story again.
>
> *Felica:* Okay, I had gone in to have a tubal ligation.
>
> *Robert:* Yeah. I know that he got very upset, but I don't remember all of the circumstances afterward.
>
> *Felica:* He found out about it from my girlfriend, subjected her to a severe tongue-lashing, accused her of helping me. He called me all

kinds of filthy names. I was obviously having a tubal ligation so that I could go out and run around and sleep around.

Robert: Yeah. It's probably hearsay. They're probably going to object to it, all that stuff you just said about his conversation with your friend. That's hearsay. Okay?

Felica: And then on the Saturday morning, which was several days afterward, because I went in on a Wednesday, I was getting ready to go grocery shopping. We got into an argument about something, and then he started calling me dirty names.

Robert: Like what?

Felica: He called me "filth." That was the word that got me. "Filth." And something just went "boing." "Boing." My spring came undone. And I just attacked him. I just went for him for maybe five minutes, yelled and screamed and kicked and slapped and scratched and did whatever I could. I wasn't even aware at the time that I was doing it. I didn't even realize I was the one screaming. It was Lottie who told me later that I was the one who was screaming. But I just lost it. He made me so angry. His reaction to this was so senseless. The reason I had it done was because I wanted it done while I was covered by health insurance. I knew a divorce was coming up. And I knew I wouldn't have the health insurance anymore. And to have it done under the insurance did not cost me anything. Because I didn't want to get pregnant again.

Robert: I don't know if I want to bring it up first, because if we bring it up then they have to bring it up and what if they had chosen not to?

Felica interprets her own misbehavior as a kind of temporary insanity and goes on, as if she had internalized the need to justify her decision to undergo the tubal ligation, to explain how that decision was itself a product of external circumstances. Robert responded by ignoring the substance of Felica's explanation, reminded her of evidentiary problems, and then suggested that it might be better not to bring up her attack on her husband. He focuses on the tactical problem while ignoring everything that his client said concerning the reasons for the attack and her characterizations of her own behavior.

Sometimes lawyers do not ignore such characterizations and, instead, validate the client's interpretation. One instance of this occurs in the following California case in which the client explained her decision to seek a divorce and described why her husband had hired a "tough" lawyer.

Client: He can't make a decision. He needs to be pushed into it. He would never have left if I didn't throw him out. Never. He would have gone on, because life was very comfortable for him. It was just fine, and he was totally amazed that I would do it. He didn't know I was discontent. After I go through this whole spiel about how I felt and what I thought, his answer to me was, "I didn't know you were discontent." My world was coming down around my ears, and that was his choice of words, because he couldn't, he really sees himself as a wonderful person.

Lawyer: Some of us like to have a good opinion of ourselves. At least some of the time.

Client: Well, I made him this wonderful person. I told him how wonderful he was, while I was hiding behind this thing I built up for myself—this smiling, gentle lady—when I was seething, until I couldn't bear it anymore.

Lawyer: So you helped create this Frankenstein.

Client: Of course, but now he's got someone else to tell him how wonderful he is.

Lawyer: Well, why not keep a good thing going?

This client attaches the conversation about the failed marriage to another discussion, the husband's choice of lawyer. Her lawyer joins in the conversation about the failed marriage and accepts her interpretation. Together they create the "Frankenstein" portrait of the self-indulgent, spoiled husband, and in so doing reach tacit agreement on the client's self-portrait as a long-suffering martyr.

Throughout their meetings with their lawyers, clients keep the question of marriage failure very much alive in their minds. They talk about the marriage in terms of guilt (their spouse's) and innocence (their own). This pattern is as observable in California, where there is a pure no-fault system, as it is in Massachusetts, where fault and no-fault options exist side by side. Even though law reform makes such questions legally irrelevant and gives lawyers an excuse to ignore or evade client characterizations, clients continue to think in fault terms and to attribute blame to their spouse. Clients use a vocabulary of personal responsibility to interpret the failed marriage, and they seem to want their lawyers to accept and use a similar vocabulary.[10] They contest the boundaries of law and seek to open it up to a broader range of concerns. Yet they do so by employing a way of speaking that is couched in legal terms. As Christopher Gilkerson argues (1992: 899), "[C]lients attempt to tell their stories to lawyers in order to persuade them that they are in the right and the other side is in the wrong . . . . Realizing their dependency on the lawyer . . . clients use the language of rights to make pleas for lawyer attention, time, and commitment."

Lawyers resist by avoiding discussion of who did what to whom during the marriage. They focus, when they are confronted with such an issue, on questions of tactics in the legal process of divorce. Client and lawyer are like performer and bored, but dutiful, audience—the lawyer will not interrupt the aria, but she will not applaud much, either, for fear of an encore. Lawyers join with, and validate, the client's vocabulary of blame only when necessary to reassure wavering clients of the correctness of their decision to secure a divorce.

THE DOMAIN OF THE PRESENT: EXPLAINING PROBLEMS AND JUSTIFYING DEMANDS IN THE LEGAL PROCESS OF DIVORCE

A different pattern emerges when discussions shift to the legal process and problems of the moment. The vocabulary of blame continues to play a prominent part in client thinking: problems in negotiations, for example, are regularly interpreted by clients as originating in their spouse's blameworthy conduct and character. But lawyers are much more active participants in these conversations than in those about the failed marriage and are frequently direct in challenging client characterizations and explanations. In Felica's case, for example, compare Robert's passive nonresponse to her earlier characterizations of Ted to his rhetoric in the following discussion of whether Ted would be willing to transfer title of one of the family motor vehicles to Felica.

> *Robert:* Have you discussed any more getting rid of the van and getting yourself another vehicle?
>
> *Felica:* Yes. I talked it over with him, and asked if he would be willing to release the van if I were to find a car.
>
> *Robert:* Yeah.
>
> *Felica:* And he said, "If he thought it was a fair deal, or a decent deal," or something. And I said, "Well, if I'm going to be making the car payments, what does it have to do with you? All I want from you is to release the van." He still wants that control.
>
> *Robert:* He's looking at everything as dollar signs. Pretty typical reaction. He's going to be defensive on all those things. Have you been looking for vehicles?

Felica's observation that Ted still wants control suggests that his reluctance to transfer title is continuous with his behavior during the marriage. Robert, on the other hand, suggests that Ted's behavior is "typical" of people during divorce and, in so doing, resists Felica's attribution of her husband's behavior to some character flaw. However, rather than trying to reach a shared position on why Ted refuses to shift title, Robert eventually changes the subject to what his client is going to do about transportation for herself. Parallel meanings are constructed and allowed to coexist. Neither lawyer nor client acknowledges, or tries to resolve, the differences. Neither is able to validate their interpretation and have it accepted as the working assumption in their interaction. Neither is able to assert dominance over the other.

Similar patterns occurred in other cases. In one, a young man provides the following explanation of why he and his spouse have been unable to reach a negotiated agreement.

Lawyer: What would happen if the two of you sat down and started talking?

Client: Well, anytime we've ever had discussions, they always turn into arguments. There are a number of other things besides the getting a job issue that I feel are inequitable in our relationship. On the rare occasion that she actually listens, she's not a good listener. When she actually listens and senses that she'd better change her ways, that may last for a week before it's back to the same old thing. And she's tied up with her hobbies. We were really broke this winter, and I tried to discuss it with her. She said I should go see a financial counselor. She one evening said, "Well, when I get my inheritance I should share that with you." And I said, "Well, that would help." But then she'd just start ranting and raving, as if I had the nerve to consider that any of her inheritance would be mine. So she doesn't mean it when she does ever make a concession. And it's very temporary and fleeting.

Lawyer: Maybe she'd make a stronger commitment to a counselor that can listen to your two points of view.

In this client's view, reaching an agreement is impossible because his wife rarely listens and never lives up to the concessions she makes. He locates cause in character and uses a language of fault and blame. Other clients provide comparable explanations for the unwillingness of their former spouse to divide personal property reasonably or to assume responsibility for their own post-divorce financial well-being. However, the lawyers involved resist explanations related to character and instead suggest that the problem is circumstantial. For them, the negotiation issue is not a matter of blame but is rather a problem of finding the right vehicle to facilitate communication.

In a few instances, however, lawyers do endorse their clients' analyses of personality as they talk about particular problems in the divorce process. For example, one California client inquired about his lawyer's view of the fairness of their offer of spousal support, and the lawyer responded by reminding him of his wife's "aggressive and dominant tendencies."

Lawyer: On a long-term basis we are talking about a woman who is a gifted artist, who is certainly commercially acceptable in the sense that she can go out and sell a substantial number of paintings. She can earn income in a desirable profession.

Client: I think she told me today she was going to work. That she had to go to work. So I presume it was that.

Lawyer: That's up in the air at the moment as to whether she's going to continue to wait tables or not.

Client: Yeah.

Lawyer: Apparently she found out how little she's earning by doing that.

> It's a desperate maneuver on her part. I have the feeling that aggressive and dominant as she tries to become, she is really getting uptight.
>
> *Client:* Well, she always gets very paranoid about financial matters.

Another lawyer answered his client's question about the lack of a response to their longstanding offer concerning the division of marital property as follows:

> *Lawyer:* I hear that she [the spouse's lawyer] doesn't communicate with her much at all. It is hard to get hold of her. She doesn't respond to letters; she doesn't answer letters and she changes her position all the time.
>
> *Client:* Really. I lived with it for a long time. I know.
>
> *Lawyer:* What's fascinating is that people don't change their basic behavior patterns once they begin a divorce. They really don't.

This lawyer's insistence on the continuity and stability of "basic behavior patterns" is unusual: lawyers generally rely almost exclusively on situational explanations. But whatever the attribution, lawyers speculate about social behavior only when it appears directly relevant to legal activity. They engage in the production of meaning strategically and in a way that implicitly defends the separation of law from society, even as they breech that separation when it suits their aims.

Lawyers deploy a stage theory to interpret and explain why opposing spouses behave as they do during the divorce. They suggest that divorce typically produces intransigence and hostility at the beginning, followed by a period of emotional confusion and then a gradual return to rationality. They emphasize the importance of understanding problems in light of the different behaviors and moods associated with each stage. One Massachusetts lawyer put it the following way when answering her client's question about why his wife got so upset when he purchased some new clothes:

> *Lawyer:* You are in the stage of divorce where she thinks she can deliver you on to the street with one pair of jockey shorts and nothing else. That's the stage you're in.
>
> *Client:* I think that's what she thinks.
>
> *Lawyer:* Everyone thinks that in the beginning. I almost get worried when a person comes in and says, "My wife has just said that she's going to give me everything." I think it's normal for her to say, "I'll leave you on Main Street bare-assed." When they don't do that, then I know the normal process isn't happening. It won't happen.
>
> *Client:* Okay.

In her explanation this lawyer describes the behavior of the spouse as common, as reflecting what "everyone thinks," and she links that behavior explicitly to the stages of a "normal process."

In other cases lawyers were somewhat less explicit in establishing such linkages. They use rhetoric such as that employed by the following lawyer to describe the opposing spouse's position on custody as a reaction to the beginning of the divorce process itself.

> *Lawyer:* Is it likely that the two of you would disagree on anything in terms of your relationship with your kids?
>
> *Client:* No, I don't think so.
>
> *Lawyer:* I think what you have is parents who have been relatively, consistently agreeable in regard to their kids and then they first get into a divorce situation. Sometimes unfortunately they can get their heels stuck in cement on something that just doesn't compute in view of their past experience. I mean all of a sudden they can't agree about anything when they've always agreed.

Clients, unlike their lawyers, employ such circumstantial explanations rarely and selectively; in discussions of the divorce process they use them to justify their own claims to particular assets or a particular division of property. One such explanation is provided by a young, working-class woman who was seeking a share of the equity in a house that her husband had built and in which she refused to live. When her female lawyer asked whether she had made any contribution to the construction of the house, the client responded,

> *Client:* I was working nights at the Hideout, regularly from six to one at night, and I just had Gail, and so I'd go home. I didn't want to get up in the morning and build a house. It was winter. Who wants to build a house in the middle of winter?
>
> *Lawyer:* I just wanted to know whether there was anything to what he said about your never wanting to build the house.
>
> *Client:* I wanted the house, but I didn't want the house at my mother-in-law's—next door.
>
> *Lawyer:* So that's what made you less involved with the project.
>
> *Client:* Plus he wasn't building the house that I wanted him to. He was just building this little house, and I wanted a bigger house. It was just a little house, no garage. It was nice, he was building a house, but it was going to be next to my mother-in-law. At the time my mother-in-law didn't even like me, didn't even speak to me, and I'm going to live next door.
>
> *Lawyer:* Self-preservation . . . .

The client's explanation for her refusal to contribute has several dimensions. First she talks about her work and her need to stay home with the children. Next she focuses on the fact that the house was being built next to her in-laws. Then she briefly suggests that the house was not to her liking before returning to its proximity to her husband's relatives. In this, as in other cases, the client explains and justifies her behavior largely by reference to circumstances beyond her control. Client and lawyer construct a mutually acceptable circumstantial explanation for what seems, initially, to be an unjustifiable negotiating position. Their dialogue moves toward closure on an explanation that the lawyer accepts as legally defensible and strategically useful.

In talking about their spouse's behavior during the divorce process, clients frame narratives of fault, blame, and excuse similar to those developed about their failed marriages. The behavior of the spouse during the divorce process is portrayed as the product of permanent character traits and personality dispositions. Yet, when their own conduct is at issue, client self-portraits again emphasize circumstance, situation, or the provocations and injuries inflicted by the spouse.[11]

Lawyers take a much more active role in constructing interpretations related to the legal process of divorce than they do when clients talk about the reasons for marriage failure. Where the meanings to be negotiated focus on the present and are relevant to the task at hand rather than on marital history, lawyers tend to join with, rather than ignore, their clients in constructing interpretations. Yet they rarely embrace an interpretation that attributes action to fixed character traits or speaks in terms of fault and blame. Instead, they emphasize circumstantial factors in explaining the conduct of both the spouse and the client.

THE DOMAIN OF THE FUTURE: GIVING ADVICE, PLANNING STRATEGY

Lawyers are most actively engaged in attributing meanings to events and behaviors when advising their clients about the tactics and strategy of the legal process itself. In so doing they signal clients that people in the throes of a divorce are particularly vulnerable to stress and emotion. They suggest that clients ought to be suspicious of their own judgment and, by implying that such judgment is likely to be unreliable, lawyers highlight the importance of depending on them for sound guidance. The construction of meaning justifies and reinforces professional authority by limiting the scope of the legally relevant and inducing clients into a wariness about one part of their own experience.

The warning that divorce clouds judgment provides the backdrop for many discussions of tactics and strategy. In one California case, the lawyer provided a vivid example of the construction of the ideology of separate spheres when he alerted his well-educated client to the danger that her emotions might get in the way of a satisfactory property settlement and advised her of the need to bring her emotions under control.

Lawyer: People have a very, very hard time of separating whatever it is—so I think for shorthand, we call it the emotional aspect of the case—from the financial aspect of the case. But if there is going to be a settlement, that's kind of what has to happen, or the emotional aspect of the case gets resolved and then the financial thing becomes a matter of dollars and cents and the client decides, I'm tired and I don't want to fight over the last $500 or the last $100.

Client: I mean, I don't want to fight and I do want to fight, right? That's exactly what it comes down to.

Lawyer: Yeah, you're ambiguous.

Client: Oh, boy, am I ever. And I have to live with it.

Lawyer: That's right. I'd say the ambiguity goes even deeper than the issue of fighting and not fighting. The ambiguity is what Irene talked about and that is—it's the real hard one—it's terminating the entire relationship. You're angry; you're pissed off. You've said that. And are you ready to call a halt to the anger? I'm not so sure that that's humanly possible. Can your rational mind say, "Okay, Jane, there has been enough anger expended on this; it is time to get on with your life?" If you are able to do that, great. But I don't know.

Client: Well, obviously some of me is and some of me isn't.

While, in this case, the divorce and the emotions associated with it seem to be fueling the client's desire to fight, in other cases lawyers caution their clients against being too trusting, too ready to make concessions, or too impatient. They warn clients that the divorce process is long and tiring; they caution against the failing courage that springs from the need to make hard choices (Kressel, 1985). Clients, eager to blame their spouses for problems in the marriage and for difficulties encountered in the divorce process, end up worrying about being too tough or unfair; many are overcome with second thoughts. In response, lawyers interpret those reactions as natural during a divorce.

Attempting to exercise power over the construction of the meaning of divorce, lawyers compare their clients' feelings or actions with what is "common" or with what they have seen in other cases. In this way lawyers again employ a vocabulary of motive based on some idea of the "normal divorce." In the following exchange concerning the difficulty of actually filing for divorce, the lawyer constructs such a norm through a variety of rhetorical devices.

Client: I think he's exhausted and I think he understands that there is no hope. He kept on saying to me, "You don't want me anymore, do you?" I said, "That's not what I am saying. I'm saying we are better off separated."

Lawyer: I suspect it's a very hard thing for you to file this petition, and I think it may be still difficult. Even when you are the one who wants the dissolution, sometimes it's really hard to do that. I know. I have another client who has been separated for a couple of years and it's coming down now where it's a matter of actually getting the divorce and he's been the one who separated. His wife has been hysterical about the divorce, but he wanted it and now when it's coming down to the time he tells me, "I feel so bad about this." And it's very natural. I mean, people feel that way. But I think that you are going to be spinning your wheels with this until you decide, until you feel comfortable that you really want to file the petition and do it.

Client: See, I don't want him in my life, but filing the petition to me is just something that I think is gross. I don't know why.

Lawyer: I can tell that you have been really having a hard time doing that.

This lawyer validates his client's expression of difficulty but moves quickly from a focus on *this* client's difficulty to the general level; he locates her feelings in an abstract statement "sometimes it's really really hard to do that." The client is assured that her reactions fit a typical pattern, one that the lawyer has seen before. In describing her hesitancy as a reaction to making what seems like an irrevocable decision, the lawyer displays confidence in his own interpretation. "I know," he says, and he bases his knowledge on a comparison of this client's feelings with those of another of his clients. He uses the term "natural" and deploys folk wisdom, "people feel that way," to establish both his expertise in understanding her reactions and the extent to which those reactions arise out of the divorce process itself.[12]

A similar focus on the divorce itself as an explanation for behavior and a similar use of the rhetoric of comparison and generalization in constructing particular explanations occurs as lawyers advise their clients about offers and demands concerning property, support, and child custody. In the following case, a relatively inexperienced woman lawyer urges her client to ask for more support than the client feels is appropriate and explains that the client's reticence arises from guilt that many "women feel" during the divorce.

Lawyer: It's going to be up to you whether you think it will really hurt him or that he will be really impoverished by this and that he can't make it, but don't forget he's going to be left with a $250,000 house when it's all over.

Client: I know.

Lawyer: Or more. And what are you going to do? You'll have freedom. A lot of women feel that way at the time and they say, "So what?" Do you feel guilty? Do you?

Client: I feel bad for him, I feel sorry that I hurt him, and I'm sick of fighting.

Lawyer: How old are you?

Client: Thirty-two.

Lawyer: You have forty, fifty, sixty years to say, "Gee whiz, why didn't I want to screw him?"

Client: Yeah, I know. Let's just get it over with.

This lawyer argues that the client's feelings though temporary are, nonetheless, extremely consequential and suggests that if her client acts on those feelings she will, in the long run, regret it. The client, in turn, accepts the lawyer's explanation for her reluctance to bargain and acquiesces in the lawyer's strategic advice.

Another example of talk concerning short-term feelings and their long-term consequences occurred in a California case in which support was again the subject of discussion.

Lawyer: Well, taking spousal support out of the house payment is not being dishonest. The main person we have to protect is you.

Client: I know.

Lawyer: Whatever you take out of this marriage has got to last you the rest of your life. You can't count on him coming along and saying, "Oh, you need money you sweet little darling. Let me help you."

Client: Right.

Lawyer: You know, "Let me make your house payment for you." "Let me pay off your house so you have it free and clear." They just are not beating the bushes out there.

Client: I don't know how you work that out.

Lawyer: Hold out a little bit longer and don't just agree to give him Grandma's undershorts and everything else, simply to get rid of him and be done with it.

Client: Well, I'm a pushover.

Lawyer: At this point I've got a lot of people like you coming in here signing things I can't believe.

Client: I've been a pushover all my life. That's my whole problem.

Lawyer: Yes. And you have to toughen up and realize you're number one, now.

Client: I'm trying. I'm trying.

Lawyer: If you stop and think, the rest of your life's out there.

Client: I know. I've really tried to be nice about it.

Lawyer: Yeah. But you can only be nice so far. We've got to take care of you the rest of your life. And too many people have come to know, "Too soon old and too late smart." And they have lived to regret the fact that they wanted to get along with their ex-husband. If getting along with him means you live at the poverty level and he lives on Easy Street, how long are you going to get along with him anyway, before you start resenting it?

Client: Not very long, I'm afraid.

Lawyer: And he's going to resent it to some extent, but he's also going to respect the fact that you did stick up for your rights.

Client: Yeah.

Lawyer: He ain't going to like it.

Client: Oh no.

Lawyer: If you don't get along with him because he's got too much and you don't have anything . . .

Client: Okay, I'll go back and tell him. This ought to ruin his whole Christmas.

In this case the lawyer emphasizes the consequences of the client's decision by repeated use of the phrase "the rest of your life." She interprets the client's feelings by referring to the experience of her "clients" and suggests that *this* client's willingness to give in just to "get rid" of her husband is similar to "a lot of people like you." She, and other lawyers, employ folk wisdom ("too soon old and too late smart") to interpret their clients' actions and to suggest more appropriate ways of behaving. In so doing, this lawyer mobilizes interpretations from Alfred Schutz's (1962) "attitude of everyday life" to support her own rational-purposive objectives. She blurs the distinction between the legal and the social that she is, at the same time, constructing. Somewhat atypically, the lawyer is able to "sell" both her interpretation and her advice. Closure is reached; an agreed version of reality is developed.

The tendency of lawyers to interpret client objectives as short-sighted, to urge them not to act on the basis of those desires, and to emphasize their legal experience as a source of expertise, is further illustrated in discussions of visitation and child custody between Felica and Robert.

Robert: The biggest mistake anybody can make in these situations in the initial stages is saying we'll let it go. That is the completely wrong idea and the reason it's wrong is that there has to be some kind of a pattern set up so that everybody gets comfortable with it. You can't get your life settled if you never know if the kids are going to be home or not. It would really wreak havoc with you, and the same thing goes for the kids, they almost know they can push you around at that point. I would say if we're going to go that way we should definitely state what nights they're going to stay with Ted and what nights they're going to stay with you and really set up a detailed program. Otherwise, it's just going to be havoc.

Felica: It seems so hopeless to do that.

Robert: No it's not. I prefer to have very strict rules set up. I've seen too many cases where they say the visitation parent can come anytime they want and so on. That does not work out well.

Felica: I will not get into that. I'm not going to have a piece of paper saying my kids can be with me Monday, Wednesday, Friday and with Ted Tuesday, Thursday, Saturday. If John wants to spend the night he'll call, Ted will say sure, and he'll come and pick him up.

Robert: I've had a case, several cases, where the visitation parent would just show up anytime and where it was up to the custodial parent and she would just say, "I don't think this is an appropriate time." One time the guy showed up at ten o'clock in the evening. We're talking about children around ten years old. She was saying, "I just don't think this is an appropriate time." He was saying, "Well, I have reasonable visitation, which means anytime," and they wind up back in court. Whereas if they had had a structured program, he would know when he could be there and not be there. That's why I favor, in the beginning, that kind of a program. Not everybody wants it. As I said, I'm not gonna tell you that you have to take that, that's just my viewpoint. What I see is problems that can crop up and why we have those kinds of agreements.

Felica: I want them to be with him whenever they want to. If they decide they don't want to go with him I want them to go up to him and say, "I don't want to go with you."

Robert: Well, just consider what I've said. Stop and think about it. Sit down in your living room or whatever and strongly consider what I've said and then give me your decision. Be logical about it, objective about it. I've seen people spend a lot of money trying to figure out what is reasonable visitation.

A later conversation about custody between Robert and Felica replays similar concerns:

Felica: I don't want to get involved in all these little nitty-gritties. I can't do it. I'm not up to it yet.

Robert: I think you are playing with a real bomb if you were to do it afterward. Let's say you gave custody of John and Max and Joel to Ted without having those little nitty-gritties, as you say, worked out. I think you would be in a very poor position, because the person who has physical custody of the kids has the ace in the hole. And what I don't want to see is you behind the ball. I want to be sure that if a situation comes up that would hurt you, hopefully you've covered that and we've resolved that, so that you don't have to go back into court. He could leave in the middle of the night with the kids. And you could say, "Well, I trust this guy." See, if you guys could really trust one another, or were really getting along, we wouldn't be sitting in front of Judge Sokol for this.

Throughout these conversations Robert portrays Felica's reluctance to get involved in negotiating specific legal agreements as a misplaced reaction to the divorce process itself, as a mistake commonly made "in these situations." He refers to the divorce as "a very dangerous time period." He invokes his experience in "too many cases," and he describes another case, in which the client's unwillingness to be specific created "havoc," as a tactic to get her to reconsider. Felica is urged to be "logical" and "objective." Through this advice Robert indicates that his client's expressed desires are neither logical nor objective, and he portrays that client behavior during divorce as emotional and irrational.

He ends by cautioning his client about an inclination to trust her husband that the lawyer himself attributes to her; he tries to frighten her out of this posture by conjuring up an image of the husband sneaking off in the night with the children. Throughout, Felica refuses to acquiesce. She resists Robert's effort to tie down every detail of custody and visitation as too legalistic and unsuited to the kind of relationship she envisions with her soon-to-be ex-husband. But Robert persists and reminds Felica of what she has earlier said about Ted and his behavior. In the end, she agrees that she cannot really trust her husband, that she has to be careful about her own desire to get things over with, and that they should go with "what we had approached them with originally. Me in the house with custody of the kids."

The focus on the temporary emotionalism that surrounds divorce, and the effort to keep emotions out of law, is a continuing theme as lawyers give tactical advice to clients (see O'Gorman, 1963; Griffiths, 1986; Erlanger et al., 1987; Kressel et al., 1983; McEwen et al., 1994).[13] In one Massachusetts case, an experienced male lawyer focuses on the transient nature of hard feelings in a discussion with an older woman client whose husband has filed for a divorce after a long marriage.

> *Client:* I think maybe it is just because of the way he's been that I'm just on my guard all the time, everything I do.

> *Lawyer:* Don't be. He's angry, probably paying more than he thought he's going to pay. He was telling you how things were going to be before and he was wrong. Just don't let him get to you. Very often what happens after some time is that the emotional aspects drop out and you wind up having a better relationship than you had.

> *Client:* I don't really feel that we're going to be friends again, but I feel that we should at least be able to be civilized with one another.

> *Lawyer:* You really can't. So many people at the beginning of a divorce just are ready to go for the throat and after some years they start remembering the better times.

> *Client:* My feeling now is that it is over, it is time to just go on.

> *Lawyer:* You just can't find rationality, though. Emotions get involved no matter who he is. It just takes time.

This lawyer argues that his client's desire for a civilized relationship with her spouse cannot be reached during the divorce. Such a goal may be realized only after the divorce is over and "the emotional aspects drop out." He compares the emotionalism of divorce with a rationality that is put aside during that process.

This juxtaposition of emotion and rationality, this image of the divorce process itself as leading people to act in ways that they would not otherwise act, is prevalent as lawyer and client make decisions concerning the timing and substance of offers, demands, and proposed agreements. One Massachusetts lawyer, for example, advised her client to postpone trying to reach an agreement with his wife because, "She's too caught up in her own anger to really think straight. I wouldn't want to come up with an agreement now that six months from now she's going to go on and try to modify. I'd rather have her settle down again and on the basis of rationality work something out."

A California lawyer suggests that an offer must be timed to coincide with one of the wife's emotional peaks.

> *Lawyer:* Now, let me tell you what's coming up in the next two months. We've got the holidays coming up. And oftentimes you find people having tough times dealing with divorce cases around the holidays. My sense is we ought to get on it quickly, so that she isn't sitting there at her Thanksgiving table. Holidays are classically depressing, even if you have your entire family.
>
> *Client:* I agree.
>
> *Lawyer:* So what I'm saying is, I think we ought to get on it, and get an offer over there, so that she has it long before Thanksgiving. In other words, you want her to receive this offer at a time when she feels the best she's going to feel about you. Okay? If she gets it at a time that she feels the worst she's going to feel about you, I don't care what's on the piece of paper, she's going to reject it.
>
> *Client:* I'll do what I can.

This lawyer makes explicit the link between the explanation of behavior and the services that lawyers can provide. By interpreting behavior as responsive to circumstances and, therefore, contingent rather than rooted in intractable personality dispositions, lawyers increase the apparent value of their services by suggesting that their own sense of timing may be decisive.

Unlike clients, who shift interpretive frames when they move from their spouse's to their own behavior, lawyers deploy situational explanations in most contexts. They consistently use the effect of the divorce itself to explain behavior. In this way they construct an image of human behavior as adaptive and adaptable; they suggest that strategic thinking is as important in the realm of social behavior as it is in the planning and execution of legal maneuvers. In this way, lawyers and clients together chart the boundaries of the legal and establish the contours of its rules of relevance.

CONCLUSION

Despite legal rules designed to "demoralize" divorce and to eliminate issues of fault and blame from the legal process, the construction of meaning in lawyer-client interaction is focused on those very issues. Clients insistently use the language of guilt, fault, and responsibility to describe and interpret the behavior of their spouse. The meanings that they construct excuse and justify their own conduct and place blame for the failure of their marriage, as well as for problems in the legal process of divorce, squarely on their spouse.

Such interpretations serve, in part, to save face and evoke sympathy. For clients, the divorce lawyer is a stranger whose loyalty cannot automatically be assumed and must to some extent be earned. By projecting blame on their spouse, clients work to reinforce that loyalty, to penetrate the objectivity and reduce the social distance built into the traditional professional relationship. Their vocabulary serves to add sympathy to fees as a way to command their lawyers' energies. The emphasis on fault and blame thus not only has a strategic function in lawyer-client relations, but also provides psychological distance from a failed marriage and contentious divorce proceedings.

This emphasis poses an awkward choice for lawyers. If they were to join with clients in the project of reconstructing the marriage failure and the moral standing of the spouse, they would be dragged into a domain that is, in principle, irrelevant to no-fault divorce, wastes their time, their client's money, and is in fact beyond their expertise. On the other hand, if they directly challenge client characterizations, or dismiss them as legally irrelevant, they risk alienating their clients or deepening client mistrust. Thus, lawyers remain silent in the face of client attacks on the spouse. They refuse to explore the past and to participate in the construction of a shared version of the social history of the marriage. When they do interpret behavior they limit themselves to conduct that they argue is directly relevant to the legal process of divorce, and they stress circumstances and situations that produce common responses rather than intentions or dispositions unique to particular individuals. In this way they deflect what is, for many clients, a strong desire to achieve some moral vindication, even in a no-fault world (Merry and Silbey, 1984). As John Griffiths argues (1986: 155),

> This contrast suggests that lawyers and clients are in effect largely occupied with two different divorces: lawyers with a legal divorce, clients with a social and emotional divorce. The lawyers orient themselves toward legal norms and institutional practices, the clients toward the social norms of their environment. Clients go to lawyers because it is otherwise impossible to secure a divorce, not because they want to invoke the legal system as a regulatory and conflict-resolving institution. That the law concerns itself with the substance of their relationship is an adventitious circumstance for most divorcing couples . . . .[14]

Lawyers and clients do negotiate about the meaning of the spouse's behavior during the divorce and its effects on strategies and tactics. In this domain asymmetry in power between lawyers and clients is most apparent. By limiting interpretive activity to their area of expertise, lawyers are able to explain the social world through the lens of the legal process. They are able to structure conversation to fit their rational-purposive ideology and to limit the impact of their clients' views of social life.

Just as the reliance of lawyers on situational explanations and their emphasis on the divorce itself as the most relevant situation in explaining behavior validates their implicit claim to expertise and authority, the focus on divorce and its explanatory power brings more of the client's social world within the lawyer's claim to competence. Lawyers can have little insight into the dispositions or character of people with whom they have had little contact; legal training provides no readily recognizable psychological expertise (Simon, 1980). However, knowledge of the divorce process and experience in dealing with people as they experience it is precisely what divorce lawyers are supposed to be able to provide. Lawyers' explanations put a premium on their own strategic judgment, and on deft manipulation of the legal process to minimize the effect of the negative behavioral consequences often associated with marriage failure. Thus, the lawyer's construction of meaning works to justify his authority and invites client dependence.

At the same time, lawyers' refusal to engage with client efforts to give meaning to the past is not without consequences. It often means that clients end up believing that their lawyers do not understand or empathize with them. Furthermore, the negotiation of the meaning of social relations may go far in explaining how contentious and difficult the settlement process becomes (Erlanger et al., 1987; MacDougall, 1984; Mnookin, 1984). Because agreements often require continuing exchanges between the spouses, whether any proposed agreement has a reasonable chance of working, perhaps even whether it can be negotiated at all, depends on the way the divorcing parties view each other. Thus lawyers' reactions to client interpretations are inexorably intertwined with disposition prospects and consequences. If the lawyer does not challenge client attributions of fault and blame, unexamined, uncontradicted characterizations may make it more difficult to persuade clients to rely on future promises of the spouse.[15] While lawyers say that behavior is more influenced by situation than by personality, insisting on that belief in the face of their clients' more personalistic construction of social relations may threaten their relationship; at the same time, ignoring it may threaten their ability to help secure a negotiated or stable outcome.

The meanings constructed and the vocabularies of motive used in lawyer-client interaction in divorce respond to the distinctive characteristics of that social relationship. Lawyers deploy the resources of professional position; they emphasize their experience and the expertise that experience provides as they try to limit involvement in the client's social world. While this limitation gives power to lawyers' interpretations, it cannot guarantee acquiescent clients. By repeatedly expanding the conversational agenda, clients resist their lawyers' efforts to limit the scope of social life relevant to their interaction. As a result, they insure both the fragility of power in lawyer-client relations and the elusiveness that characterizes the meaning-making process. Thus, in divorce as elsewhere, law, and the images of social life with which it is associated, are deeply embedded in an unequal, yet volatile and conflictual, social relationship.

3

Negotiating "Realism" and Responsibility in Lawyer-Client Interactions

In the world of no-fault divorce, the legal process formally has limited functions—dividing assets and future income, fixing custody and visitation, and, occasionally, protecting physical safety and property (Jacob, 1988: 5, 7–8; Weitzman, 1985: chap. 2). Nonetheless, if they are to provide effective representation on each of these issues, lawyers must understand their client's goals, expectations, and objectives (McEwen et al., 1994: 169). But interpreting clients' interests is a known quagmire (Kressel et al., 1978). Clients often do not appear to know what they want, or may not want what they "ought" to want. They seem to change their minds in unpredictable ways, or they may not change their minds when it is, from their lawyer's point of view, strategically wise to do so. Moreover, they may find it difficult to distinguish between lawyers who are trying to impose their own vision and those who are trying to develop a shared set of goals, expectations, and objectives (Simon, 1984).

In this process, lawyers indeed may seek to impose a particular understanding of what is in the client's interest. Or, when it comes to identifying and defining client goals, they may be permissive. That is, while they are intensely concerned that the client adopt what they define as "reasonable" goals (McEwen et al., 1994: 166), within the rather broad parameters of that notion, lawyers may not be directive.[1] But if the meaning of "reasonable" is, in fact, quite open and leaves ample room for negotiation, both lawyers and clients may nevertheless find that what is reasonable is limited by what is legally possible. Within that definition the final "choice" is, at least rhetorically, generally left to the client (for a contrasting view, see Simon, 1991). However, before that choice can be made, considerable energy must be devoted to the construction of the meaning of what is "realistic" in divorce. Defining and identifying "realistic" goals, and orienting and reconciling clients to the world of the legally possible, occur during complex negotiations of meaning in which struggle, if not overt conflict, is frequent.

The mutual construction of such "realism" takes two forms in divorce cases. On the one hand, lawyer and client may, over time, develop a set of goals and expectations that capitalizes on the lawyer's knowledge of the legal world and the client's knowledge of her own social world. The working meaning of "realism" is not dictated by one or the other, but built by them together without the need for either to alter the other's view in many important respects. On the other hand, lawyer and client may not share a common view of what is realistic, and each may seek to advance a particular interpretation (White, 1990). Here, meaning may be as elusive as it is in other areas of the divorce process. Yet the effort to define what is realistic is at the heart of the complex lawyer-client interactions we observed (Mnookin and Kornhauser, 1979). Even if successful, that view is not so concrete and tangible that, once achieved, it can be taken for granted and easily maintained. It is always in danger of slipping away as events from the client's social world intrude into the deliberations, and as lawyer and client together gather information about the goals, expectations, and strategies of their adversaries.

In this chapter we examine how lawyers and clients negotiate the working meaning of "realism" in divorce. We consider, in particular, the strategies and tactics employed as they try to identify and settle on their joint objectives in the legal process of divorce. We also describe strategic and tactical enactments of power as lawyers and clients negotiate about who is going to do what in the case and, through that negotiation, allocate responsibility for the management and progress of the divorce.

In examining the ongoing and fragile negotiations of "realism" and responsibility between lawyers and clients, we focus first on the factors that underlie differences in the vision of both lawyers and clients, and then on the strategies and tactics employed to promote particular versions of reality and particular ideas about responsibility. Clients, of course, have greater difficulty than lawyers in becoming oriented to what is conventionally regarded as legally possible (see Blumberg, 1967; Macaulay, 1979; Mann, 1985). Some of their difficulty is obvious. Often they seem to their lawyers to be emotionally off-balance, angry, depressed, anxious, or agitated. They may appear to have trouble understanding what they are told, believing the information that they get, and focusing on the alternatives that are presented to them (Johnston and Campbell, 1988: chaps. 4–5). They may be impelled to strike at or "pay back" their spouse in ways that alter the posture of the other side and make their goals more difficult to attain.

Second, clients may seem to expect more of the legal system than it can deliver under even the best of circumstances (see Merry, 1990: 179). What lawyers see as "unrealistic" expectations may range from saving the marriage to transforming the spouse, but they are most likely to be centered on financial affairs. Clients tend to reason upward from needs, rather than downward from resources, and they have great difficulty in dealing with the gap between the two. Additionally, clients may be slow to realize that many legal entitlements are not self-executing (Scheingold, 1974: 23). The judge at a hearing on temporary support, for example, may say that the client is entitled to $100 a week, but that does not guarantee that the client will receive anything. Some clients resist accepting their lawyer's definition of what is possible because they cannot believe that the law actually is what it is and because they do not fully understand the costs of achieving their objectives. Vindication, the last dollar of support, meticulous estimates of property value, a neat and precise division of property, a visitation scheme that covers a very wide range of contingencies, and equitable arrangements that govern the future as well as the present may be theoretically possible, but even approximations require extensive services that middle-class clients generally cannot afford.

Lawyers, of course, are less encumbered in developing a view of what is conventionally regarded as legally possible. Nevertheless, it is not all clear sailing for them. Their understandings may be habitual and unreflective; they may uncritically subsume the particular within the general. Moreover, in any particular case, they may face three kinds of information problems. In order to form a view of the legally possible that avoids unreflective categorization of cases, they may need to know things that clients sometimes *cannot* tell them, such as what their goals are, as well as things that clients sometimes *will not* tell them, such as their feelings.[2] In addition, there are things that clients sometimes try to tell lawyers that lawyers do not recognize or understand (Simon, 1991: 221; Alfieri, 1991a: 2123–24; Cunningham, 1989: 2464–65). For example, in a case we discuss in Chapter 5, a female client could not decide whether she wanted to settle or litigate, and could not make the lawyer understand that she had great difficulty in negotiating a settlement with her spouse because she did not feel that she could trust him to fulfill any commitments that he made.

It would, however, be a mistake when thinking about divorce cases to assume that clients are emotional cripples and that the personalities, problems, and politics of lawyers do not color the meaning they assign to realism or their responses to their clients' definitions.[3] In fact, lawyers may not be astute, attentive, or experienced enough to catch the client's message (Alfieri, 1990). In addition, they may be so alienated, overworked, or worn down by practice that they do not have the patience or stamina to negotiate effectively with their clients.

However serious these problems, the problems lawyers encounter as they seek to fit their definition of realism with their client's desires and understandings may be even more serious. Lawyers' abilities to interpret the social world of their clients depend on the raw information they receive from clients, the interpretations that clients present, and the interpretations or reinterpretations that lawyers themselves make. All of these steps are complicated and, as we saw in Chapter 2, pose difficulties for lawyers (Alfieri, 1991a: 2131–45). Occasionally, information is presented without an overt interpretation. For example, a client may simply state, "He did not give me money for tuition." More often, however, the information the client does provide is reconstituted through the client's experience, perception of self, and particular vocabulary of motive into highly interpreted material: "He had no interest at all in furthering my education."

The nature of lawyer-client communication means that lawyers must continually sift through and evaluate the interpretation of the social world presented by the client in order to reconstruct an understanding that they can effectively use in promoting the client's interests (Alfieri, 1991a; Cunningham, 1989: 2482–2483).[4] In this effort they may, from time to time, be assisted by information that comes from other sources, such as opposing counsel or relevant documents. For the most part, however, lawyers must depend on their own experience and judgment.

DEFINING THE LEGALLY POSSIBLE

Lawyers use an array of strategies to try to construct a particular meaning of what is "realistic" and to persuade their clients to adopt a particular definition of what is, in their view, legally possible. Of course, their knowledge of legal rules and process, and the information that they have about specific players, such as other lawyers, judges, and mediators, provide powerful arguments (Wilkins, 1990). In addition to their feel for the legal system and for the dramatis personae, lawyers, particularly specialists in family law, benefit from their experiences in prior cases. Having "heard it all before," they frequently look beyond words and positions articulated to what they believe are more fundamental concerns (Luban, 1981: 454). On the other hand, unless they have been through the process before, clients' only sources of information about the nature and limits of divorce law are their own lawyer and anecdotes related by family and friends.

Lawyers, at least initially, often join with their clients' positions and appear to be sympathetic to their stated goals and objectives. However, they quickly introduce their clients to what they claim is realistic by invoking their own understanding of legal norms and their own expectations about what courts would do were they to go before a judge (Simon, 1991: 214–16). Clients are told that it does not make sense to "insist on something that is far out of line from what a court would do."

In addition, lawyers use delay and circular conversation to convey messages about what is legally possible. They engage in a form of passive resistance, maintaining the form of the agency relationship while subtly altering its substance. Rarely are expectations overtly branded as unrealistic in a judgmental sense; instead, most lawyers patiently, but insistently, remind their clients of the constraints that they claim the law imposes on both of them (Griffiths, 1986: 160).[5]

The behavior of clients mirrors that of their lawyers. Expectations about lawyer performance are generally not made explicit. Clients typically do not specify what they want their lawyers to do or how they want their lawyers to behave (Simon, 1991: 215; White, 1990: 46–48). In fact, one of the chief difficulties lawyers and clients must contend with is their mutual aversion to confrontation. In the face of continued client demands for the "unreasonable," lawyers restate technical or strategic difficulties, try to recast reasonable goals into acceptable outcomes, or simply change the subject. They do not directly tell their clients that they are being unreasonable (Griffiths, 1986: 160).

In the face of lawyers' insistence that they accommodate themselves to the "reality" of what the law allows, clients persist, at least initially, in expounding their needs, explaining their notions of justice, or reiterating their objectives. But generally they do not insist that their lawyer make a particular demand, argue a particular position, or even endorse their view. Where dissatisfaction is great, the usual client response is "exit" rather than "voice" (Hirschman, 1970).

Although defining the legally possible is one of the divorce lawyer's basic devices in efforts to exercise power in lawyer-client interaction, others include rhetorical devices, technical language, and role manipulation. Perhaps proceeding from experience in the law school classroom, lawyers conjure up a "parade of horribles." In this scenario, clients are informed that if they continue to seek one goal or another, they will suffer a series of negative consequences of continuing and mounting severity. Alternatively, lawyers tell stories about other clients who have persisted in similar courses of action, pursued understandable but unrealistic objectives, and suffered disastrous results.

While technical language is rarely used as a strategy to confuse clients or make them feel dependent on professional expertise, clients tell us that it has this effect nonetheless. In addition, some lawyers invest, or try to invest, their views with persuasive authority by puffing up their status in the legal community. They cast themselves as the "dean" of the divorce bar, or as one of its most experienced and astute practitioners, or as an insider with special access to the judge and other functionaries.

Most lawyers keep their clients at a social distance. In California, where approximately 50 percent of the clients in our study consulted a therapist as well as a lawyer during their divorce, lawyers work hard to construct a boundary between legal and social worlds and restrict their efforts to the legal side of divorce while leaving the management of the client's personal difficulties to someone else. The exceptions, however, are striking. One lawyer in Massachusetts routinely engages in behavior common among friends, but atypical in lawyer-client interaction. She reveals extraordinary biographical detail to her clients, talking at length about her own divorce, health, finances, housing, and the eating habits of her children. This lawyer violates the standard normative under- standings concerning appropriate professional distance, becoming friend and therapist as well as legal adviser.[6] These multiple roles enable the lawyer who adopts them to use therapeutic moves and appeals to friendship to shape her clients' definitions of the legally possible and, at the same time, blunt any critique of her performance.

Clients are more limited in the resources that they can mobilize to persuade lawyers to accept their view of what is realistic or possible (Alfieri, 1991b). Their inherent advantage is their knowledge of their spouse and generally superior ability to estimate the spouse's reaction to offers or demands. Lawyers are sensitive to this comparative advan- tage and often try to exploit it. As a lawyer put it in speaking with one of his clients: "That's what I'm inclined to do here, unless you're of the opinion you would rather start at sixty-forty. I mean, you know Joan and you know how she would react." This lawyer seems willing to alter his favored pattern of negotiation—starting with an inflated demand—in the face of the client's superior knowledge. For that instant, the social world of the client, rather than the world of law and legal experience, defines the parameters of the reasonable and the legally possible.

In addition to deploying their knowledge of their own social world, clients frequently assert their views, or resist their lawyers', through rep- etition and denial.[7] Lawyers may talk about the unreasonable or the unobtainable, they may predict this or that outcome, but clients need not, and frequently do not, acquiesce. Rather, clients become quiet or change the subject, only to reintroduce the same topic later. What may seem to the observer to be wasted motion and circularity, may really be a tactic in an ongoing negotiation. Finally, clients on occasion fight back by withholding information, sometimes explicitly, sometimes not (White, 1990: 48–52). They use this tactic when they want to exclude the lawyer from some field of inquiry, often because they consider an issue out of bounds or would be embarrassed by some disclosure (Mar- gulies, 1990).

The negotiation of what will count as realistic between lawyer and client is time-consuming and repetitive, yet still often incomplete or unclear in its results. Whose definition of reality prevails is often impos- sible to determine. Even as decisions are made and documents are filed, how those decisions and documents relate to lawyer-client conver- sations about goals and expectations can be mysterious. It is, however, precisely by attending to this mystery that one can understand the fragility of power and the elusiveness of meaning in their interactions.

ALLOCATING RESPONSIBILITY

Unlike the effort to define reasonable and attainable goals, the task of securing the client's objectives initially appears to be neither opaque nor ambiguous. The steps that must be taken to get on with the case are routine. Particular, well-defined procedural requirements must be satisfied to secure various kinds of court assistance. Knowing and executing the necessary steps are conventionally regarded as the lawyer's responsibility (Rosenthal, 1974: 15).[8] Many involve details of procedure beyond the experience of even the most sophisticated client. Most of the remaining steps involve various kinds of negotiations with the other side. Where the lawyer believes tasks are more easily or more cheaply carried out by the client himself, such an assignment ought to be straightforward. Some activities are clearly the exclusive preserve of the lawyer—preparing the pleadings, conducting hearings and trials, for example. However, other aspects of divorce that could be shared or assigned to the client often are not.

In general, lawyers try to maintain control over negotiations with the other side, except in discussions about personal property. They do this by insisting that these negotiations take place on a lawyer-to-lawyer basis. To lawyers, these professional exchanges are a core element of legal services in divorce, an arena in which their professional experience and competence are more nearly actualized than in helping clients comprehend the legal process or figure out their financial prospects. Nevertheless, some clients, perhaps fearful that their interests will not be adequately represented, want to negotiate directly with their spouse.

But whatever the explicit assignments of responsibility, divorce cases are not self-executing. It is not always clear what needs to be done, who is going to do it, and who is responsible for assuring that it gets done. Either lawyer or client might not take the steps that she ought to take, has agreed to take, or been urged to take. In this context, enactments of power, either in assuming or assigning responsibility, are, like those in the negotiation of the legally possible, often unclear or confused.

One reason legal action in divorce does not proceed in a clear and orderly way is simply that individual and organizational agendas are beyond the control of any single party to the case.[9] However, the divorces that we observed suggest that the fundamental reason cases do not proceed steadily or smoothly is that lawyers and clients on the same side encounter, from each other, various levels of procrastination, vacillation, disapproval, withdrawal, and repression (Binder, Bergman, and Price, 1991: 237–56). These moves involve indirect enactments of power and indirect tactics of resistance (Scott, 1990: 29–33). Rarely do lawyers or clients acknowledge that they are not going to do what they said they would do, or that they are repressing their inclination to say something they are not going to say. The effect of these covert enactments of power becomes manifest only after a price has been paid; these enactments are more powerful on that account (Scott, 1990: 202–03).

One of the surprising aspects of the lawyer-client relationship in divorce proceedings is the rarity of the imperative mode. Put quite starkly, clients almost never say to their lawyers something on the order of, "I am the client, I am paying the bill, now do this."[10] This finding is not a comment about a form of speech. It is not that clients just find a more diplomatic way of issuing a command. Rather, in the face of disagreement, clients do not assert their prerogative to tell the lawyer what to do. Such a finding would not be so remarkable if the professional in question possessed scientific or technological expertise such that a layperson would be out of order were he to issue commands against the professional's technical judgment. However, in the context of divorce, many of the judgments over which conflicts occur do not reflect technical considerations; rather, they are questions of timing, motive, and interpretation for which the lawyer may have no comparative advantage. Indeed, insofar as the resolution of those questions depends upon a feel for the behavior of the spouse, the client's qualifications may well be superior.

Lawyers are no more inclined to command than are their clients (Simon, 1978). Power, if it is to be effectively deployed, must be more subtle and indirect. As a result, lawyers urge, cajole, flatter, use rhetorical tricks, provide unqualified or contingent advice, predict harm, discomfort, frustration, or catastrophe, but they almost never say, "I am the professional, I am the expert, now do this." Furthermore, although lawyers frequently fail to act, they rarely invoke their knowledge and experience as grounds for refusing to act.

The avoidance of imperative modes suggests that the expressive forms used are intuitively sound. Both lawyers and clients apparently recognize that, were they to behave as if they were hierarchically empowered, they would undermine the legitimacy of what is generally considered to be a cooperative enterprise (Simon, 1984: 485). But sound as the conventional forms may be for defining the limits of overt power, an unwillingness to issue commands opens a wide territory for subtle and latent maneuver.

As in many human endeavors in which progress is not externally imposed or organized, procrastination in divorce cases is frequently the weapon of choice.[11] Almost all of the actions that need to be taken to move a case from initiation to conclusion can easily be avoided. Procrastination may occur when neither lawyer nor client does anything, although each thinks that the other is committed to action, and it may occur when the action taken is different from what was agreed upon.

Procrastination's effects may be increased by the haze that eventually settles over the question of who had responsibility in the first place.

Procrastination may be purposeful and self-conscious. It may also be structural, built into the way that lawyers organize their practice. Lawyers in small- and medium-sized firms are extremely reluctant to turn prospective clients away. As a consequence, they frequently order their workloads in some form of queue. In the doctor's office one waits in line to see the doctor. In legal matters, the wait is not to see the lawyer, but once having seen him, to have him attend to your case. The outcome of such a regime is clients who press their lawyers to keep their cases moving, or clients who are frustrated and angry at the lack of progress.

Additionally, lawyers sometimes lose interest in cases, especially when the other side is intransigent about settlement and the client does not have the resources to pay for full-scale adjudication. Just such a stalemate led a California client to tell us:

> I'm hung up over the matter that it's not wound up yet. And nobody is eager to wind it up. They are not concerned about finishing the deal, closing the book. And I just find it really bizarre for lawyers to be like that and let it linger on and on. It's like it's stashed in another pile and I can't figure out why they are not doing anything.

On many occasions, rationalizations for inaction are offered that may simply excuse poor organization, inattention, or bad work habits. Matters do not receive attention because the lawyer alleges that she is concerned about provoking the other side, trying to conserve the client's money, or trying to get the client to take more responsibility for his own life.

Competing loyalties are another reason for procrastination. Blumberg's (1967) well-known article, "The Practice of Law as a Confidence Game," dramatically alerted us to the influence of the work context on lawyer allegiances. But his theory was developed in the organizationally tight confines of a lower criminal court, where defense lawyers are highly dependent on their continuing relations with judges and prosecutors. These kinds of continuing relations are inherently less important in the divorce context. Because divorce lawyers in the sites we studied are most often general practitioners, they practice in many courts and deal with a shifting cast of actors. Nonetheless, many of these lawyers went to great lengths to stay on good terms with the lawyer on the other side, even if this meant not prosecuting their client's case to the extent they had promised (Griffiths, 1986).

However, procrastination can also originate in sound strategy. Lawyers frequently do not do what they have agreed to do, or implied they would do, because they disapprove of their client's agenda, disagree over questions of timing, or are deterred by cost. In these circumstances divorce lawyers are especially affected by their view of their client's emotional situation. Are the client's emotions under control? Is he able to function as a reasonable litigant? Has the psychic divorce kept pace with the legal proceedings, or should the latter be delayed until the client achieves a more stable emotional perspective?[12]

Clients also may have sound reasons to procrastinate. While they frequently do not agree with their lawyers, they may not want to contest an issue with them directly (White, 1990: 45). A client may be in this posture because of information she is unwilling to share with the lawyer, because she may be embarrassed by her own ambivalence, or because she may be inclined to trust her own, rather than her lawyer's, judgment or intuition.[13]

Moving from procrastination to other strategies and tactics in the allocation of responsibility leads, as it were, from the core to the periphery, from routine practice to more exceptional activities. For instance, repression, or the failure to state goals or views of which one is very much aware, occurs from time to time.[14] We encountered vacillation and indecision in three different sets of circumstances: first, when both negotiations and adjudication appeared seriously flawed; second, when either the lawyer or the client viewed the other as unstable or unpredictable; and third, when one or the other apparently lacked the ability to order and rank alternatives. These occasions do not involve overt assertions of power; rather, power drifts or context or personality disables lawyers or their clients from grasping the reins of power.

In the abstract, the lawyers we studied espoused an ideology of shared responsibility (see Simon, 1984: 486–89). They said that they try to divide the labor with their clients such that, once they provide the client with the capacity to understand the technical requirements and the relevant distillation of their professional experience, lawyer and client together can set overall strategy and plan tactical moves. Sometimes behavior conforms to this ideology; most of the time it does not. As one lawyer told us,

> The client seems willing to take my advice. I would say, "We've got an agreement. This is as good as you're going to get in court, and I think it's not worth the risk of going to court." And I think she would say, "Okay, fine." On the other hand, if I said, "Look, I think you can do better in court, and I think it is worth the ordeal, which it will be, to go in there," and I think, "Okay, let's go in there and let the judge decide." She would agree to that, too.

This is not joint consultation. These are the words of an "expert" who assumes his advice will be heeded. This language can be interpreted as a reflection of power derived from professional position, power that lawyers have because they are lawyers. It is, however, unclear what precise claim this lawyer is making—that the client will do as he says because he is a lawyer, or that she will do as he says because, being a lawyer, he has the knowledge and experience to warrant her reliance on him. In either case, the client is on foreign terrain, terrain where the deployment of knowledge and experience may be resisted in various ways. That resistance complicates and enriches enactments of power in lawyer-client relations even as it makes it difficult, for both lawyer and client, to determine who is responsible for what.

In the next section we examine negotiations concerning realism and responsibility within a single case. By attending to a single case, we hope to demonstrate the forms that power and resistance take in lawyer-client interaction, to show how clients remake the advice they receive as they consume professional services, and to illustrate changes over time in the way meanings are constructed and power is enacted.

THE CASE OF THE UNSUPPORTED WIFE

The narrative that follows involves the divorce of Kathy, a client whose case we followed, and Nick, her husband. Kathy retained Wendy, a solo practitioner, and Durr, Wendy's paralegal, to represent her. When our observations began, Kathy had already conferred once each with Wendy and Durr. We observed four conferences between Kathy and Wendy and one between Kathy and Durr. In addition, we conducted five interviews with Kathy and three with Wendy.[15]

Kathy is a housewife and part-time secretary living in California. She had been married for twenty-eight years when Nick, a local government official, initiated divorce proceedings. They had four grown children, one of whom was living at home. Kathy tried for many months, without success, to bring about a reconciliation with Nick.[16] Besides the family house, where Kathy lived throughout the divorce proceedings, the couple's assets consisted of their pensions, modest collections of sculpture and rugs, two small savings accounts, two vehicles, and assorted personal property.

Wendy began her legal career in 1963, a time when women lawyers in her community were rare. Throughout her career she has been primarily involved in family law, first working for the government, then in a firm, and now alone. Although she says she has an unusual understanding of the emotional dimensions of divorce, particularly with respect to women, she is nonetheless ambivalent about this practice:

> I kept getting these family law cases and I really kept fighting it and I really didn't think I wanted to be a family lawyer because it is really a miserable business. But one day I woke up and I thought, "Well, I've been through it myself and I really know what these people are going through and how they are hurting and somebody has to do it."

Wendy believes she has a distinctive way of practicing family law. Her theory is that, in addition to possessing all the expertise of a certified family law specialist, she provides superior service because she can recognize and validate the emotional trauma typically experienced by people in divorce. She is able to provide this service because she had been divorced, because she is a woman and thereby naturally empathizes with the situation of rejected women, and because in Durr she has a superior support structure, available at all hours, willing to listen to anything, and knowledgeable about the intricacies of law enforcement and social service resources.

To illustrate the construction of meaning and the dynamics and trajectories of power in the negotiation of "realism" and responsibility between lawyers and clients, we present this case chronologically, beginning with our first observation.

First Lawyer-Client Conference

The first conference we observed was unusual because of the presence of Nick, who had not yet retained a lawyer. The stated reason for the conference was to discuss the division of marital property. Wendy opens the meeting by asking Nick what his thoughts are concerning the property division: "Did you have a proposal for how you wanted to divide it?" Nick responds in a disarming way:

> To me it's real simple. If she's going to ask for whatever, I'm not contesting anything. I don't care about what happens with that. I've given her the car, half the house, if it ever sells, whatever part of my retirement or whatever part I own, she can have it. I'm not trying to keep anything from her. To me it's simple. Just come up with whatever you feel is right and that's it.

This response is both passive—Nick says he is willing to do whatever Wendy feels is fair—and, at the same time, hostile. He talks about Kathy as if she were not present, and acts as if there really is nothing to discuss; everything is already settled. He appears both in control and ready to settle on whatever basis Wendy proposes.

Wendy appears to accept this pose and moves quickly to discuss how to determine the worth of the assets. She suggests that Nick obtain an evaluation of the pensions. She delegates to Kathy the tasks of determining the value of their life insurance and of finding an appraiser for the sculptures. These tasks are, in her words, "little executory things." Kathy accepts her assignment without comment.

But signs of trouble quickly emerge as Wendy and Nick discuss various items of personal property. While Nick acknowledges that rugs exchanged in barter for his labor during the marriage are community property, he nevertheless feels that he has a privileged claim to them because he had to hold two jobs to obtain them. Before Nick leaves the conference, Wendy reminds him and Kathy of the nature of the process that they are embarking on. "[In] most divorces nowadays," she says, "although there are a lot of emotions involved, and allegations of 'he said' and 'she did,' and things like that, it really comes down to an accounting problem."

We see here the beginning of the negotiation of the meaning of what the legal process of divorce can do for the participants and, at the same time, an instance of the construction of the ideology of separate spheres. The "reality" that Wendy constructs undervalues emotions, although she presents herself as a lawyer who cares, a lawyer who understands the emotional trauma of divorce. Even for a lawyer as emotionally sensitive as Wendy purportedly is, everything must be assigned a value or else it is of no consequence. There is little explicit resistance; neither Nick nor Kathy openly contest the version of legal reality that Wendy presents. Yet as soon as Nick leaves, Wendy predicts that Nick will "collapse" when he realizes the net difference between his and Kathy's pensions, and "scream bloody murder and hit the ceiling" when Kathy and Wendy make a comprehensive property proposal to him. Her warning that the legal process is really about accounting, not emotions, begins to have some bite.

Kathy responds by acknowledging that Nick has a problem with his temper. Yet the conference closes with Kathy defending Nick. She says that Nick is really "a nice man," and she expresses her hope that the divorce process will not "take that away from him." Wendy again tries to introduce a note of "realism" that she claims is based on her experience with the legal process of divorce: "I hope we can do it with a minimum of animosity. But there's bound to be a little resentment." The reality of the divorce process is not just that it is an accounting problem, but that the best that one can hope for is a "minimum of animosity" and "a little resentment." While Kathy says she understands what Wendy is saying, she nonetheless insists that the reality of the legal divorce is not, and will not be, her reality. "I hate it," she says, "I hate the whole thing" (the divorce and the divorce process).

Thus, almost before this case begins, the meaning of realism and responsibility is on the table. In the domain of responsibility, the lawyer tries to get the client and her husband to do the drudge work, ostensibly to save money. In the domain of what is realistic, Nick's feelings about moonlighting, the reality of his hard work—namely, that the first job is to support his family and the second is for himself—are at war with his recognition that the law draws no such distinction. And Wendy warns the pair that they can indulge their emotions as they wish, but in the end emotions must give way to the "accounting problem."

Yet Wendy also recognizes that legal reality does not square easily with the social reality that both Kathy and Nick experience. She knows that displacing emotions is not easy and predicts that Nick's volatility will take over when he comes face to face with the economic reality of divorce.[17] In making this prediction, Wendy claims to know Kathy's social world in a way that Kathy cannot claim to know the legal world that Wendy represents. Thus lawyer and client together paint the picture of a spouse whose first reactions to new developments are likely to be extreme. The client's contribution to this joint effort is based on first-hand experience with her husband's temperament; the lawyer's more cynical and pragmatic view is based on what she has seen in similar cases.

In her final comments about Nick and the divorce process, Kathy resists and distances herself from the adversariness that Wendy represents. Power slips away; shared meaning is elusive. Wendy will not be able to dictate a single, uncomplicated version of reality. Although there is no easy acquiescence, Kathy recognizes that she is now in an alien space where the procedures and traditions that will govern her divorce are not freely chosen. Whatever the possibilities for movement within this space, the legal divorce is legal precisely because it is law's to give. Entering the divorce process, Kathy encounters rules that, while self-evident and taken for granted by others, are not of her own making. She must deal with professionals who have well-established routines, no matter how foreign she finds these routines and no matter how hard she resists. Her freedom of action, though considerable, is constrained. Her resistance, however resourceful, will become meaningful only as a reaction to the hierarchically structured legal world.

First Interview with Client (Four Days after the First Conference)

Kathy speaks easily to us about the breakdown of her marriage. She believes that counseling might have saved her marriage, but says that Nick would not take part. She found out that Nick had filed for divorce only when a friend noticed the announcement in the local newspaper. Nevertheless, she admits that she still "has a glimmer of hope that maybe he will come to his senses." Kathy initially consulted a lawyer (not Wendy) reluctantly:

> *Kathy:* So I went to the lawyer and I waited and waited and waited, and I thought, "Boy, it's sure taking him a long time to do something about this." So I called him one day. Like three months had passed and I thought I surely should have heard something by now. Well, he says: "Oh, I just found this sitting on my desk and the papers were there."
>
> *Interviewer:* You mean he had forgotten completely about the whole thing?
>
> *Kathy:* Yes.

Kathy chooses "exit" (Hirschman, 1970) and switches to Wendy, who has a reputation as "a go-getter" and someone who will "really fight for her clients." Moreover, Wendy makes Durr, a paralegal, available to Kathy, a move that suggests she will not be just another lost file.

This interview provides both a graphic illustration of a failure in responsibility for case progress with the first lawyer, and intimations of difficulties with the current lawyer in defining reality and assigning responsibility. Kathy tells us that she wants to get her "fair share," which to her translates into the house, the opportunity to escape from her dead-end secretarial job, and something to even out their incomes. Yet she has not been asked to make her goals clear to her lawyer.[18] On the other hand, for Kathy, silence may be a kind of power and protection. Unarticulated goals cannot be labeled unreasonable and dismissed.[19]

First Interview with Lawyer (Six Weeks after the First Conference)

To Wendy, gender is the touchstone to tactics and strategy in divorce, and it explains her acute interest in power.

> *Interviewer:* Do you see a difference in your role with women clients?
>
> *Wendy:* Women have a problem. They've been a housewife all these years. When the other attorney starts pushing a woman who's been a housewife for twenty years to go out and get a job, it really angers me. They have to realize that if they were suddenly told they could no longer practice law it would really be just devastating. I'm very protective of these women, especially because I feel they are going to make a life change that is going to affect them the rest of their lives, and, as a result, I want them to take their time. I mean I don't want them making any rash decisions when they are under such an emotional strain. So I will cover for my clients. I will drag. I will delay.

Wendy likes to think of herself as exercising maternal power over, and on behalf of, her clients. She seeks to protect them from aggressive lawyers who underestimate what women go through during a divorce. In addition, by controlling the pace of the divorce, she says that she serves interests that the client, in a rush to closure, does not know she has.

> *Interviewer:* What if a woman is married for twenty years, so she's in her middle forties, and her kids are off in high school?
>
> *Wendy:* The courts here feel she should become a useful, productive member of society. I don't agree with them. I think that a woman who has been a career mother and wife all these years has put in her time. If she had been in the army she'd be retired. But they don't look at it from that standpoint.

At this point the lawyer's view of what is desirable departs from the reality of law itself. Wendy presents herself as powerful because she knows both the reality of the everyday world of law and the reality of the everyday lives of women.

Interviewer: What kind of expectations do these women come to you with?

Wendy: Well, I think most of them see movies or read books where the husband is going to pay for the divorce, and they are going to get alimony and they are going to get the house.

Wendy seeks to empower herself by suggesting sharp distinctions between the "realities" she knows and the world of fiction in which her clients live. Her job is to construct a world of harsh realities in which husbands refuse to pay alimony and houses get sold as just another piece of community property.[20] Here she has struck at the core of the procrastination dilemma. Clients may not be emotionally ready to face what the lawyer sees as legal and economic realities. The supportive lawyer ought then be prepared to "cover, drag, and delay." But for how long? And who is to decide how long is long enough?

While exposing the ambiguous nature of delay, Wendy's actions show the indirect and elusive nature of some enactments of power. Interrogatories had been served and yet she has not looked at them. Have they been ignored as part of a conscious strategy of delay, or have they been shunted aside because of other, more pressing work? Has Wendy told Kathy about the interrogatories? Is this a lawyer's self-protective move, or a deliberate decision to let the client heal emotionally before she is dragged back into the minutiae of the case? Has the lawyer focused on the situation of this client, who has by this time been separated from her husband for nearly three years, or does she assume that all similarly situated middle-aged women should be treated alike? Is this an instance of benevolent maternalism or simple neglect, of an enactment of power or the power of inattention?

Second Interview with Client
(Eleven Weeks after the First Conference)

Kathy begins by saying, "I don't know what's going on. Not a heck of a lot is going on. We're just getting paperwork done." Although the required attention to financial detail was "a pain in the neck, you sure know where you stand when you are finished." When asked about her attitude toward the pace of the case, Kathy said:

> I think I'm reaching a point now where I either want to get it over with or something else better happen. I just can't stand this anymore. I just feel like I'm floating around in space. I don't care if I clean my house. I don't care about anything. I'm not normally like this.

Despite her sense of urgency, Kathy had not said anything to Wendy about "the pace at which things get done." She believes that Nick is also anxious to get the case going, especially because his living conditions are "terrible." Yet at the same time that Kathy wants the marriage to be over, she continues to be upset by its breakup.

> I have a feeling that if we could have had counseling together that this is a marriage that could have been saved because it was a good marriage, it was a strong marriage, and I just feel like God, why are you doing this? But it is a need in Nick. I can really see that. But I haven't changed the way I feel. I really miss him very much. It's [the feeling of rejection] the worst thing I've ever dealt with in my life.

At this point, the social world of the client and the legal world of the lawyer appear to overlap, in terms of determining the client's financial needs. But in the more important matter of the client's emotional posture and whether or not to get on with the case, there does not appear to be any connection between lawyer and client. It is not that the lawyer has prevailed in a contest over timing and progress and is now simply "in charge." Instead, the question of timing and progress is an unexplored, unaddressed irritant—a weakness, not a strength, for a lawyer who imagines herself as mother-protector. Kathy wants to go in two directions at once. The status quo is intolerable. She wants her husband back and she desperately awaits the miracle that will return him to her life. But she fears this will not happen and is consequently resigned to getting on with the case. The problem in constructing a joint reality between lawyer and client is that, while the client tells this all to the interviewer, she fails to tell the lawyer.[21] As a result, the case hardly moves at all.

Third Interview with Client
(Twenty-three Weeks after the First Conference)

In a short interview, Kathy several times expresses her belief that substantial progress should have been made in her case, and disappointment that it had not:

> I expected a lot to happen before I went on vacation, and I thought, "Nothing is happening." So I paid my bill and I went on my vacation and came back and still nothing has happened. I expect it to be final pretty soon or something, but there's been nothing from a lawyer. I really have not talked to those people for a good five months maybe.

Although she still seems worried that progress in the case would carry her further away from her marriage, she is increasingly reconciled to the fact that there is no alternative:

> I don't really want things to get going, I mean I have mixed feelings about the whole thing. But when I talk to my kids, they say, "Mom, just don't hold out any false hopes, so why don't you just get it over with?" And I think, "Okay, they are right. It's time to stop this stuff."

This interview shows that the silence over case progress persists. The client's views are clear to us, if not to the lawyer. She wants to get on with the case unless her husband is coming back, which she understands is not really going to happen. But the lawyer is doing nothing to push the case along.

Kathy avoids confronting the reality of a lawyer who is not paying attention to her case. Instead, in the face of her own inability, or unwillingness, to do more than pay her bill and hope that something will happen, of her inability and unwillingness to enact the power of the principal to command her agent, she acquiesces in the ambiguity of inaction. She is complicit in a process characterized by drift and inaction, by unarticulated assumptions and unclear expectations. Is her case again lost in her lawyer's office, out of sight and off the agenda? Or is Wendy acting on a theory that the best indicator of this type of client's readiness to proceed is when she affirmatively asks the lawyer to get on with it? Either alternative would involve a passive enactment of power by the lawyer: the difference between them is that the first is about responsibility (the lawyer is not doing what the client wants because it does not suit her), the latter about "realism" (the lawyer believes she knows the state a client must be in before progress is feasible and that she knows how to identify it).

Fourth Interview with Client
(Twenty-five Weeks after the First Conference)

This interview occurred in a brief interlude before the second lawyer-client conference. Kathy reports that she and Nick "were never going to be able to talk to each other again if something did not happen pretty fast," so she made an appointment with Wendy. She tells us that she hates the process of haggling over small amounts of money or items of property: "it's just so picky." At this point, the harmony of the earlier conversation between Wendy, Nick, and Kathy has disappeared. As Kathy feared, the divorce process is bringing out the worst in Nick. Legal realities are fast contaminating her social world, and, despite the fact that she is paying the bill, she feels powerless to make things happen with her lawyer.

Second Lawyer-Client Conference
(Twenty-five Weeks after the First Conference)

> *Wendy:* Okay, from what I understand, Kathy, you want to get going on this again.
>
> *Kathy:* I do. Nick is getting to the point where he will hardly talk to me and I don't want that to happen. I still would like to remain friends if we can.

Wendy's opening comment suggests that the client is responsible for the hiatus in case progress and has now decided to get things going again. Since we know that is not the case, Wendy is either smoothly shifting blame for the dead time to Kathy or trying to get a fix on her client's emotional readiness to get on with the case. Yet Kathy chooses not to hear or feel the blame. Her "I do" suggests that she hopes to preserve something from the marriage by moving forward to end it.[22] Her wishes are finally made clear; what had been until now unspoken is finally put into words.

However, the conference still does not overtly grapple with the issue of how to get the case moving. Discussion turns to the net value of the house, the value of other significant items, and the relationship of spousal support to property division.[23] The shift of attention from the status of the case progress to financial detail may be Wendy's way of trying to make progress. She quickly gets to what is for her the heart of the case, namely how Kathy can keep her house. Wendy is not optimistic about the house and is, at one point, rather cavalier in suggesting that Kathy should consider "moving into a mobile home." Given Kathy's age, low income, and skill level, the question of spousal support would seem to be as important as the house, yet it is raised only as an item for future negotiation. Wendy is not ready to confront this issue and Kathy rather passively follows her lawyer's lead.[24] Kathy's fleeting assertion of power is quickly lost in "accounting."

Third Lawyer-Client Conference
(Thirty-one Weeks after the First Conference)

This conference is the defining moment in negotiations over both "realism" and responsibility. It is focused on three questions: who is going to conduct the negotiations; what the lawyer's and client's goals are concerning the house and support; and, if the goals are not clear, how they are to be determined. Kathy begins with a report of her discussions with Nick about the house. She had presented him with four scenarios: (1) sell the house, (2) sell the house in two years when they would be eligible for favorable tax treatment, (3) buy him out, and (4) trade the house for two condos.

After a discussion of all the asset values, Wendy tells Kathy that it would take about $20,000 to buy out Nick's share:

> *Wendy:* I don't know whether you want to tell him, because you seem to be negotiating fine, or I can call his attorney and say, "Well look, we have certain costs of sale and everything when you sell the house. Because you will be selling it eventually. Therefore we figure the net equity is so much, and in adding the items that you should get versus what I should get and everything, I figure that $20,000 is approxi-

mately . . ."—I'll be glad to make a copy of this for you, in fact, so that you can take it along and show him if you wish.

Kathy: Yes. And this way [imagining what she will say to Nick], "You don't have to pay any support."

Wendy: All right. Well, whatever, however you want to do that. But shouldn't you be getting support from him? Are you getting support from him?

Kathy: He's paying the house payment.

Wendy: Well, I think even after you get divorced you are going to need some continued help from him. If he's making the house payment now and you are going to have a $20,000 second to pay on it, to him, how are you going to do that? You know a little practicality around here won't hurt. You've had a long marriage and therefore you are entitled to support and obviously you can't make enough on your own to support yourself and become self-supporting. Now you can rent out rooms, take in laundry, and things like that, but let's look at it from a practical standpoint.

Kathy: No, I threw my iron away.

Wendy: Whatever you take out of this marriage has got to last you the rest of your life. Prince Charming just has not been known to come along and sweep up my clients.

Kathy: There's a lot of frogs out there, though.

Wendy: A lot of toads, even more than frogs. Not only that, but if they sweep you up and take you to the castle it's because they want you to sweep it up. So it is a practical matter that we have to figure out. This is really your best opportunity to keep this one [house] if you can. As you said, you are probably going to have to rent out a room or take a second job, if you want to do that, or turn to robbing banks. Your husband is just going to have to get used to the fact that you are his forever insofar as responsibility for support is concerned. I mean, he may get rid of the body, but he ain't going to get rid of the responsibility. You are going to have to get support from him. You just don't make enough money.

Kathy: He's not going to want to hear that.

Wendy: Well, he's not going to want to hear it because people don't hear what they don't want to hear. But it doesn't work that way. He is stuck with you.

The question of who will do the negotiating surfaces early in this conference. It is rather clear that this lawyer, unlike most, does not want to do it. She compliments Kathy on her performance to date, even though that performance has produced no concrete results. Then she says she could talk to the other lawyer, but in the middle of the imaginary conversation that she would have with the lawyer she switches to the voice of her client—"in adding the items that you should get versus what I should get"—indicating, at least indirectly, that she is not really going to have any such discussion with the other lawyer.

The focus then shifts from the house to support. Kathy does not think that her husband will agree to pay support. Wendy does not accept that picture of the future. Regardless of the disposition of the house, Kathy cannot support herself and should not delude herself that someone ("Prince Charming") is going to come to her rescue. Reality is again juxtaposed with fantasy, the world of the legally possible to the world of fairy tales.

Wendy asserts that the job is to convince Nick that he cannot evade his responsibility simply through denial. Despite the force of both the argument and the language in which it is expressed, this enactment of power misses its mark, is evaded, and is left unaddressed. Kathy does not contradict Wendy on the issue of need, but she never agrees that support is a fixed objective.

In a sense, two static versions of reality are at war with one another. Both Wendy and Kathy agree that Kathy needs support. Kathy does not think that Nick will agree to provide it, but she does not express this view forcefully enough to make her lawyer explain how to go about getting it. Again, no one seems in charge. This case, like most of the cases we observed, does not move in a linear fashion. Important questions are raised, discussed, but then left hanging; positions are advocated to an audience that seems all too able to tune them out.

This condition is most clearly reflected in the discussion concerning the disposition of the house. The conference began with Kathy talking about four different schemes that the client and her husband had discussed. In response, Wendy ultimately presents a series of ten alternatives, some of them intelligible, some of them not.[25]

Those alternatives, however, are neither generated logically from some set of empirical and normative assumptions nor presented all at once; rather, they seem to be the product of Wendy's stream of consciousness engagement with the problems of the house and support. That Kathy, even if she took notes, could keep any of this straight as she set off to deal with her husband, is doubtful. In the middle of her discussion with Wendy she confessed that the conference "gives me ideas, but I get totally confused when I thought I really knew what I was doing. I mean I really thought I had that thing [the house question] wired."

Despite her rather haphazard presentation of alternatives, we see in the following exchanges that Wendy does have a negotiation strategy in mind, however unusual it appears to be.

Wendy: You may need to talk to him some more before you come up with a conclusion and see if he's interested in any of these.

Kathy: That sounds like quite a few alternatives.

Wendy: Quite a shopping list right there that you can go over with him and kick around. Maybe one of these will be acceptable.

Kathy: Yeah, maybe.

Wendy: And, if it is, then we can work things out. Well, anyway, do some talking and see what you come up with. If you want me to step in and talk to the attorney, I think . . .

Kathy: You may have to . . .

Wendy: I'd be glad to.

Kathy: Because, as I say, I'm not that knowledgeable and I just hope that I can . . .

While there is considerable confusion and circularity, there is also some forward movement in this conversation. But it is still not a directed movement, and neither Wendy nor Kathy seems to have the case in hand. Power drifts. Wendy extends a halfhearted offer of help, yet Kathy is reassigned the responsibility to negotiate even as she admits that she is not sure what she is doing. Wendy and Kathy seem to agree that without spousal support Kathy has no income security. But Kathy still does not believe that her husband will agree to provide support. Despite Wendy's pressing concerns about the risks of life without at least the possibility of support, she gives Kathy carte blanche to relinquish such a claim, a remarkable position for a lawyer who, as we will see, believes her professional role is to stiffen the "backbone and spine" of her women clients. This negotiation about the realism of client goals is, from Wendy's perspective, a negative enactment of power: the major theme seems to be that it is the client's life, hers to mess up if she pleases.

Wendy provides virtually no professional contribution, no explicit direction, despite her decades of family law practice. All she can do is list alternatives, as if to say, "Here is a set of outcomes that are technically feasible; see if your husband will buy any of them." Perhaps this is a subtle way to ascertain Nick's opening position, but it sounds more like an invitation to consider anything that he finds acceptable.

Wendy sends Kathy out to negotiate with Nick without any advice about psychology, structure, stakes, moves, tactics, or order of alternatives, and without any background about what a judge would be likely to do if a settlement is not achieved. Moreover, Wendy offers no justification for this assignment of responsibility. Why, the client might wonder, does my lawyer exclude herself from negotiations with the other side?

This phase of the case is difficult to interpret. Have we encountered a lawyer who speaks a politically correct language of "protecting" women, but whose behavior is in fact disorganized and ineffective? Or is she, to the contrary, deftly sending Kathy out to negotiate with Nick, knowing that little will be accomplished, but believing that only these frustrating encounters with him will lead her to redefine their relationship in realistic terms, which then will form the basis for sound negotiations?

What is going on in Wendy's mind, if there is any one authentic version, does not make any difference to our larger point about the nature of power in professional relationships. Whether Wendy is a very poor, or a very crafty, lawyer does not affect the proposition that lawyers and clients are not fully conversant with each other's agendas, that their interactions take the form of negotiations in which meaning is elusive, and that direction and influence flow back and forth between them, and even away from them both.

Fourth Lawyer-Client Conference
(Thirty-seven Weeks after the First Conference)

This conference may be viewed as something of a corrective to the preceding one. Wendy takes a strong position about goals, reinforces her view by describing a court's likely attitude, and establishes a practical plan for conducting the next stage of negotiations. However, because of Wendy's lack of preparation, the conference gets off to a bad start:

> *Wendy:* Okay. Let's see. Where's your file, do I have it here? What are we here for?
>
> *Kathy:* I wish I knew what I was here for.
>
> *Wendy:* You were going to go back and talk to your husband, I believe.
>
> *Kathy:* Yes, I did. He just said anything I wanted to do, do it.
>
> *Wendy:* What can we do? There are several alternatives. I'm trying to remember because this was November 3, so it's been six weeks.
>
> *Kathy:* You mean you can't remember that long?
>
> *Wendy:* I don't understand.
>
> *Kathy:* Gee, I can.

The image in this initial dialogue is not of a lawyer who has taken charge, but rather of one still unable to grasp her client's pressing needs. Those needs are indicated when Kathy says she wishes she knew what she was "here for." Wendy hears that comment as if Kathy had forgotten something, rather than understanding it as a general statement of Kathy's continuing doubts and disorientation. Moreover, Wendy quickly becomes the disoriented one, unable to grasp why the client would care that she remember the earlier meeting.

Subsequently, the conference moves on to review the conversations that Kathy has been having with Nick:

> *Wendy:* And so you haven't told him the sad facts of life, that you are going to have to continue to have money?

Kathy: I have not told him anything like that. I figured the less I said the better.

Wendy: Whether you sell the house or not, you'll probably be entitled to some support. What do you want to do?

Kathy: I don't know what the best thing to do is. I honestly don't. That's where I'm at a total loss. I do not know what the best thing to do is.

For the first time in their interaction, Wendy asks Kathy directly what she wants to do. But Kathy does not respond. Instead she substitutes the question of what is "best" for the question of what she wants. In so doing she seems complicit in the drift that characterizes this case. Her response suggests that any objectives she may want to construct demand knowledge that she does not possess.

In Kathy, Wendy confronts a client unable or unwilling to articulate goals despite the negotiations she has been conducting with her husband for months. Wendy responds by upping the ante concerning the issue of support:

Wendy: Well, it's really your decision because you have to live with it for the rest of your life.

Kathy: I know.

Wendy: If I make that decision and later on you are unhappy about it you are going to say, "Well, why did she choose this road to go?" I think probably, unless you let him know he's going to have to pay support, you may be working on a false assumption. He's going to have to know that whether you keep the house or sell the house or whatever, he's going to have to pay you support.

Kathy: I really wish that I didn't have to take anything.

Wendy: I understand that. But let's be practical. You have all these basic expenses that there is nothing you can do about. You cannot meet them. You cannot make enough money to do so.

Kathy: You know I'm just a wimp.

Wendy: If you were a brain surgeon I'd tell you to tell him to go buzz off and waive it. But you can't do that. You don't make enough money, and I'm really concerned about how are we going to take care of you. You have to have income from him, too. There is just no other way that you are going to get around it.

Once past the formulaic lines about whose decision counts, Wendy goes beyond the "we could do this or we could do that" stance that she took in the previous conference, and insists that the client demand the necessary spousal support. The world of the client's wishes is now vividly contrasted with that of practicality. Wendy insists that the client face a "reality" that, from her lawyer's experience in divorce, she knows best.

As the lawyer becomes more strident, the client seems to lose all decisiveness—she has no idea what to do, and refers to herself as a "wimp." This apparent indecision may reflect resignation rather than weakness, a paralysis induced by knowledge that she will not get what she requires. In Wendy's insistence that there are no alternatives, what might look like a power grab seems more like the hard sell (see Simon, 1991: 217) phrased in a caring language—"how are *we* going to take care of you."

The negotiation concerning goals and their meaning and the allocation of responsibility between Wendy and Kathy takes on new dimensions when recent financial experience is reviewed:

> *Wendy:* So what he's paying you is certainly a fair amount based on his income. But I still think you need more on top of that. Didn't I tell you that you needed a couple of hundred dollars more than he's giving you already? Is he paying the taxes and insurance or are you paying them?
>
> *Kathy:* No, I'm paying it.
>
> *Wendy:* So he's paying about $400 a month.
>
> *Kathy:* Uh-huh.
>
> *Wendy:* That's ridiculous. Here we go again. He should be paying more now.
>
> *Kathy:* I know. I've almost gone through the savings account.
>
> *Wendy:* Why have you let him get away with this all this time?

Conscious or not, Wendy is engaging in classic scapegoating: "Why have you let him get away with this all this time?" Unappealing as this behavior may be, it is a forceful attempt to shake the client out of her reluctance to ask for support. Thus, in negotiating the meaning of the client's post-divorce financial situation, Wendy now appears ready to employ whatever tools it takes to get her message across.

In the following exchange we see one way Wendy tries to do so. This attempt takes form through a juxtaposition of Wendy's self-proclaimed practicality with Kathy's increasing willingness to play the role that Wendy is assigning to her.

> *Wendy:* What do you do if the roof falls down? You have to have a new roof put on.
>
> *Kathy:* I don't know.
>
> *Wendy:* Well, you have to think about this. It's a very practical situation.
>
> *Kathy:* I've never really given much thought to me.
>
> *Wendy:* Well, I understand that and we've already talked about being number five and now you are number one. You really have to start

thinking about what's best for Kathy. What are you going to do? And I'm really awfully concerned.

Kathy: Well, I will, I'll tell him. But, I can hear it now.

Matters of real significance are contained in this brief exchange. Wendy appeals to Kathy to begin to look out for herself. Wendy seems to acknowledge that Kathy's difficulties spring from her view of herself, as well as from simple naiveté about the hard realities of living by herself. Kathy needs help to look out for herself, and if she cannot muster the courage to confront her husband about his responsibilities, her financial future will be bleak.

The client initially resists: she cannot think about the confrontation without cringing. Yet, in the end, she imagines herself doing what Wendy has asked her to do while, in the same instant, fearing Nick's expected outrage. A concrete proposal and a plan for negotiations is then worked out for the first time.

Wendy: What we will give him, no interest, $22,000 payable in five years out of the sale of the house, and it would be secured by a second trust deed on the house. But at least if we make this kind of offer, now, if you like I can instead write a letter to his attorney making this offer. Generally, this is the way people do it, involving the attorney. But I know the two of you have been trying to keep the costs down and have been able to negotiate. So if the two of you can do it, that's just fine.

Kathy: Well, I will go back to him and tell him exactly what we've said here.

Wendy: This way you've at least made an offer, so you've gotten things moving a bit; I mean this thing is really kind of mired down and it's silly for us every six weeks to get together and go over the same figures again and have the same conversation.

Kathy: I know. And I'm such a dunce when it comes to anything like this.

Wendy: Okay, give him a $20,000 note payable in five years, secured, and tell him that you need support of a minimum of $500 a month. It should be more than that. Tell him that I said that's rock bottom, and I'm appalled that you haven't been getting more.

This climactic exchange is both clarifying and confusing. It is clarifying in that the lawyer and client finally have been able to negotiate a proposal and have agreed on a definite plan for its delivery. They have settled on an understanding of what is realistic and a division of responsibility simultaneously. However, the exchange is confusing because they discuss two very different versions of the proposal. The first version includes a $22,000 transfer, to be made from the proceeds of a sale and no support. The second version involves a $20,000 transfer, no sale, and includes support. Kathy says that she can remember "that," but which "that" is she to remember?

The exchange also suggests that Wendy is well aware of both the inefficiency of Kathy's past efforts at negotiations and of the repetitive and circular nature of their exchanges. Thus she acknowledges that it would be routine at this point to send the demand in writing to the other lawyer. But rather than make that effort, she makes only a half-hearted offer to take over the negotiations.

Is Kathy just a helpless victim of a lazy lawyer or, even now, are circularity and repetition her way of exercising power? At some level is she aware that, as long as she keeps the divorce process from reaching closure, the possibility of reconciliation with Nick remains? Who is "using" whom and for what purpose? Is Kathy a passive consumer, or an agent whose apparent passivity produces an intended circularity and repetitiveness that Wendy now recognizes?

At the end of the conference, it is apparent that Kathy is still unconvinced that there will be any spousal support in her future.

> *Wendy:* Once he finds out that you have to get spousal support, he may say "You'll rot in hell before I'll give you a nickel." Then you can tell him, "Well heck, my attorney's heard that one before, umpteen hundred times." But that's not true. You will get money from him. There's just no question.
>
> *Kathy:* I'm sure of that. I mean, I'm sure he's not sure of it.
>
> *Wendy:* Right. But I'm just telling you if we go to court, you are going to get money from him. You will probably get more. He's been getting away with murder and we've been letting him do it, but no more Ms. Nice Guy.

In this exchange, Wendy mobilizes the conventional authorities, "what the court will do" and "what other clients have experienced," in an effort to persuade Kathy to accept her view of reality. She should receive support because a court would grant support; she will regret the day she bargains for privation, as have other women. The client leaves and will talk to her husband—but what will she say? Neither lawyer nor client really know.

Second Interview with Lawyer (Immediately Following the Previous Conference)

The interview focuses both on Wendy's view of Kathy as a negotiator and the court's probable attitude toward support.

Interviewer: Did you expect her, the last time that she talked [to the husband] to say the things that she's now going back to talk to him about?

Wendy: I really figured at that point she would take it to him and we would have it wrapped up. It's not really a terribly satisfactory thing having her negotiate it like this because she is not getting her fair share. And if she had said, "Okay, you can handle it," she'd be getting quite a bit more than she's going to be settling for. If I had it my way, we'd have been in court six months ago with an order to show cause to get a little more spousal support.

Interviewer: Do you think it's possible that she thinks if she lives with this situation and behaves in a nice fashion, that he'll give up the idea of the divorce?

Wendy: No. But I think a lot of women delude themselves into feeling that if they are nice and fair then if they run into financial trouble, their ex-husbands will help them financially. And I try to get across to them that that is not going to happen.

In this conversation, Wendy rationalizes her failure to take charge of the negotiations by portraying herself as the powerless victim of a client who will not let her act: had she been able to act, Kathy would receive more spousal support. But Wendy still refuses to recognize that what Kathy may want from Nick is emotional rather than financial support. The "reality" on which Wendy focuses is not the continuing emotional tie between Kathy and Nick. Instead, Wendy, constructing the ideology of separate spheres, is now in full "accounting" mode.

Interviewer: What do you think a judge's attitude would be about spousal support?

Wendy: There's no question. She's been married to him for a long, long time. He's making much more money than she is. She's established her ability to earn an income and established a need. So there's no question a judge would order her support. And she would easily get $500 a month.

The meaning against which Wendy evaluates the posture of the case is shaped by her view of what the court would do. This places her in the unpleasant position of having to admit that their negotiating strategy is not working. As Wendy puts it, "I just don't think I'm going to get her enough money. But is there ever enough?"

Fifth Interview with Client
(Forty-three Weeks after the First Conference)

Kathy had come to the office to see Durr, but also spoke to us about Nick's response to the support proposal and her reaction to his response.

Kathy: Wendy wanted me to go back and tell him [Nick] that I wanted to stay there two years or something and that I needed *x* dollars a month.

Interviewer: Did he have a specific reaction to that?

Kathy: Do you really want to know what he said?

Interviewer: Yeah, what did he say?

Kathy: He said, "Christ, I'm not going to do that." And I said, "Well, I'm just telling you what the lawyer said."

Kathy's response is as telling as her husband's. She does not argue for support on the merits. She puts all responsibility for the demand on her lawyer. She is not asking for this arrangement that infuriates her husband; she is simply a messenger relaying information from a professional. The understanding that her lawyer thought she had finally negotiated with Kathy was, in Kathy's presentation to Nick, only an expedient, a way to end an unpleasant conversation.[26] That Kathy's social world was highly conflicted was made clear in this interview.

Interviewer: Do you think he is trying to push you to the wall?

Kathy: Well, I don't. I told him one time, I said, "I'm really scared. I am scared because I've been a wife and mother for a heck of a long time and all of a sudden I'm thrust out there." And he's always made fun of my stupid little jobs, as he called them. Now, all of a sudden, my stupid little jobs have got to be my livelihood. And I'm scared. I'm really scared.

One side of Kathy is that she is a vulnerable, untrained worker in a tough job market, with no prospects for improvement and no second line of defense. But despite her worry about the future, Kathy's definitive position seems to be: "You know, I'm not going to ask for the money. I really am not."[27]

Kathy's marriage was eventually dissolved and a settlement agreement incorporated into the judgment one year and seven months after the first conference. She kept the house. Her share of community property was stated to be worth $27,000 more than Nick's. In consideration of Nick's forgoing any claim based on this unequal distribution, Kathy irrevocably waived any claim to spousal support.

Third Interview with Lawyer
(Fourteen Months after Judgment Was Entered)

This interview was, for the most part, devoted to securing background information about Wendy's education, career, and her goals in divorce practice. Her goals have a distinctly therapeutic if not political cast (yet they were hardly apparent in Kathy's case):

Nobody wins. It's not a question of winning. It's how much can you take out with your sanity and dignity intact. I try to encourage women that living well is the best revenge and that they can't look back over their shoulders and worry about what he's doing with whom. They have to go on. And I guess the major satisfaction we've gotten out of it is to see some of these women come in who are just so awful, I mean you have to scoop them up in a basket. I mean, the women who come in here say: "Give him everything. He's going to kill me if I don't." Or the husband tells them, "You are not going to get anything after all because the kids are grown and you don't deserve any support." And who believe their husbands because they have been conditioned to. And how we can bring them in here and they are absolutely spineless creatures that are just spread all over the floor and build them back into something with a spine and a backbone and finally realize, "I'm a human being and I have rights." They learn to stand up for themselves. It really is a real sense of accomplishment.

Wendy sees herself acting for women who have been intimidated or conditioned by their husbands to accept less in divorce than the law would secure for them. However, transmitting technical information about the law to such clients is not enough. Rather, their self-identity must be reconstituted so that they understand that they deserve that to which they are entitled. In the end, Wendy imagines that she produces not only optimal outcomes, she also produces new women. Did she believe that she had wrought this transformation in Kathy's case?

Interviewer: Did you find her an easy client, a hard client, to work with? Sort of typical or not typical?

Wendy: I would say the biggest problem with that case was that it was one of those hurry up and wait. There would be a lot of activity and then there was nothing.

Interviewer: Why do you think that was? Do you think she was ambivalent about the divorce?

Wendy: Yes. I think that they still kind of cared for each other quite a bit and I think that there was a lot of trouble letting go. And a lot of hurt. And I used to hurt her feelings so much because I called her Kitty all the time because she struck me as a Kitty. A very soft person and to me that's a Kitty. And I mean I would often call her Kitty and she would look so crushed—"My own lawyer doesn't even know my name." I do know your name, but you are just a Kitty to me. So I tried to be really careful and call her Kathy. Kathy is harsher and to me she was just such a very sweet person. I really felt very sad about that case because I liked her so much as a person. So it was kind of sad the way it worked out. But I think she was happy with the results in the long run. I get some cases where I just wish they would go away and get somebody else because this is costing them too much for what they are getting.

To remake clients requires powers no divorce lawyer possesses. And

Kathy was by no means remade into a new woman. In fact, Wendy candidly admits to playing on, and compounding, the client's difficulty of self-assertion.

CONCLUSION

The case of the unsupported wife suggests that power in lawyer-client interaction is not the straightforward phenomenon generally depicted in the literature, but a more subtle and complicated construct enacted in often ambiguous and conflicted behavior. Some of the more important respects in which power in lawyer-client relations differs from the conventional picture are that it is enacted through implicit negotiation as well as overt action; that motives, goals, and data are often deliberately concealed; that power can be elusive, even to the point of disappearing; that assertions of power may be resisted openly or covertly (Scott, 1990: 136–38); that the locus and nature of power change over time; and that lawyer-client differences, even on matters of great moment in a client's affairs, rarely result in open confrontation.

In the case of the unsupported wife there were substantial and important changes over time in the construction of meaning and play of power. But those changes were by no means linear. Subjects would appear and disappear quite unpredictably from the negotiating agendas of lawyer and client. Indeed, in some sense Kathy and Wendy traveled along different and separate trajectories throughout the case. Power was enacted and performed, yet it was often difficult to say who, if anyone, was "in charge," or who, if anyone, was directing the case. Power was at once shaped and reshaped, taken and lost, present and absent.

When power is considered to be dynamic and fluid rather than solid, stable, and centralized, the subtle negotiations over what is realistic and who is responsible for what that are seen in the case of the unsupported wife are to be expected. Indeed, comparable negotiations occur in all cases we observed. This view of the nature of power in the professional relationship does not, however, predict two dimensions of lawyer-client interaction that we also observed—the avoidance of confrontation even in the face of disagreement over important issues, and the reliance by clients on exit, rather than confrontation, as a response to dissatisfaction.

Divorce clients are typically the weaker parties in their relationship with their lawyers. The weaker party in a relationship that reflects a major disparity in power does not often directly confront the stronger. Slaves, prisoners, and wives subjected to patriarchal hegemony have realized that effective resistance, even effective symbolic resistance, may have to be indirect, subtle, elusive, and ambiguous (Scott, 1990). In divorce, lawyer and client negotiate meaning, but they do so on uneven terms. We have pointed out the entrenched position of lawyers—their turf, their rules, their vernacular—and the enhanced vulnerability of clients—high stakes, high affect, and inadequate resources. Avoidance and exit become the ultimate recognition of legal hierarchy, the final expression by someone in a structurally inferior position who cannot fight, but will not surrender.

4

Law Talk in the Divorce Lawyer's Office

The negotiation of meaning and the exercise of power in lawyer-client relations occur against a background of legal norms and procedures that, in turn, provide the broad boundaries within which lawyers and clients construct a picture of the legally possible. Those norms and procedures define what will be useful in putting together persuasive legal narratives by establishing what is both relevant and realistic. In the preceding two chapters we have seen how lawyers and clients in divorce cases work within these boundaries to negotiate the meaning of marriage failure, develop explanations for the behavior of people going through divorces, exchange ideas of what is reasonable in terms of expectations and objectives, and decide on a division of responsibility for the management and progress of the client's case. We have seen the importance of what we have called the ideology of separate spheres, in which law is distanced from society and portrayed as a domain of reason and logic.

Yet the nature and meaning of law's norms and procedures as well as the character and motivations of its central actors are themselves neither self-evident, readily apparent, nor fully specified in that ideology. Each has to be interpreted and made concrete in the context of the ongoing interactions of lawyers and clients in specific cases. Lawyers have to construct stories and give examples to explain how law works and why it works as it does. In so doing, they have to translate legal rules into the vernacular and negotiate with their clients an acceptable sense of how those rules apply to the case at hand.

While, in the interpretive tradition, attention has been given to the legal construction of social meanings (Merry, 1990; Yngvesson, 1993), the encoding and decoding of such meanings in judicial doctrine (e.g., Dalton, 1985), and the difficulties lawyers and clients have in making their interpretations comprehensible to each other (Hosticka, 1979; Alfieri, 1991b; Cunningham, 1992), few scholars have focused on the crucial problem of understanding how law itself is made socially meaningful (see Greenhouse, 1986; Engel, 1984; Yngvesson, 1993). Few have examined the way understandings of law are created in and through legal practice.

In that process, lawyers understandably play a major role. Lawyers are important intermediaries between clients and the legal system precisely because of their greater knowledge of and experience with legal norms and procedures (Parsons, 1954). Thus it should not be surprising that in much of their conversations with clients, lawyers provide knowledge of how particular legal processes work and of ways the law might be used in the clients' favor. They place "familiar metaphors of legal procedure . . . in everyday moral and relational contexts . . . in an effort to both make 'common' sense of law and to extend its authority into everyday situations . . ." (Yngvesson, 1993: 71). As a result, they help make legality socially meaningful. They play an important role in shaping mass legal consciousness and in promoting or undermining the sense of legitimacy that the public attaches to legal institutions (see Brandeis, 1933; Shapiro, 1981).[1]

The role of lawyers in making law socially meaningful and in informing citizens about the legal process itself has been an important, complex, and controversial issue in legal ethics. The organized bar has imposed a special ethical obligation on lawyers to respect and encourage respect for the law and existing legal arrangements.[2] As a result, lawyers were traditionally subject to disciplinary proceedings for making derogatory comments[3] about courts, judges, and other lawyers. Recently, however, there has been some relaxation in the official strictures, giving lawyers more leeway in what they may appropriately say about the legal order and its various agents and officials. Disciplinary rule has, with some exceptions, become professional admonition.

Some scholars believe that despite the rarity of disciplinary proceedings against those who criticize legal processes or officials, lawyers generally act as apologists for existing legal arrangements (see Gordon, 1984a).[4] Lawyers' activities, ethics, and understandings of appropriate professional roles are thought to reflect the legitimating assumptions of the legal system. In this view, one would expect lawyers to communicate to their clients a traditional, formalist picture of law—one that differentiates law from power, that emphasizes the determinacy of legal rules, the objectivity of legal decision making, and the fairness of legal judgments.[5] As they participate in the construction of the ideology of separate spheres, lawyers would be expected to translate their abstract association of law with reason and logic into a particularized description of the virtues of legal reasoning and of the actions of particular legal officials.

Such behavior would not only legitimate existing legal arrangements, but would also provide an account of, and a justification for, the professional authority with which lawyers are themselves vested. Given this picture of law, the authority of lawyers would be derived from both their specialized knowledge and their commitment to disinterested client service (Carr-Saunders and Wilson, 1933; Moore, 1970). Legal problems are understood to be technical (Rosenthal, 1974: 7–28), and clients on their own are assumed not to have sufficient knowledge to cope adequately with them (Moore and Tumin, 1949). When lawyers articulate the legitimating assumptions of law, they portray success in the legal system as dependent on expert knowledge and the shrewd application of legal rules. What the client buys when he gets legal help is some of that expert knowledge. In this view, the construction of particular meanings for law is part of the play of power in lawyer-client relations.

Recent critical scholarship starts with a picture quite similar to the one embraced by the organized bar: it assumes that lawyers present and defend a traditional understanding of law when they speak to their clients (Simon, 1984). Critics argue, however, that lawyers should not do so. Instead they want lawyers to help demystify the law by exposing the inconsistency and arbitrariness of legal doctrine to their clients (Kelman, 1987) and, in so doing, to undermine the legitimacy of existing legal arrangements (see Gabel and Harris, 1982–83).[6] They want lawyers to teach clients that rules are used by legal officials as instruments to achieve personal and political purposes or as post hoc rationalizations (Gabel and Harris, 1982–83). Rights and responsibilities cannot be deduced from pre-existing rules because rules are so numerous, complicated, and ambiguous that they can accommodate almost any result.

The replacement of legal formalism with a less rule-centered interpretation of law is part of the effort of critical scholars to reform lawyer-client relations and to provide an alternative to traditional understandings of professionalism and professional power (Gordon and Simon, 1992). Critics assume that undermining formalism will contribute to the reorganization and reorientation of the legal profession and to the diminution of the power of lawyers over their clients. Stripped of the illusion of rule determinacy, clients will demand a more active role in the management of their own legal problems; lawyers will be free to come to terms with the constitutive effects of their activities; and, finally, lawyers and clients working together can break down the artificial boundaries separating law and politics. As Peter Gabel and Paul Harris (1982–83: 376) put it, lawyers should help their clients to "reconceptualize the way the legal system itself is organized."

Such reconceptualization should be possible because conversations between lawyers and clients are frequently about the nature, operation, and efficacy of legal institutions and the characteristics, motivation, and competence of legal actors. They range from perfunctory recitation of rules governing the divorce process to complicated explanations of particular results. While discussions of the legal system—what we call "law talk"—occur throughout lawyer-client interaction in divorce, they are not spread evenly. Law talk tends to occur when prompted by significant events in the course of litigation. It is, in addition, more likely to be initiated by a client inquiry than volunteered by a lawyer. Finally, what is perhaps most striking is the relative uniformity in law talk among the many different kinds of lawyers in our sample. Differences in geography, experience, type of practice, and degree of specialization are not associated with differences in the way law is presented to clients in the divorce lawyer's office.

LAWYERS, CLIENTS, AND THE MEANING OF LAW

We begin our discussion of the ways the meaning of law is constructed in lawyer-client interaction by examining one case, involving a client whom we call Jane, and her husband, Norb. Both were in their late thirties, and they had no children. Their marriage had been stormy, involving both substantial separations and infidelity by the husband. This divorce was Jane's second; there were no children in the first marriage either. She had received extensive psychological counseling prior to and during the case. Both Jane and Norb had graduate degrees and worked full time; financial support was not an issue. They owned a house, bank stocks, several limited partnerships in real estate, his retirement benefits, and personal property. The house was an unconventional building to which the husband was especially attached.

Jane and Norb initially tried to dissolve their marriage by engaging a mediator and did not at that time individually consult lawyers. Their mediator was himself an established divorce lawyer with substantial experience in divorce mediation. At the first substantive session, the mediator stated that he did not think that further progress could be made if both the spouses continued to live together in the house. Although she considered it to be a major sacrifice, Jane volunteered to move out of the house after her husband refused to leave. Thereafter, she visited the house occasionally, primarily to check on plants and pets.

Over time, however, this arrangement upset Norb. Rather than raise the problem at a mediation session, he hired a lawyer (Paul) whom, Jane later said, Norb himself had characterized as "'the meanest son-of-a-bitch in town.'" Subsequently, Norb and his lawyer secured an ex parte order restraining Jane from entering the property at any time for any reason. The restraining order ended any prospects for mediation and Jane, on the advice of the mediator and another lawyer, hired Peter.[7]

Subsequently, a hearing about the propriety of the ex parte order was held by a second judge. The issues at this hearing were whether the order should be governed by a general or a divorce-specific injunction statute, what status quo the order was intended to maintain, and whether Norb's attempt to secure the order violated a moral obligation undertaken when the client agreed to move out of the house. The second judge decided against Jane on the first two issues, but left consideration of the bad faith question open to further argument. The client's therapist (Irene) attended the hearing and the lawyer-client conference that immediately followed. At that conference the therapist stressed that contesting the restraining order further might not be in Jane's long-term interest even if it corrected a present legal wrong.

In this case Peter described and interpreted the legal process of divorce largely in response to questions or remarks by Jane. In many of their conferences she asked for explanations of some aspect of the legal system's procedures or rules. While most of her questions concerned the details of her own case, several were general. Thus, she invited Peter to explain the way that the legal process operates as well as to justify its operation in her case. His explanations were interspersed in the discussion of major substantive issues, particularly concerning what to do about the restraining order and how to proceed with settlement negotiations:

> *Jane:* How often does a case like this come along—a restraining order of this nature?
>
> *Peter:* Very common.
>
> *Jane:* It's a very common thing. So how many other people are getting the same kind of treatment I am? With what, I presume, is very sloppily handled orders that are passed out.
>
> *Peter:* I did talk to someone in the know—I won't go any further than that—who said that this one could have been signed purely by accident. I mean, that the judge could have—if he looked at it now—said, "I would not sign that," and it could have been signed by accident. I said, "Well, then how does that happen?" And he said, "You've got all this stuff going; you come back to your office, and there's a stack of documents that need signatures. You can do one of two things: you can postpone signing them until you have time, but then it may be the end of the day; the clerk's office is closing, and people who really need this stuff aren't going to get the orders. There's someone else that needs your attention, so you go through them, and one of the main things you look for is the law firm or lawyer who is proposing them. And you tend to rely on them."

In this exchange Jane expressed her own disappointment with the legal process, characterizing it as "sloppy." Instead of defending it or providing a limiting interpretation, Peter reinforced her disappointment. He stated that a legal order of immense consequence to Jane may have been handled in a way that in several respects is inconsistent with the ideology of separate spheres, in which law is presented as a rational system: it may, Peter speculates, have been signed "purely by accident." Moreover, he claimed that he received this information from "someone in the know," someone he refuses to identify. By this refusal, he implied that the information was given improperly, in breach of confidence.

Furthermore, Peter's description of how judges handle court orders suggests a high level of inattention and routinization, rather than an exercise in reason and logic. Judges sign orders without reading them to satisfy "people who really need this stuff." While the judge is said to ignore the substance of the order, he does pay attention to the lawyer or law firm who requests it. The legal process is thereby portrayed as responding more to reputation than to substantive merit. Thus, Jane is introduced to a system that is as hurried, routinized, personalistic, and accident-prone as the social world from which it claims to be distinct and which it seeks to regulate.

Throughout this case, the theme of the importance of insider status and access within the local legal system is reinforced by Peter's references to his personal situation, including his close ties to the local district attorney:

> I just came back from lunch with the district attorney. And, of course, the question might be: "How often does this happen?" And I'll say, "With some degree of regularity." And someone might say, "Who else do you guys eat with when you meet?" And I'll say, "Nobody."

He then reminded Jane that on occasion he serves as judge pro tem in divorce cases. Jane responded by inquiring about a case that she had observed earlier:

> *Jane:* How did you decide the case of the overextended New Vista attorney?

> *Peter:* No, New Verde attorney, New Beach. The other attorney, the overextended . . .

> *Jane:* I love the Perry Mason titles.

> *Peter:* Oh, let's see. There were four matters. He stipulated to the child custody. I gave the wife all the attorney's fees she asked for and made a notation that the request was less than I knew it cost to prosecute the action. I held him in contempt for not paying the doctors, and . . .

> *Jane:* You didn't put him in jail, I presume.

> *Peter:* No, I didn't put him in jail. I would have if they had asked me to. And the fourth one was the child support. In chambers, they had asked for $275, and I gave them $300. And he wanted to pay what? $25 a month, or something.

> *Jane:* Hard-nosed judge. Whew.

Later Peter says that he knows one of the judges involved in Jane's case well enough to tell him off in private ("I'll tell you when this is over, I'm going to take it to John Hancock and I don't think he'll ever do it again") and that he supported the other's campaign for office. These references suggest that a lawyer's capacity to protect his client's interests depends in part on his special access to the system's functionaries who will react to who he is rather than what he represents.[8]

Moreover, the kind of familiarity with the way the system works that insiders possess is all the more important in divorce cases because the divorce process is extremely difficult to explain even to acute outsiders.

> *Jane:* Tell me just the mechanics of this, Peter. What exactly is an interlocutory?

> *Peter:* You should know. It's your right to know. But whether or not I'm going to be able to explain this to you is questionable. It's sort of simple in practice, but it's very confusing to explain. I've got an awful lot of really smart people who I have represented—who've asked me after the divorce is over, now what the hell was the interlocutory judgment?

The communications about law and the legal system that we have been discussing so far are, for the most part, explicit. The message is in the message. But there is also a way in which the language forms that this lawyer employs to describe the legal process also communicate something about the process itself. Although Peter is articulate and knowledgeable, his reactions to many of Jane's questions are nevertheless circuitous and confusing. Interviews with clients, as well as our own observations of lawyer-client conversations, suggest that Peter's style is quite common. Instead of direct description, lawyers frequently use analogies that seem to obscure more than they reveal. This practice, of course, may be seen as a simple problem of communication. Yet it also suggests that law and legal processes are themselves so dense and erratic that they pose a formidable barrier even to well-educated and intelligent laypeople. An example of this impenetrability is seen when Jane once again presses Peter to explain why the restraining order was imposed and he responds:

> I like Mike Cohen (the judge who imposed the restraining order); I respect him; he's a hard worker; and I think he's very, very honest; I supported him in his campaigns, so on and so forth—but I have had difficulty understanding how he thinks. I have an analogy that I thought of today. While my jury panel was on a break, I went in to watch him, and there was a district attorney that he was questioning. They were going to sentence some guy—it was a probation revocation—they were going to sentence him to county jail. The district attorney had earlier argued that he ought to be sent to the state prison. The judge turns to the district attorney and says, "Well, now, when I send him to county jail, I want to do this, this, this, this, this, but this is my problem; I don't know if I can do this, do this, do this." And the district attorney started to help him solve his problem, then said, "Wait a minute; I don't know what I'm doing. I don't want him to go to county jail; this guy belongs in state prison. You just said you were going to think about sending him to county jail, and now you want me to tell you how to do it; I think you're wrong, and I'm not going to tell you how to do it wrong." Now those weren't his exact words, but then Cohen had some more chin music and then contin-

ued it for another day, so that he could think it over. And he had an excuse. He said, "Well, I need some more evidence on this." And I talked to the district attorney afterward, and I said, "It was so clear to me what was going on. It was as though you, as one side, say, 'Judge, the way I see this case it's a matter of five plus five plus five divided by three equals five. Now, you have made a tentative ruling where you say, five plus five plus five equals fourteen. Now, you want me to tell you how you come up with a right answer after you've made the first false conclusion. And I can't do it.'" And that's what happened.

This answer implies, in its own confusing way, that the restraining order, like the county jail sentence, rested on a "first false conclusion." What that conclusion is, Peter never does say. But in the course of constructing the parallel narrative about the sentencing hearing, he suggests that the mind of the judge is unfathomable, that the judge did not know the limits of his own powers, that the district attorney, at least for a moment, did not know his own interests, and that in the end, time had been wasted pursuing a course of action based on a mistaken premise.

Moving from the restraining order to the question of how a settlement could be reached, Jane asks why her lawyer did not acknowledge to the other side what he had shared with her, namely that a court battle might end in defeat. In response, Peter might simply have said that it is poor strategy in a negotiation to tell the other side that you recognize that you may lose. Instead he says:

I'll explain it in my usual convoluted way, using lots of analogies and examples. When a lawyer writes to an insurance company, representing a person who's been injured in an automobile accident, usually the first demand is somewhat higher than what we actually expect to get out of the case. I always explain that to clients. I explain it very, very carefully. I don't like to write letters of any substance without my client getting a copy of it, and inevitably, I will send a copy of it to my client with another letter explaining, "This is for settlement purposes. Please do not think that your case, which I evaluate at $10,000, is really worth $35,000." And then months later when I finally get the offer to settle for $10,000, I will convey it to my client, and they'll say, "Well, I've been thinking about this, and I think that you're right; it really was worth $35,000." I then am in a terrible position of having to talk my own client down from a number that I created in the first place and that I tried to support and convince them about—of course, they wanted to be convinced, so it was easy. That's the difference between a letter that you send to your adversary and what you communicate to your client. They're two different kinds of communications. The way I evaluate the case is the way I did when Irene was here. This is an objective evaluation for your use, and there is this tension and conflict in every representation. You have hired me to represent your interests. I do that in two fashions. One, I tell you the way I truly see the picture, and then I try to advance your case as aggressively as I can. Sometimes—almost always—those are inconsistent. The actions, the words, and so forth are inconsistent.

Like the example of the county jail sentence Peter used earlier, this example is also drawn from an area of law unrelated to divorce. His point is the hypocrisy of orthodox settlement negotiations. Even if warned, he claims, clients are likely to confuse demands and real values. That is their error because in the legal process words and goals, expressed objectives and real objectives, are usually "inconsistent."

For clients, this is a difficult and disappointing message. They come to the divorce lawyer's office believing in the efficacy of rights in the legal system, only to encounter a process that not only is "inconsistent," but cannot be counted on to protect fundamental rights or deal in a principled way with the important matters that come before it. As Merry (1990: 170) puts it, "Although the consciousness of legal entitlement is pervasive and powerful and draws ordinary people into . . . [the legal process], with experience they reinterpret that entitlement as something to be won with struggle."[9] In divorce cases that experience begins with the construction of the meaning of law that occurs in the lawyer's office.

In his case, Peter provides no reassurance in the face of Jane's surprise and disappointment that her rights are neither absolute nor secure in the legal process.

> *Jane:* I just really cannot quite believe this. Part of me is still incredulous. It's nothing else than property rights. I don't even have the rights of a landlord, to go to a home that I own 50 percent of, to make sure it's not being destroyed. I don't understand that. I always thought that, in some way or another, if one's human rights were not protected, one's property rights were.
>
> *Peter:* No.

As they continue to discuss how the legal system deals with property, Peter repeatedly uses the word "arbitrary" to describe the valuation process:

> Okay, it's $9,500 to $10,200. That would have been probably $1,000 less if the appraisal were three to four months ago because the decline in interest rates has increased the present value of pensions on an actuarial basis. I'm not sure I truly understand why that's true, but it is. And so, in a way, that's an arbitrary value that's been placed, just like these appraisals are arbitrary. You may think of it in terms of $1,250, but if that's what it takes to settle this case, to give up that in an exchange for what are really illusory values on some of this other stuff—on three of the things, the values are really arbitrary: The value of the house, any real property appraisal, is arbitrary; the value on the retirement is definitely arbitrary; and the value on the limited partnerships is very definitely.

Peter reinforces this point about arbitrariness when he expresses his sense that fairness may not even be a goal of the divorce process. For him, the meaning of law is not to be found in equity or justice, and this understanding must be taken into account in planning case strategy. They discuss what they ought to demand in trying to negotiate a settlement:

> *Jane:* That's as much as can be expected, I believe. Am I right in that?
>
> *Peter:* I think so, too. I think that that effects a good settlement. Well, it effects an equal division. I don't know—is a legal settlement a fair settlement? It gets the legal aspects of the case over.

Later in this same conversation the relationship of law to fairness and justice is discussed more explicitly. At that point Jane muses about her goals and describes her expectations about the legal process of divorce.

> I'm a liberal. Right? A liberal's dream is that you will find social justice, and so here was this statement [the lawyer's letter to Norb outlining their position on the illegality of the restraining order] that it was possible to fight injustice, and you were going to protect me from horrible things like judicial abuse. So it was really nice.

To Jane, "justice" demands that the error of the restraining order be righted. For Peter, however, that kind of justice simply gets in the way of what for him is the real business of divorce: to reach a property settlement, not to right wrongs or vindicate justice. There is a particular kind of justice that the law provides, but it is not broad enough to include the kind that Jane seeks. For her, justice requires some compensation, or at least an acknowledgment that she has been treated unjustly. When she finally gets her lawyer to speak in terms of justice, he admits that it cannot be secured through the legal process.

> *Jane:* But as you say, if you want justice in this society, you look somewhere other than the court. I believe that's what you were saying.
>
> *Peter:* Yeah, that's what I said. Ultimate justice, that is.

Legal justice is thus juxtaposed with ultimate justice. The person seeking such a final accounting is clearly out of place in a system that focuses much more narrowly. To fit into the legal system, clients must reduce their conceptions of justice to what the law can provide. But perhaps the language of justice serves, for this client, a purpose that is neither as abstract nor as disinterested as her words suggest. Jane identifies justice solely with the vindication of her own position. She never refers to a more general standard. Thus the failure of law to provide justice is, for her, a failure to validate her position. The language of justice also serves to bolster her image of herself as an innocent, rather gracious, victim of an evil husband and his untrustworthy lawyer.[10] This language serves finally to exert moral pressure on Peter to validate Jane's sense of herself even as he attempts to explain the limits of the legal process.

In total, the meaning of the legal process constructed in this case involves an open acknowledgment of human frailties, contradictions between appearance and reality, carelessness, incoherence, accident, and built-in limitations, all of which seem at odds with the ideological separation of the legal from the social, a separation from which law is said to derive its legitimacy. The meaning constructed is both cynical and realistic.[11] In the remainder of this chapter we illustrate the ways in which this cynical and "realistic" picture appears in other cases.

INTERPRETING THE LEGAL PROCESS OF DIVORCE

How do other lawyers and clients talk about the law, particular laws, or legal processes? What characteristics are attributed to law and the legal system? Before addressing these questions it is important to note that there is a rather regular progression in law talk—a constant narrative structure.

The Significance of Rules

Almost all divorce cases start with the lawyer's brief explanation of divorce procedures as they are laid out in statutes.[12] This law talk is full of explicit references to rules. Lawyers describe the rules that frame the process, establish its limits, and provide alternative routes. However, the written law is only a starting point. It fades rather quickly as the interaction progresses. Descriptions and characterizations of the legal system now occur mainly when clients like Jane ask why a particular result occurred or what results might be predicted. In response to these unsolicited inquiries, lawyers rarely make explicit reference to rules.[13] Rules and their relevance are taken for granted by lawyers who generally act as if clients already shared their empirical understanding of the legal process. As a consequence, at this point in the interaction, lawyers do not take the time to introduce their clients to the subtle manner in which rules permeate the legal process.

Although the trained ear would recognize that their formulations are clearly rooted in an understanding of rules, lawyers often talk about what can or cannot be done, or what is or is not likely to happen, without explicitly noting that their views are shaped by statutes or court decisions. Typical of such implicit rule references is the response of a lawyer to a client's inquiry about what would happen to child support if his income were reduced:

> You should keep in the back of your mind that if your financial situation changes in the future the judgment can be modified. That's not a

problem. It is not etched in stone. Anything to do with a child is always modifiable by the court.

How and why judgments in court "can be modified" is not explained. The client is not told whether that possibility is a result of the ease with which lawyers escape from earlier agreements, or of the sympathy that judges display toward children, or of the rules governing support, custody, and visitation. This failure to identify rules and highlight their relevance prevents clients from having access to law's public discourse and the resources for argument provided by an understanding of rules. In addition, it helps lawyers maintain a monopoly of those resources and focuses client concerns on the professional skills and capacities of their particular lawyer.

Lawyers, in fact, talk to clients in much the same way that they talk to each other.[14] There is no acknowledgment that clients may not already understand the salience of rules. The normal conventions of lawyer-to-lawyer discourse are not translated for clients, and there is no concerted effort to bridge the gap between professional and popular culture.

Even when rules are explicitly noted, there are few references to or discussions of their determinate power. Perhaps not surprisingly, lawyers and clients do not talk about the legal process of divorce as rule-driven or rule-governed. Nor do they usually construct an explicit evaluation of the rules themselves. However, when rules do at times emerge as part of the explicit conversational foreground, they are generally disparaged; contrary to the assumptions of both the organized bar and critical scholars, lawyers rarely defend the rationality, importance, or efficacy of legal rules. They rarely seek to anchor their power in claims to technical, legal knowledge.

As a result, it is common for lawyers to mock rules as irrelevant or useless in governing the behavior of legal officials involved in the divorce process. Rules, according to one California lawyer, do not give "clear-cut answers. If they did we wouldn't even have to be talking." A Massachusetts lawyer spoke more generally about the irrelevance of rules in describing the way the local court system operated: "There really are no rules here, just people, the judge, the lawyers, the litigants." Another maintained that the scheduling of cases reflected the virtually unchecked power of the bailiff:

> When you get heard is up to the court officer. He's the one who controls the docket. They don't have a list prepared and they don't start at the top and work down. They go according to his idea of when people should be heard.

Other lawyers extended the argument about the ambiguity or irrelevance of rules to more important aspects of the legal process of divorce. Several suggested that judges refuse to be guided by rules of evidence and that such rules therefore have no bearing on the way hearings are conducted.[15] In Felica's case (discussed in Chapter 2), her lawyer explained that he would not be able to prevent the opposing spouse from talking about his client's alleged adultery even though such testimony would be technically inadmissible according to the literal rules:

> I think we just have to realize that it is going to come out. We just have to take that as a given. You know, they teach you in law school about how to object to that kind of testimony: "I object, irrelevant," "I object, hearsay." But then when you start to practice you realize that judges, especially in divorce cases, don't pay any attention. They act as if there were no rules of evidence.

Still other lawyers expressed frustration about the ineffectiveness of rules governing filing periods, establishing times in which responsive pleadings are to be submitted, or governing the conduct of discovery. Moreover, statutes concerning property division are, as lawyers tell it, often irrelevant to actual outcomes. Lawyers in both Massachusetts and California regularly criticized judges for failing to pay attention to those statutes or to the case law interpreting them. As one Massachusetts lawyer told her client in a case involving substantial marital property,

> In this state the statute requires judges to consider fifteen separate things, things like how long you were married, what contributions you and Tom made, whether you have good prospects. It is a pretty comprehensive list, but I've never seen a judge make findings on all of those things. They just hear a few and then divide things up. Things generally come out roughly even, but not because the rules require it.

What lawyers do make visible as they respond to their clients' questions are the personalities and dispositions of actors within the legal process and the salience of local norms rather than legal rules. Emphasizing people over rules, law talk acquaints clients with a process in which judges exercise immense discretionary power.[16] The message to the client is that it is the judge, not the rules, that really counts. What the judge will accept, what the judge will do, is the crucial issue in the divorce process.

With respect to property settlements, Massachusetts clients are reminded that since all agreements require judicial approval there is, in effect, "nothing binding about them. The judge will do what he wants with it." Another lawyer explained that in dividing the marital property, "the judge can do as he chooses." Still another lawyer informed his client of what he called the "immense amount of power and authority" that judges exercise and suggested that the particular judge who would be hearing his case would use that power "pretty much as he deems fit."

A second way in which lawyers denigrate rules is by characterizing them as unnecessarily technical. They claim that, as a result, even judges and lawyers frequently do not know what they mean. Still a third criticism of rules focuses on their weakness in guiding or determining behavior outside the legal process. Lawyers construct narratives about the limits of law.[17] They acquaint their clients with the limited efficacy of legal rules and caution them not to rely too heavily on rules or court orders. This is particularly the case when lawyers are trying to discourage their clients from pursuing a certain course of action. Thus, in a California case, the lawyer's response to the client's concerns about her husband's continuing refusal to obey a restraining order issued against him was to stress the futility of going to court to obtain a contempt order:

> *Lawyer:* So what you would like is what? You'd like phone calls if he needs to . . .
>
> *Client:* Limited to the concern of the children or medical bills, and never mind giving me all his heartache trouble.
>
> *Lawyer:* He's in violation of the court order [restricting contact with the spouse], but to take him to court, it can be done, I'm not saying that we won't do it. It's a matter of proving contempt. We can prove it, but then what do you get out of that? You don't get anything.

"You don't get anything" suggests that since rules and orders are not self-executing, they do not necessarily govern behavior or resolve problems. This lawyer is schooling his client in what has been called the "gap" problem, the extremely loose coupling between legal rules and social behavior (Abel, 1973: 184; Sarat, 1985).

The same emphasis on the limited efficacy of rules is conveyed in the following discussion where a Massachusetts lawyer talks to his client about the irrelevance of joint legal custody. The client brings substantial preconceptions about the meaning of joint custody to this exchange. The lawyer's effort is to disabuse him of those preconceptions, to emphasize that what matters is the ongoing relationship between spouses rather than the posture of official arrangements:

> *Client:* The custody order I would like to be requested is joint custody. That means, and correct me if I'm wrong, that I shall be aware and informed, and be able to have input in my daughter's life as well as she would have the right to be aware, informed and have input in my daughter's life whether my daughter is there with her or here with me.
>
> *Lawyer:* There's no such thing as court ordered joint custody. In a realistic sense, real sense of joint custody. You are thinking of it as if there is. Just like it's a court ordered step. You get custody and she has visitation rights. That means definite things. You have the custody and you control the child's life: she becomes a visitor. On joint custody that's something that is worked out between the two individuals who right from the start are able to deal with the child with no major problems. They would deal with the child in a normal manner.

This lawyer's comparison of court orders and what really happens suggests a parallel between the ineffectiveness of rules governing the behavior of those who are part of the legal apparatus—lawyers, court officers, judges—and the limited power of rules to control the behavior of people outside the legal process.[18]

The Critique of Legal Officials

When attention is turned from assessment of rules to evaluation of the behavior of actors in the legal process, the construction of meaning continues in a critical, even cynical, mode. In their characterizations of judges, for example, lawyers tend to think in comparative terms, often noting that different judges react differently to similar combinations of facts and rules. Thus law talk turns discretion into difference. The legal process is said to individualize results, not on the basis of the idiosyncratic fact patterns or the litigants' particular needs, but as a reflection of the propensities of the individual judge. In one case, for example, the lawyer suggested that he might have difficulty getting the judge to accept a particularly favorable division of property. As he explained,

> Some judges wouldn't care. I could do it by representation. Just present the papers to the judge, tell him what we've done, and he'd shake his head and sign an order and we'd be all done. Judge Max doesn't let that happen. Most other judges would not even ask questions other than saying something like "Are you satisfied?" But this judge will very likely want to ask her if she indeed understood the agreement before she signed it and he'll want to run through the thing.

As another lawyer put it, "There are no 'for sures,' you are dealing with the antithesis of science at the other end, with opinion, viewpoint."

While some judges are considered better than others, and better judges are deemed "smart" or "experienced" or "savvy" or "reasonable," the clear tendency of the talk about judges is to call into question their skill, dedication, and concern. In the lawyers' vocabulary, no word is more prominent in describing judges than "arbitrary." Judges are portrayed in ways that suggest that they are capable of making decisions on grounds that have nothing to do with facts or rules. As one Massachusetts lawyer said in explaining to his client what to expect in a hearing, "You have to be careful in terms of how you do certain things because you can really prejudice the judge against you by bringing up certain issues in a certain way."

In another conversation, a lawyer encouraged his client to adopt a particular demeanor in the courtroom:

> *Lawyer:* But you sit there somewhat respectful. Do the same thing in this courtroom, okay? Hands in front of you are just fine, or on the table just fine. I don't care, but don't cross your legs.
>
> *Client:* [Crosses legs.]
>
> *Lawyer:* I asked you not to do that. If you do it I'll probably nudge you

in the shoulder and ask you to stop crossing your legs. Okay? No arms over the back of the chair. Okay?

Client: [Sits up very straight.]

Lawyer: That's all right. You look nice and neat and scared that way, that's okay. But sit up with your arms and hands in front of you; I don't care where they go, but in front of you, and without the crossed legs. Okay? And then one other thing I ask of you. Don't go like this [puts head on his desk], or anything, but don't go like this. Okay? No matter how tired you are tomorrow morning I want you to look pretty alert. It's best if you can just remember to keep your hands on the table or in your lap, and you'll be all set. Okay? Why? Why am I asking you to do this? Only because the judge will be looking at you. Okay? And he's going to make a decision, a fairly important one, and I don't want that decision to be influenced just by the way you sit.

Client: Like, he doesn't care.

Lawyer: Well, he might, if he doesn't like you. Okay? And even if he doesn't like you but you look concerned and you're interested, he'll probably go your way anyway. Judges are people, and we might as well play the odds rather than have some surprises develop just because the judge doesn't like the way you're sitting.

Client: Some would do that?

Lawyer: Yup, some do.

In explaining why he must talk about such things as posture and appearance, this lawyer is guarding against the possibility that the judge's decision may be "influenced just by the way you sit." The client seems surprised, even incredulous, but his incredulity does not seem to disturb his lawyer who uses it as an opportunity to reinforce the story he is telling.

While this is an extreme case, law talk is peppered with references to extralegal factors that influence judges, including their backgrounds and experiences. Thus one lawyer cautioned a female client that her chances of arranging joint custody for her child were not great because

> [j]udges don't have a real good sense of what to do about this. It is a very male-dominated view, because most of the judges are in their forties and fifties or over. In their day, when they were practicing lawyers, you either get custody or you don't. So they don't quite know what to do with joint custody.

While judges are influenced by minute details of client dress and behavior in the courtroom, they are also alleged to be incapable of grasping the nuances and subtleties of legal arguments, uninterested in the details of particular cases, and inclined to act in ways that make their decisions difficult to understand. As one Massachusetts lawyer said in explaining a judge's ruling:

I don't think he's totally oblivious to some of the more obvious things. The more subtle things I'm not sure he's catching on to. And he's not exercising his authority to allow us to delve into a lot of the more subtle things. Perhaps the judge doesn't want to rule on the motion for sanctions because he wants you to get your evidence. He wants to hear enough so that he can grant you your divorce. There is the possibility that he can see at least the obvious things down below him and those are enough for him. And that he doesn't care about the subtleties and that those things that are so obvious to him are all he needs. He wants to give you what we want to obtain. Now that's a possibility, and we shouldn't discount it yet. However, as much as I hope and pray that that's just what he's doing I'm not all that optimistic on it either. And I wouldn't guess that he was doing that based on his reputation. Based on that reputation I have my doubts that he is that bright, that he's that aware of what's going on. But if he is, we should be aware that he might be.

This lawyer's critique is enhanced by the rhetorical play on the words obvious and oblivious. At the same time, the general criticism is softened by the suggestion that the judge's limitations may work, in this case, to the client's advantage.

In other cases, judges are said to lack the requisite qualifications or knowledge to make the decisions that the law requires them to make. As one California lawyer put it in explaining why he was not optimistic about a favorable ruling on a complicated property issue, "You've got a judge with a 110 IQ who is sitting there, and he says, 'Hey, I don't want to hear all the goddamned complications. Let's do it the simplest way.'" Or as another lawyer suggested:

> Here's the problem. What they really ought to do in domestic law is every judge who hears domestic law ought to have, literally a CPA, or somebody familiar with financial data, prepare for him or her something before the case to say somehow there is magic going on here. Judges don't think even logically to say, "Where's the money going to come from?"

However, criticism of judges does not end with issues of competence and qualification; it also includes issues of motivation, sensitivity, and concern. Many judges are said to be lazy, insensitive, concerned more with their own convenience than with the issues, and generally uninterested in "justice." As one lawyer put it, they "don't want to make tough decisions." The talk of this and other lawyers indicates that the ease of making decisions is a major influence on the judiciary.[19] It suggests that the inattentiveness, insensitivity, and incompetence of judges must be taken into account in deciding how to process cases.

These explanations describe the legal system as idiosyncratic and personalistic. The value of lawyers, and hence their claims to power in relation to their clients, is rooted in a kind of insider knowledge that is unavailable even to well-educated, well-read clients. Such interpretations suggest that the skilled lawyer is someone who knows the back corridors of legal institutions, the personalities of judges, and how to present client desires in such a way as to appeal to the judges' proclivities. They highlight a "private knowledge" the full details of which cannot be shared with clients, and, at the same time, serve to shift responsibility for bad results from lawyers to powerful and unapproachable legal authorities. This dimension of lawyers' power is ironically rooted in demystification. But power grounded in such knowledge seems fragile and fleeting. Instead of the solidity of technical, expert knowledge of august, carefully worked out, timeless rules, divorce lawyers can claim no more than a studied familiarity with a set of institutions and practices that inspire fear rather than awe and bewilderment rather than respect.

When attention is turned to interpreting and explaining the behavior of other lawyers, the most generous characterizations describe those lawyers as "reasonable." The comment of a California lawyer was typical:

> It's a problem. But, he [the client's spouse] has to deal with Joe Jordan, too, and he has to deal with him on a personal basis and he can change attorneys, but Joe Jordan is a reasonable person. I'm glad he chose him, frankly. Because there are other attorneys I would rather he not have who would go ahead and tell him to do these things. But I think Joe Jordan is reasonable and I hope he can give him a lecture and really tell him about contempt.

Opposed to the reasonable lawyer is, among others, the "hypothetical maniac." According to one California lawyer, such legal mania tempts all lawyers, though only a few succumb:

> And he may say, "Well, what's a little leak in a roof," and then all of a sudden if it gets out of hand you've got to go to a judge to determine what is a little leak in the roof. The real core of all these things is you can become a hypothetical maniac as I call it. In law school we used to laugh because there was always a guy in the back who would raise his hand and say, "Now what if the person was a diabetic and crossed the street and a hemophiliac was coming left, but the hemophiliac belonged to a club"; and you sit in your chair and think, "My God, this guy's a maniac in the back row." Well unfortunately in the practice of law you are guarding yourself from malpractice and you are also thinking, "My God, the one time I don't alert somebody she's going to walk out the door and it's going to happen." And it happens just enough to make you real sensitive. So, what I think lawyers would be better off doing is telling the client about the probability scale. If there was some way of telling them, "Hopefully this won't be a problem, hopefully your roof won't blow off."

In still other cases, lawyers affirm and further unravel the dangers of dealing with certain lawyers who are excessively preoccupied with "technical" matters:

What your husband's lawyer has just done—it's a technical point and I am absolutely right; there's no issue on it; in fact, it's never come up before because no one would ever question it. What they've done is, in the midst of negotiation, gone off to the side and have your husband's lawyer telling him something which he then tells you, which then would jeopardize any of this. In other words, the lawyer—your husband's lawyer—didn't even have to tell him. It's nothing in which there are decisions to be made.

The message is that clients are not well served by lawyers who alert them to every possible eventuality no matter how remote.[20] To do so only makes negotiations more difficult and increases the probability of a contested hearing.

Political agendas are also alleged to lead to unreasonable lawyer behavior. The most commonly expressed criticism of this type targets "feminist" lawyers:

> *Client:* What's Claire's [the wife's lawyer's] track record on these things [willingness to reach negotiated settlements]? What's her normal way of operating on these things?

> *Lawyer:* What I know about Claire is that she can be very reasonable. On the other hand, it is my opinion that her feminism has been distorted in terms of how it relates to divorce law. Therefore, if there's any rhetoric from your wife about what spousal support is supposed to be, Claire will foster and cultivate that, rather than be real with her. Claire is an ardent feminist and often confuses the issues of when to say enough is enough.

The distortion introduced by feminism encourages the wife to ask for more spousal support; to "foster and cultivate" is to convert "rhetoric" into concrete demands. The reasonable lawyer, on the other hand, separates political belief from professional practice (Simon, 1984) and knows when to say "enough is enough."

Other lawyers are even more direct in calling into question the professionalism, integrity, and ethics of their opponents. One of the most dramatic instances of this occurred in a Massachusetts case in which the husband's lawyer was repeatedly frustrated in his efforts to obtain discovery from his client's wife:

> *Client:* He said we'll produce these things in seventy-two hours.

> *Lawyer:* He also defended her. He actually tried to make arguments as to why they weren't answered. All of them, I assure you, counterfeit as they could be. There was nothing of substance to those arguments and I found it most distasteful. And I shouldn't be telling you this I suppose. The ordinary client I wouldn't tell it to, but as far as I'm concerned his arguments are quite distasteful to me as an attorney in my profession.

Later, the same lawyer laments that the actions of the other lawyer are

> . . . Incredible. Whether he's just a plain pain in the ass, or whether
> they have some sexual affinity, which I'm not even intimating,
> whether they have a religious affinity, whether they just like each
> other, whether he just wants to push his client's story whether he
> knows it's true or not, whether he's irresponsible, whether he is some-
> one who will circumvent the law and the rules to obtain any result
> that he can, whether he doesn't even know what he's doing, whatever
> the reasons, the facts are that he's been doing what he's been doing
> and that's what we're dealing with. I think it's a monster.

This lawyer employs powerful, but contradictory, rhetoric. He
acknowledges that lawyers should not criticize other lawyers and should
avoid mudslinging in general, yet he does both at length. He notes that
his adversary's motives are irrelevant to planning case strategy even as
he elaborates various interpretations of those motives. Nowhere does he
consider that the behavior that he finds so frustrating might arise from
responsible professional practice or from a well-intentioned effort to do
justice. The legal process of divorce is presented as a game where rules
are abused and ignored by major participants.

Justice and the Legal Order

How do lawyers and clients talk about the efficiency, fairness, and social
utility of law in general, and about the legal process of divorce in particular? Again one begins by noting the relative absence of positive characterizations. Lawyers, at least in the divorce context, do not defend the
legal order in which they participate as either critical scholars would
predict or the organized bar would prescribe. Instead, law talk suggests
distance between lawyer and legal order, with the former portrayed as
struggling valiantly within the confines of a process that seems neither
equitable nor just.[21] In numerous instances, moreover, lawyers suggest
that their clients are being "victimized" rather than well served by the
legal process. Law talk thus initiates the client into a jaded professional
world, disabused of the illusions of formalism.

Money, clients are advised, is the chief determinant of legal results.
Legal rights are "absolute" to the extent that clients "want to invest the
time, effort, energy, and money" necessary to assert or defend them, but
clients also are often advised that they cannot afford to do so. As a
result, lawyers often suggest that clients should settle for less than the
client initially perceives as fair. As one Massachusetts lawyer explained
to a client in a hotly contested divorce in which the wife's wealthy family
was paying her lawyer:

> I'm not just making this up. I'm telling you very frankly it appears as
> though he's [the wife's lawyer] doing a $10,000 case. That's just the
> way it is. You can't afford a $10,000 case. Can't do it. And that's part of
> the injustice of the American legal system. I'm not going to do as

> much work as he is at the moment. I can't. I'm just not equipped to do it. If you were to give me $10,000 I would drop everything and work forty hours a week, but I can't based on what you can afford.

This lawyer attributes the "injustice" of the "American legal system" to the law's inability to compensate for economic differences. At the same time, he shifts responsibility for any possible failure from his own performance to the client's limited means while he both suggests the wisdom of putting more money into the case and disclaims an interest in having the client do so.

Cost is not the only factor that lawyers point to in their critiques of the legal order. Clients are also introduced to a system in which backlog and delay are pervasive, where rights are eroded by wars of attrition carried out over extended periods of time:

> It is wearing and tearing. Just how much wear and tear can you take? You've seen more than most divorce victims of how the courts work. And so you should have a pretty good idea of what it's going to be like. It's going to be dragged out. After the trial, even if you win, there's going to be a lot of stuff dragged out after that.

The repeated references to a "dragged out" process and to "wear and tear" suggest that the pace of litigation is one of the factors that turns litigants into "victims of how the courts work."

Courts are not the only objects of this criticism. The theme of the needless infliction of distress is found in a Massachusetts lawyer's evaluation of the state legislature, which established a longer waiting period for no-fault than for fault divorces:

> They feel that if you go in and fight that's going to prevent people from going through divorces. They're worried that if you make divorce too easy everybody's going to go through divorce. I don't personally see it that way. I just don't see the need of putting people through the anguish. It's a tough decision, but I think that once people make it they're going to stick with it. I don't think they're really accomplishing what they think they are. They're causing more pain than they should.

A costly, slow, and painful process might be justifiable if it were fair, reliably protected important individual rights, or responded to important human concerns. Law talk is, however, full of doubts about whether the legal process even aims at meeting those goals. Lawyers inform clients about the distance between law and society, not just because of the limited efficacy of legal rules, but because of the law's tightly limited concerns. This indoctrination is especially important because there frequently is a clash between the client's ultimate objectives and the lawyer's description of what the law can actually do; often, the client's agenda is broader than the law's alleged competence.[22] Lawyers construct an ideology of separate spheres by pointing out the limited nature of legal justice and encouraging clients to come to terms with this reality by lowering their expectations and by implicitly directing them to look elsewhere for consolation.

CONCLUSION

The common conversational practice of debunking legal formalism and equity, thereby flattening the ideals of legal justice and fairness, would seem to call into question the very role and authority of divorce lawyers themselves. As clients hear that rules are not central to the divorce process, sooner or later it must dawn on them that the purported technical expertise of lawyers and their presumably sophisticated knowledge of rules are really only of limited value. However, while law talk stresses the peculiar patterns of individual legal actors and relegates rules to the background, it prepares the way for an alternative defense of professional power: one based not on rules but on local knowledge, insider access, connections, and reputation (Blumberg, 1967).

Lawyers suggest that their most important contribution is knowledge of the ropes, not knowledge of the rules;[23] they describe a system that is not bureaucratically rational but is, nonetheless, accessible to its "priests." Lawyers frequently go to great lengths to impress clients with their range of contacts and importance on the local legal scene. Such references take many different forms. One Massachusetts lawyer, trying to reassure his client in a difficult case, noted:

> By the way, the judge has been appointing me on all the guardianship and guardian ad litem cases up here where an attorney is needed from out of town. So maybe that is a sign that he likes me. And maybe that's a sign that he's inclined your way anyway.[24]

While the client's emotions may be said, in the ideology of separate spheres, to have no place in the legal process of divorce, this lawyer suggests that the emotions of legal officials make an important difference in determining how cases are dealt with. Other references to the importance of personal reputation and affective ties are even more blatant:

> Now I think I have a good reputation with the registrar of probate here. Judge Murdoch is married to, no, what am I saying, Judge Murdoch's sister is married to Bob's wife. My God, try again. His sister is Bob's wife. Okay. They talk all the time. Bob likes me very, very much. We get along very, very well. And I have a good reputation in this court and I think it's going to get through to the judge.

It is not reputation in some general sense that counts, but reputation "in this court." This specificity typifies law talk in the divorce lawyer's office; that talk is laced with references to how things are done in particular courts and with comparisons suggesting that no two courts (or even no two judges) operate in the same way. The legal system, thus portrayed, is localized, governed by peculiar and specific practices rather than by universal norms and therefore requires extensive familiarity with the local scene. Both the unrepresented client and the inexperienced lawyer are pictured as being at a real disadvantage.

While creating doubts about the legal process, divorce lawyers give clients reasons to rely on them by emphasizing the importance of their insider status. In this posture, the interests of the professional depart from those of the legal system.

In a legal order whose legitimacy is said to rest on the claims of formalism, procedural justice, and, to a lesser extent, on those of equity, the law talk of the divorce lawyer's office is replete with "rule skepticism" (Frank, 1949). Moreover, while it acknowledges the importance of discretion, and of the particular proclivities of the actors who exercise it, it is highly critical of their motives, capacities, commitments, and concerns. If the presentation of a formalist front, or of a legal system whose officials are fully committed to doing substantive justice, is necessary to legitimate the legal order, then the presentation of the legal process at the street level may work to unwind the bases of legitimation that other levels work to create.[25] While critical scholars are devoted to proving the proposition that legal rules are indeterminate and to enlisting practicing professionals in the project of demystifying and exposing the claims of legal formalism (Singer, 1984), divorce lawyers seem routinely to be engaged in this same project as they counsel clients.[26] In this way law is given meaning and professional power is constructed through the routine, albeit complex, exchanges between lawyers and their clients that accompany the legal process of divorce.

5

From Adversariness to Resolution:
Lawyers, Clients, and the World of Deals

In this chapter we examine the way meanings are constructed and power is exercised as lawyer and client assess the strategies and tactics necessary to move from contention to the resolution of the divorce. Given the portrait of the legal process described in Chapter 4, lawyers and their clients must confront the question of how divorce disputes should be managed. This concern is central in most of the cases that we observed, and it is an issue that may recur as lawyer and client discuss each of the major issues in a divorce case. Generally the question is whether the client should attempt to negotiate a settlement or insist on resolution by a judge. This question is sometimes posed issue by issue and sometimes across many issues.

While, at least at the outset, many clients think of the legal process as an arena for a full adversarial contest, most divorce disputes are not resolved in this manner. Although not all lawyers are equally dedicated to reaching negotiated agreements, most of those we observed advised their clients to try to settle the full range of issues in the case (see also Griffiths, 1986; Erlanger et al., 1987). This advice highlights what Kenneth Kressel (1985: 59) labels a "professional dilemma." As Kressel (1985: 59) explains, "While the official code of conduct prescribes a zealous pursuit of the client's interests, the informal norms and the realities of professional life prompt compromise and cooperation."

This is not to say that these divorces were free of conflict, for the negotiations themselves were generally quite contentious.[1] Although some of the lawyers we observed occasionally advised their clients to ask for more than the client had originally contemplated, or to refuse to concede on a major issue when the client was inclined to do so, most seemed to believe that it is generally better to settle than to contest divorce disputes. Against this backdrop we describe the ways in which lawyers and clients together construct a sense that settlement is the appropriate alternative. We examine the process through which lawyers explain to their clients how settlement works and then persuade them of the wisdom of negotiating a resolution of their cases rather than going to trial.

As elsewhere, the construction of meaning and the exercise of power in settlement are neither linear and definite, nor easy to identify. Clients often resist the pro-settlement message of their lawyers and deploy various tactics of resistance to keep alive the possibility of contested hearings or trials. Thus the selling of settlement is a risky business for lawyers. Lawyers worry that as they advise clients to negotiate, compromise, and settle they will be seen as selling out rather than providing zealous advocacy. Craig McEwen et al. (1994: 164) argue,

> [A]ttorneys must constantly demonstrate their identification with a client's interests and needs. Lawyers thus may build client trust by accepting and supporting a client's world-view. At the same time, however, lawyers must try to act as objective and skeptical advisors. The skeptic's role often means telling clients things they do not want to hear and urging compromise, thus placing in jeopardy the clients' trust in them as vigorous allies.

In their interactions with clients divorce lawyers try to manage that risk in two ways: first, by stressing that the ultimate decision about, and responsibility for, settlement rests with the client; and, second, by describing negotiation as an adversarial process in which lawyers look for an edge and advance their clients' interests even as they seek a consensual outcome. Even in the search for consensus, law is made meaningful as an arena where advantage rather than equity, opportunism rather than fairness, is the order of the day. Thus settlement is cast as a different kind of combat, but as combat nonetheless. Settlement is presented as a search for advantage unencumbered by the formality and rigidity of adjudication. In this presentation, the legal process seems continuous with, rather than distinct from, the social world. As a result, the meanings constructed in the divorce lawyer's office exist in tension; contradictory messages exist side by side, fostering ambiguity rather than clarity, elusiveness rather than solidity.

Settlement is, of course, pervasive in both criminal and civil justice (Mather, 1979; Feeley, 1979; Kritzer, 1990). Most litigated cases are processed without contested hearings on ultimate issues. Thus negotiated settlement is the norm against which contested hearings can be seen as a deviation (Melli et al., 1988). However, despite its relative rarity, formal adjudication is quite significant. It is the prospect and anticipation of what judges or juries would do were cases tried that provide the impetus for settlement activity both before and after cases have been formally filed in court (Ross, 1970; Sudnow, 1965). Efforts to resolve disputes without adjudication are said to take the form of "bargaining in the shadow of the law" (Mnookin and Kornhauser, 1979). So common is negotiated settlement that

[o]n the contemporary American legal scene the negotiation of disputes is not an alternative to litigation. It is only a slight exaggeration
to say that it is litigation. There are not two distinct processes, negotiation and litigation; there is a single process of disputing in the vicinity
of official tribunals that we might call LITIGOTIATION, that is,
the strategic pursuit of a settlement through mobilizing the court
process . . . . Galanter, 1984)

While the pervasiveness of settlement is widely recognized, the
meaning of settlement for lawyers and their clients, and the meaning of
law that is constructed during the settlement process, seem far less
clear. In criminal courts, cases are settled through negotiations in which
defendants are offered consideration in the form of reduced charges or
sentences in return for pleas of guilty. That the overwhelming majority
of criminal defendants accept such offers and waive their constitutional
right to trial by jury may reflect the fact that most of those who are formally charged are factually guilty (Feeley, 1979), or that the costs in
terms of ultimate penalties are generally less than the opportunity costs
imposed by the process of adjudication itself (Feeley, 1979). In civil
cases the prevailing image is of a complex bargaining process in which
parties make offers and respond to demands in an incremental and
sequential effort to identify a number, a settlement figure, that falls
within each party's range of acceptability (Priest and Klein, 1984; Posner, 1973). This image suggests that the bargaining process involves a
rational, cost-benefit calculation of the conditional probability of success at trial, in which transaction and information costs may play a key
part in explaining whether cases settle (Priest and Klein, 1984).

Scholars have tried to understand what accounts for the "selection"
of cases for trial or the "survival" of disputes in the litigation process by
examining a variety of factors that might affect such calculations (Grossman, et al., 1981). Galanter reviews such efforts and identifies several of
the most prominent explanations (Galanter, 1987: 202–3). He suggests
that efforts to reach negotiated settlements may fail (1) where the "settlement value" is insufficient; (2) where one of the parties is trying to
show some external audience that "no stone has been left unturned"
(Galanter, 1987: 202–3); (3) where the case is so complex and the likely
adjudicated outcome so "indeterminate" that parties can find no zone
of agreement; (4) where one of the parties is concerned about the
impact of a present settlement on bargaining credibility in future cases;
or (5) where a party "wants to adjudicate in order to affect the state of
the law" (Galanter, 1987: 202–3).

In most litigated cases lawyers play the major roles in communicating, bargaining, and working out negotiated settlements.[2] The nature of
such settlements is often affected, if not determined, by their own interests, relations, or positions within bureaucratic organizations (Eisenstein
and Jacob, 1977; Utz, 1978; Nardulli, 1978). Moreover, there is some evi-

dence that settlements are influenced in important ways by the relative experience or expertise of the lawyers representing the adverse parties (Genn, 1987), by the mix of attorney negotiating styles (Williams, 1983), and by the compatibility of lawyer goals and role orientations (O'Gorman, 1963; Kressel et al., 1983). In these efforts to understand why cases do or do not settle, little attention has been paid to the consequences of lawyer-client interaction in constructing the meaning of settlement and in making it the preferred alternative (for exceptions, see Kritzer, 1990; McEwen et al., 1994).

In order for settlements to be reached, clients must authorize their lawyers to enter into negotiations and must sign off on the agreements that are concluded on their behalf. Some suggest that client acquiescence is obtained through a carefully orchestrated process of manipulation in which lawyers conspire against their clients to get them to accept an agreement that they neither initially wanted nor subsequently believe to be fair (Blumberg, 1967). Others suggest that lawyers and their clients often have conflicting interests in the settlement process, with lawyers, especially those working on a contingent fee basis, seeking quick settlements that may maximize the return on their time but result in a lower settlement than clients might otherwise have obtained (Rosenthal, 1974; Johnson, 1980–81; Rowe, 1984; Kritzer, 1991, chap. 5). The prevailing image is of the lawyer selling settlement to reluctant clients who would prefer to seek vindication of rights or who want to use the legal process as a tool of vengeance and retribution (Leff, 1970).

This chapter examines negotiations between lawyers and clients about the settlement process. It describes and analyzes the way lawyers introduce their clients to the "world of deals" (Galanter, 1984) that comprises the litigation process, as well as the way clients react to that introduction. It examines the construction of legal meaning in the course of discussions of the strategy and tactics of case disposition. What reasons do lawyers give for preferring negotiated resolution to adjudication? How do clients understand and respond to these reasons? What, in their view, is a desirable settlement? To what extent are desirable settlements also interpreted as fair? What are the problems and pitfalls of the negotiation process? Are clients reluctantly drawn into agreements they would otherwise prefer not to make?

The question of disposition, of how the case will be resolved and of the procedural mechanisms and strategies for reaching a satisfactory result, was raised early in most of the cases we studied. It was, in addition, a recurrent theme throughout conversations between lawyers and clients. In those conversations the lawyers' message is overwhelmingly pro-settlement. They consistently emphasize the advantages of informal as opposed to formal resolution. Adjudication is presented in an unfavorable light, as an alternative to be avoided (see Chapter 4). Thus the image of the lawyer as "shark," eagerly stirring up trouble, fanning the flames of contention, does not describe the lawyers we observed (compare O'Gorman, 1963).[3] This is not to say that lawyers are uniformly cooperative or that they advocate meekness and acquiescence or "peace" at any price. Such is not the case. Negotiations in the cases we studied were usually adversarial and were described by lawyers as a process of "hard bargaining" (Genn, 1987).

The pro-settlement message is one that clients are quite prepared to hear. Most, but not all, of the clients we observed either were initially disposed to accept a negotiated solution or were quickly won over. There were, however, a few cases in which clients initially insisted on a strategy of total victory, of vindication at any price. In those cases lawyers appealed to the client's long-term self-interest or to their desire to reach final closure as a way of making settlement seem more acceptable. In their efforts to move clients toward settlement, especially in those cases where clients were most reluctant, the lawyers we observed tried to walk a fine line. Their advocacy of negotiations, with the resulting necessity of concession, ran the risk of provoking in their clients the perception of blurred loyalties. Lawyers were very aware of the possibility that clients might question their loyalties, and, as a result, they emphasized that negotiations would be quite contentious (McEwen et al., 1994: 157). They portrayed their role in those negotiations as one of zealous advocacy for their client's interests, while emphasizing that settlement was, all things considered, the best route to realize those interests.

WHY SETTLE?

Efforts to construct the meaning of settlement generally begin with lawyers' arguments about and descriptions of its advantages and benefits. Lawyers rarely wait to be asked about strategies and methods of case disposition. They introduce the subject themselves as they discuss how to deal with particular issues or formulate general strategy. Such discussions often involve rather direct contrasts between negotiation and adjudication.

As we saw in Chapter 4, the case of Jane and Norb involved just those kinds of contrasts. In that case two issues seemed to preoccupy both lawyer and client: whether to ignore or contest the restraining order and what position to take concerning disposition of the family residence. Much of their interaction was devoted to discussing the restraining order—its origins, morality, and legality; the prospects for dissolving it; the lawyer's stake in contesting it; and the client's emotional reaction to it. Substantively the order was not as important as the house, which received much less attention and generated much less controversy. Both issues, however, forced the lawyer and client to decide whether they would retain control of the case by engaging in negotiations or cede control to the court for hearing and decision. Peter definitely favored negotiations:[4]

> What I would like your permission to do then is to meet with Foster [the other lawyer], see if I can come up with or negotiate a settlement with him that, before I leave his office or he leaves my office, he says, "We've got something here that I can recommend to my client," and I can say, "I've got something here that I can recommend to my client." My feeling is, Jane, that if we reach that point, both lawyers are prepared to make a recommendation on settlement to their respective clients, if either of the clients, either you or Norb, find something terribly disagreeable with the proposal that the lawyers have come to between themselves, then the case just either can't be settled or it's not ripe for settlement. But we would have given it our best shot. But, as you know, I'm very concerned about wasting a lot of time and energy trying to settle a case where two previous attempts have been dismally unsuccessful.

The major ingredient of the settlement system as described by Peter is the primacy of the lawyers. They produce the deals while the clients are limited to initial instructions and after-the-fact ratification. As McEwen et al. suggest (1994: 165), "Clients are distanced from settlement activities by the reliance on lawyers as intermediaries for exchange and interpretation of information. Frequently, in response to the sense of exclusion, clients demand the time and attention of their lawyers, wondering what has happened or, more likely, not happened and why."

Peter's phrase "we would have given it our best shot" is crucial in expressing both this expectation of reliance and feeling of exclusion. The "we" seems to refer to the lawyers rather than to Peter and Jane. Indeed, lawyer efforts could come to nothing if either client backs out at the last minute. The settlement process as described thus has two dimensions—a lawyer-to-lawyer phase, in which an arrangement is worked out, and a lawyers and clients phase, in which the opposing lawyers join together to sell the deal to their clients. If the clients do not accept the settlement package, the only alternative is to go to trial. Furthermore, if the professionals are content with the agreement they have devised, dissatisfied clients not only have nothing to contribute but also had perhaps better seek psychotherapy. As Peter states:

> And if we have to come down a little bit off the 10 percent to something that is obviously a real good loan—9 percent—a percentage point on a one-year, eighteen-month, $25,000 loan does not make that much difference to you. And that's worth settling the case, and I'll say, "Jane, if we're going to court over what turns out to be one percentage point, go talk to Irene [Jane's therapist] some more." So that's the kind of a package that I see putting together.

Despite her lawyer's enthusiasm, Jane is reluctant to begin settlement negotiations until some attention is paid to the restraining order.

While she acknowledges that she wants a reasonable property settlement, she reminds her lawyer that that is not her exclusive concern. She
resists closure and insists, at least for a moment, on expanding the law's
agenda. In so doing, she contests the rigid separation of economic and
emotional concerns that her lawyer is in the process of constructing:

> Yes, there's no question in my mind that that property settlement is my
> first goal. However, that doesn't mean it's my only goal. It's just my first
> one. And I have done a lot of thinking about this and so it's all run-
> ning around in my head at this point. I've been looking very carefully
> at the parts of me that want to fight and the parts of me that don't
> want to fight. And I'm not sure that any of that ought to get messed up
> in the property settlement.

Peter responds by acknowledging that he considers the restraining
order to be legally wrong and that he believes it could be litigated.
Thus, he confirms his client's position and inclination on legal grounds.
Yet he dissents from her position and opposes her inclination to fight
on other grounds. First, he states that the restraining order, although
legally wrong, is "not necessarily . . . completely wrong" because it
might prevent violence between spouses. This complicated position is a
clear example of a tactic frequently used by lawyers in divorce cases—
the rhetorical "yes . . . but." The lawyers we observed often appeared to
be endorsing the adversarial pursuit of one of the client's objectives
only to remind the client of a variety of negative consequences associated with it. In this way lawyers present themselves as both an ally and
an advisor embracing the wisdom of a long-term perspective (McEwen
et al., 1994: 164).

Second, Jane's lawyer is worried that an effort to fight the restraining order would interfere with the resolution of the case, that is, of the
outstanding property issues. Although Peter considers the restraining
order to be a legal mistake, its effect would end upon final disposition
of the house. In the meantime, his client can either live with the order
or pay for additional hearings. He believes that it would be unwise for
her to fight further not only because the contest would be costly but
also because it would postpone or derail negotiations about the house
and other tangible assets. Thus, when Jane asks whether the issue of the
restraining order has been raised with her husband's lawyer, Peter says:

> Well, I've talked to him. My feelings are still the same. They're very
> strong feelings that what has been done is illegal, that I want to take it
> to the Supreme Court. I told Foster off. I basically told him the con-
> tents of the letter. I said that I think that Judge Cohen is dead wrong,
> and I would very much like to litigate the thing. On the other hand, I
> have to be mindful of what Irene said, which is absolutely correct,
> "Does that move us toward or away from the ultimate goal, which is
> the resolution of the case?"

The lawyer's position in this case can be interpreted as a preference for negotiations over litigation based on his determination that this client has more to lose than gain by fighting the restraining order and also fighting for the house. In this view the lawyer is neutral about settlement in general and is swayed by the cost-benefit calculation of specific cases. Thus there is a conflict between Jane's desire for vindication on what Peter perceives to be a peripheral concern and his interest in reaching a satisfactory disposition on what for him is a much more important issue.

Time and again in our study, we observed lawyers constructing an ideology of separate spheres as they attempted to focus their client's attention on the issues the lawyers thought to be most significant. While the disposition of the house in this case will have long-term consequences for the client, the restraining order, as unjust as Peter understands it to be, is in his view a temporary nuisance. His sense of justice and of the long-term best interests of his client lead him to try to transform this dispute from a battle over the legality and morality of the restraining order to a negotiation over the more tangible issue of the ultimate disposition of the house and other assets, which he believes can and should be settled.

In attempting this transformation, Peter constructs a rhetorical alliance with Jane's therapist: "I agree with Irene that fighting the restraining order is not the best way. It's probably the worst way. Negotiating hopefully is the best way." Peter's reliance on the therapist is noteworthy because it is often assumed that a therapeutic orientation is antithetical to the adversarial inclination of law and the legal profession (Eckhoff, 1966).[5] Yet in this case the lawyer uses the therapist to validate his own position. The legal and therapeutic ideologies seem to him to be compatible; both stress settlement and disvalue formal contests. Perhaps this reflects either a more general erosion of the distinctiveness of the legal form or a convergence of legal and therapeutic models of divorce.[6] However we interpret this observation, it is clear that this lawyer, and most of those we observed, construct an image of the appropriate mode of disposition of a case that is at odds with the conventional view, in which lawyers are alleged to induce competition and hostility, transform noncontentious clients into combatants, and promulgate a "fight theory of justice."

The client's own ambivalence toward settlement continues throughout her interactions with her lawyer. In discussing a letter that Peter had prepared to send to the other lawyer outlining their position on the restraining order, Jane says:

> *Jane:* So it was an important letter, and I didn't realize how much I wanted to continue fighting until I read the first portion of this letter. It kind of let me feel that finally I'd found a knight in shining armor.
>
> *Peter:* Ouch.

The transference reflected in Jane's reference to a "knight in shining armor," a female client's substitution of her male lawyer for her failed husband, may not be unusual in divorce cases, but nowhere in our sample is it as explicit as it is here. A minute later this client substitutes a different metaphor when she asks:

Jane: Are you familiar with Chief Joseph?

Peter: No.

Jane: He was a Nez Perce Indian, and he fought the troops of the U.S. government for years and finally he saw that his whole tribe would be killed off and the land devastated so he put down his weapons. And I think the full quote is something like: "From the time the moon sets, I will fight no more forever." I went away that day, that Monday, feeling that this fight had to end, and that's still what I feel. One of the thoughts I had that afternoon was that—probably it came a lot from what Irene had to say—that I've been arguing with this man for a good many years of my life. First in the living room, then involving family and friends, then involving therapists, and now involving attorneys. How many forums am I going to spend arguing with this person? And I really want the war to end. So that's my basic conflict. I feel I've been treated unjustly. I feel there's a very good case here, but I don't want to fight any more. And that's what this really is about—a continuing war. So a part of me is still very much with Chief Joseph—I don't want to fight any more. There are other and better things to do with this life.

Jane may have to live with her ambivalence, but her lawyer needs a resolution of this issue. Peter seeks this resolution by allying himself with the "don't fight" side of the struggle. Her advocate, her "knight," has thus become the enemy of adversariness. Through him the legal system becomes the champion of settlement. Ironically, the client's ambivalence serves to validate the lawyer's earlier suggestion that he might be wasting his time and her money trying to settle this case because she might refuse at the last minute to agree to a deal.

Jane and Peter reach closure on the fight/settle issue when he again asks whether he has her authority to negotiate on the terms they had discussed and repeats his earlier warning that this is their last chance for a settlement:

Well, we are now coming full circle to where we were this morning, which is fine, which is where we should be. I will make my best effort to effect a settlement with Foster along the lines that you and I have discussed and the specific terms of which I can say to you, Jane, I recommend that you sign this. The decision, of course, is yours. If you don't want to sign it, we're going to go ahead with the litigation on the restraining order and probably a trial. Things can change. We can effect a settlement before the restraining order, which is highly unlikely, or between the time the restraining order issue is resolved and the actual time of trial, maybe there will be another settlement.

I'm not going to suggest or advise, after this attempt, that either one of us put any substantial energy in another try at settlement. I just think it's a waste of time and money.

Peter's reference to "coming full circle" reflects both the centrality of the dispositional question and the amount of time spent talking about issues the lawyer considers to be peripheral. Jane, on the other hand, has aired her ambivalence and resolved to try to end this dispute without a legal contest. Both her ambivalence and her eventual acceptance of settlement are typical of the clients we observed. Having invested the time in letting Jane talk through her reservations, Peter secures what he wanted, both an authorization to negotiate and an agreement on the goals that he will pursue.

Another example of the way lawyers and clients construct the meaning of settlement is provided as a lawyer and client talked about division of personal property; here the lawyer stressed the importance of avoiding a formal, contested hearing by saying,

Whatever arbitration system you choose is better than the judge. I'll tell you what the judges are doing recently. It's garage sale time. You come to them with a list of items and they simply say, I'm holding a garage sale at the house on Saturday; you're in charge.

Lawyers repeatedly suggest that the insensitivity and inattentiveness of judges must be taken into account in deciding how to process cases. Settlement is, in this way, given meaning as the lesser evil, as well as in terms of its own direct benefits. This message is hard for clients to avoid or miss:

Lawyer: The rules are essentially different if you don't involve the court. In court you usually get a much more rigid decision.

Client: And so you're saying, it's really in my best interest to stay away from a trial.

Lawyer: It's in everyone's best interests. It's very costly. The judges are not tolerant of subtleties or innuendoes. All they want is they want you out the door, and the rulings are usually gross. They're gross rulings. They don't consider and factor in the subtleties of what the people are trying to do.

In contrast, negotiated settlement is portrayed, and praised, as an open, flexible process in which clients' individualized needs and desires can be accommodated. The word "creative" is repeatedly invoked by lawyers to characterize the negotiation process. Clients are told that as long as they are resolving their differences through negotiation,

You certainly can come to any agreement that you want. And of course it's preferable to have you decide all these things. All I want you to do is to keep in mind all the things that have to be decided. And not to put yourself into a situation where you're going to be struggling along

for money because you agreed to an amount that's too low. So there
are different kinds of things that can be built in. You can have part of
it be alimony to terminate at a certain time, maybe two years after you
leave law school or something like that. You can have it continue for
some longer period of time. Whatever you think is what you want. The
child support should continue until the child is either eighteen or
until he finishes college.

The idea that clients have a range of options and can agree to whatever they want, that as long as they are negotiating they retain control,
is, in the descriptions presented by lawyers, perhaps the major procedural advantage of the settlement process. Some lawyers seem, in fact,
to get quite carried away as they focus in on that advantage. One California lawyer told his client that "Anything anybody can think up in a
divorce you can do." Another responded to his client's question about
how much control she and her husband would have over the division of
their marital property by saying "complete control." Still another said
that in the settlement process, "we could do anything we want. We're
boss of the world there."

The pro-settlement orientation of lawyers is not just articulated in
terms of client control. Considerable emphasis is placed on the advantages of negotiation in terms of speed and cost. Settlement is presented
as much quicker and much less complicated than adjudication. As a
Massachusetts lawyer explained,

> *Lawyer:* When we talk to clients here we say, "If you take it all to trial
> you can't get on with your life for a long period of time. So it's quicker
> to go this route."
>
> *Client:* If we reached a settlement it might be a trade-off because if we
> were to sit down and talk we could get court approval sooner too.
>
> *Lawyer:* Yes. Let's say we reach a settlement next week. John and I talk
> and we resolve everything. We really don't have any problems. We
> could schedule a pretrial conference, write out a letter to the court,
> and go in and say, "We're all set ready to go. There are no issues."
> He'd say, "Fine. Set up a trial date." We could go in, you would take
> the stand and say your blurb that you're going to be required to say,
> and get off. We tell them what the exact settlement is, that we still
> agreed on this. It could be very simple.
>
> *Client:* Sounds good to me.
>
> *Lawyer:* Hopefully John will give me a call and we can sit down and
> come up with a settlement or see if there's going to be any contested
> issues. Hopefully there will be only one or two. It will take us a very
> short time to resolve as opposed to all of the issues that we could go
> into. If it's a completely contested trial, then we've got to go through
> custody and visitation and support amounts, insurance and debts, the
> whole nine yards. I'm hoping that we can cut out most of that.

Not only does settlement help clients get on with their lives, it also is much less costly than adjudication. Lawyers are often quite direct in pointing out that they stand to make more money on cases that go to trial. As one California lawyer put it,

> It's self-serving for me to tell you to turn over $5,000 to me. You see what I am saying. I am in an awkward position in terms of vested self-interest to tell you to go in and try the case.

Other lawyers emphasize that the prospect of expensive legal fees should be used to convince their opponents to try to reach a negotiated agreement. For example, after a prolonged discussion of the advantages of settlement and the difficulty of getting negotiations started, another California lawyer said:

> I think you ought to say to your wife, "I want you to know what is going to happen if we can't work something out. Win or lose we're about to spend a lot of money on lawyers. Whether it's your money or my money, somebody's gonna spend probably ten thousand bucks on lawyers. So what I want you to do is to go make a concrete proposal to me." That usually works.

Still other lawyers underline the costliness of adjudication by refusing to give a fixed price estimate if the case goes to trial. While the expense of settlement is presented in relatively certain terms, the open-endedness of the costs associated with contested hearings and trials is used to persuade clients of the economic rationality of the former.

> *Lawyer:* Settlement helps control the costs. We know what we're getting into. On the other hand, as to the expense of the trial, I can give you an estimate. I may be 100 or 200 percent off. It's very difficult.
>
> *Client:* This isn't Las Vegas odds.
>
> *Lawyer:* I can estimate accurately within a range of what I will have to put into this case, but I can't accurately estimate the amount of time that I'm going to have to put into the response to everything they do. I know, for example, if someone asks how long will it take to examine a witness, I can say fifteen minutes, half an hour, forty-five minutes, or an hour, but I can't predict how long the other guy is going to cross-examine. Assuming that the trial would take a day or less, which I think it would, I would guess that it would take two days to prepare for the trial, sixteen hours to try it, that's eight hours and twenty-four hours and then afterward two days to wrap up the loose ends. That time would not be spent in concentrated blocks. It would be spread out so a minimum of five days at $800 a day, $4,000 for a trial. It could be twice that amount, it could be $8,000. So maybe we are looking at a top range, I can't be held to this, but realistically ten would be my guess on the high end.
>
> *Client:* Um-hum.
>
> *Lawyer:* Possible up to fifteen I just can't imagine, although theoretically there is no limit. There is always something you can fight about

and if it gets down to the pots and pans, there's no limit. The limit to the amount of the attorney's fees is the size of the marital estate.

Client: All right.

Many lawyers suggest that it is important in divorce cases to avoid the ugliness of litigation especially where the spouses will have to continue dealing with one another about the children.[7] The prospect of continuing relations must, in their view, be taken into account in planning strategy and figuring out how best to dispose of cases (compare Macaulay, 1963, and Yngvesson, 1985).

One lawyer expressed the common view when he explained to his client at the start of her case,

> I don't like to view it [divorce] as an adversary proceeding. You guys are husband and wife, you've got kids. You are going to have a relationship for the rest of your life because of the children, so let's try to get you to agree on something.

Other lawyers argued that searching for revenge or for vindication is inappropriate given the context of continuing relationships and, in so doing, attempted to "demoralize" the divorce process. As the following lawyer put it,

> If you have children, you will be dealing with each other for as long as you have those children. You cannot start on a basis of "Let's go to court now to find out who's right," and then deal with each other in the future. That's not the solution. When you were married and you had disagreements, you didn't decide to take the other one to court. Well, unless somebody is trying to rip off the other person, and I mean literally, by either hiding assets or lying about income, there's no reason why people can't work it out together.

Ultimately, however, it is not the alleged flexibility of the negotiation process, its speed and cost-saving qualities, or its suitability given the prospect of continuing relations that lawyers emphasize in promoting settlement (Kritzer, 1991). It is instead a bottom-line judgment that the client will get more through negotiation than could be obtained by going to trial. Here we see the adversarial emphasis that recurs throughout discussions of settlement. As one lawyer put it, "We'll negotiate so long as you are getting the upper edge."

Lawyers present negotiated settlement not as a way of achieving equity or fairness between the parties, but as a way of maximizing their clients' advantages in the divorce process.[8] This requires a comparative assessment of the prospective outcome of such a settlement and the likely result if the case went to trial. One example of such a perspective is provided by the following exchange.

> *Client:* This agreement you're talking about, is this strictly property, or would it be property and more support?

Lawyer: It needs to be everything; it needs to be support, the way the property is divided, the way the obligations are divided, and child custody and child visitation. It covers all the issues.

Client: So what we would need to do is redo one and have both parties agree to it?

Lawyer: Right. And the only reason to sign an agreement is if you feel you're getting more than the court would give you in a trial, or if you're really anxious to get it done, which he is. There's no reason to sign an agreement if you think the court's going to do better, unless you absolutely don't want to go to court, or unless you really just don't want to spend the attorney's fees. If you can see that the court is going to do better for you than your signing, you don't have to sign away all your property. That's what I'm trying to say. Or sign something that you don't want to sign. There's no reason to.

The search for comparative advantage through the settlement process has important implications for the meaning of law, the norms of that process, the tactical advice that lawyers give clients, and the way lawyers describe their own role in the negotiation process. This search means that lawyers have to secure a clear sense of what the client would regard as a desirable outcome. This, as we have seen, can be a difficult task. Client's objectives often appear uncertain; their goals appear unclear; their sense of an appropriate resolution seems to be not well settled (see McEwen et al., 1994: 169). What this means is that lawyers spend considerable time trying to elicit from their clients what is, from the client's perspective, very difficult to articulate. What appears to lawyers to be a problem brought on by emotional upset and confusion may, however, be a form of resistance. The failure to articulate goals may be a way of contesting the effort of lawyers to impose an instrumentalist logic on the divorce process.

The construction of the meaning of settlement thus begins with a discussion of the comparative advantage of settlement over trials. In this process lawyers praise negotiation and emphasize the costs, delays, and problems of the adjudication process. These pro-settlement arguments provide the backdrop for more detailed discussions of the mechanics, techniques, and strategies of negotiation.

THE NORMS OF SETTLEMENT:
HOW SUBSTANTIAL IS THE LAW'S SHADOW?

While most lawyers praise settlement for its flexibility and creativity, they also acquaint clients with its hypothetical limits:

An agreement is totally creative between the two of you. The two of you can agree to anything you want to, as long as it's not illegal. The judge is going to say fine, and it can be as lopsided as you want to make it. The judge will say fine if you both think it's fair and both of you agree to it.

This lawyer, while emphasizing the "totally creative" aspect of the settlement process, reminds his client of major constraints that tend to restrict that creativity. The first constraint is the need to secure the agreement of the spouse. While parties "can" agree to anything, there is, of course, no assurance that agreement will be reached or that total creativity means total satisfaction. A further constraint is found in the looming presence of the law. Law sets boundaries; law keeps creativity in check. What the judge will do is crucial. While this lawyer downplays the role of the judge, and in so doing suggests that the judge will not protect people from even "lopsided" agreements, others portray this last constraint as more substantial.

The settlement process as presented to clients is both open and limited. Lawyers are quick to characterize demands and offers, as well as client expectations and goals, as reasonable or unreasonable; in so doing, they suggest that there are norms and customs that govern the settlement process. These norms and customs are known to lawyers by virtue of their experience and expertise, and along with the client's goals, they establish a sense of what an optimal settlement would look like. In most cases the articulation of the norms of settlement comes in response to client questions or requests for predictions.

Clients regularly and repeatedly seek reassurance about the progress of, and prognosis for, their cases. They look to their lawyers to forecast the future and to provide information about their prospects if they go to trial or reach a negotiated settlement. In trying to figure out how to respond to an offer, or what kind of demand to make, clients often ask, "What would a judge do?" or "What's the rule of thumb?" As one client put it while pressing her lawyer to make a prediction about the division of the equity in the marital property,

> I don't have the expertise to know what to expect. I need to know from you what it means if we fight, what it means in terms of attorney fees, what it means in terms of emotional wear and tear. Then I need to know if there is any chance of winning or your educated guess about what the court would say.

This is a vivid and important statement about the power/knowledge nexus in relations between professionals and their clients. The clients' "need" is for information and for interpretation that would give that information meaning. In response to such needs, lawyers paint a picture of the "normal" divorce settlement. Their sense of what is normal provides a standard for judging what should be asked or accepted in the negotiation process. Thus in conversations between lawyers and clients there are frequent comparisons of particular offers or demands with what is expected in the normal divorce.

Lawyer: The normal visitation schedule would be, especially for a thir-teen-year-old kid, and what's the other one, seven or eight?

Client: He's eleven.

Lawyer: Eleven. They are old enough so the court is going to look into what they want. If they want more visitation or less visitation, that is something the court is going to consider. They are getting up there where they know what they want. But normally the court is going to say visitation every other weekend, Friday at 6:00 to Sunday at 6:00; alter-nate holidays; a week during Easter; maybe a month, six weeks, two weeks, four weeks, whatever in the summer time.

Client: That's great, if we can arrange something like that. Because right now she's really restricting me, like I almost have to be confined with her looking over my head. Not that I don't mind communicating in case there's something that comes up and she has to contact them, but it's like I have someone looking over my head and such limited time that I can't enjoy them or even be part of their life. Even if we could write something up where I have them on a Friday evening at 6:00 to Sunday at 6:00, but I don't have to take the option of doing that every single weekend.

Lawyer: Well, normally you can just put in there husband has the right, and you set forth what it's going to be, every other weekend from Fri-day at 6:00 to Sunday at 6:00, upon forty-eight hours advance notice to the wife so she's not left in the air, well is he going to get them this weekend or is he not. I mean you have an obligation to let her know. I mean that is a normal thing. But I don't see any problem with expand-ing the visitation rights that she's tried to limit.

In another visitation case "standard" is substituted for "normal."

Client: All right, now I have a picky one about summer vacation.

Lawyer: Yeah.

Client: The way this thing is phrased, the day they get out of school to the day they come back.

Lawyer: No, I think it should be one week after and one week in the end.

Client: Yeah.

Lawyer: Yeah, I agree. That's the standard.

Client: That's the standard?

Lawyer: Standard, absolutely.

Client: And Barbara [the other lawyer] knows that?

Lawyer: She may. But that's standard.

In still other cases frequent references are made to rules of thumb. In the following two examples rules of thumb are invoked to try to fig-ure out offers concerning the duration of spousal support.

Lawyer: Well, he'll want an ending date on the spousal support. A real basic rule of thumb, and again that depends on a lot of factors, is about half the length of a marriage. Let's say if you've been married twenty years, you could say ten years. It's fair.

Client: Right. Well what about the eight years? We had originally talked six.

Lawyer: We had originally talked six. As I told you, there's kind of a rule of thumb about half the length of the marriage, and that's all it is is a rule of thumb. I mean you look at the circumstances, you look at a lot of different things. You've been married what, seventeen years, so that's what he's looking at there.

In explaining what is normal, standard or consistent with rules of thumb, lawyers often refer to other cases they have handled and invoke a kind of localized "common law" of divorce. As one Massachusetts lawyer said in a discussion of the disposition of the marital home,

> To give you an example how these things usually work, I did a divorce a while ago where the marriage was the same length, more children, and the house was divided two-thirds, one-third, with the husband getting one-third. It was the same type of proportionate financial contribution, and I think that two-third/one-third split would be reasonable.

However, the general reference for what is normal is not just the lawyer's experience in other cases. Anticipation of what courts or judges would do in *this* case plays an even larger role. While some lawyers make definite, concrete predictions, most are elusive and indefinite. They often begin their answers by saying "it depends" or "anything can happen." Nevertheless what is clearly communicated to clients is that what will happen in settlement negotiations is in large part determined by what the court would do if the case were tried. They are told that it does not make sense to take a position and "insist on something that is far out of line from what a court would do." Clients are told that while what a court would do is "not totally determinative of the outcome of negotiations," it is "certainly relevant."

Jane's case provides one rather typical example. When her lawyer answered her question about whether she should fight to keep possession of the marital home he predicted that the court would order the property sold:

> Why not fight for a settlement that ends up giving you the house? The only reason that I can think of is because it will involve a fight; that it will be protracted; and, in my judgment, a court could just say, "Okay, Norb, this was your idea; you take the limited partnerships at the investment value." I think it's more likely that the court would order them disposed of, get a real value, and then say, "I'll retain jurisdiction to affect the distribution," which means that you're not only hung up with a hopelessly slow judicial system, but also a hopelessly slow real

estate market. But, in principle, I don't see that Norb has a better claim to the house than you do.

In another case where there was an issue of how much to offer in the way of a division of the marital property, the client, a male college professor, worried that, "I still don't know how intimidated I should be by what potentially she could ask for." In response his lawyer reassured him of the reasonableness of their position by reference to her sense of what a judge would do.

You know that she could ask for everything. And, my reading of this court's recent decisions and the way the judges have gone in terms of property division is that that will not happen. And I maintain that position right now. That she will not get the whole house. Starting on the premise that the court's going to say, you start with fifty-fifty, and you go from there. You see how the scales are weighed considering the factors that we talked about before, educational background, employability, your work background, your experience, that sort of thing. All of those. Conduct of the parties, which isn't a factor here, thank god, you know all these things get thrown onto the scale and if she doesn't have as much education, well the scale's going to tip a little more in her favor.

In still another case a lawyer justified his advice concerning an offer of spousal support by directing his client's attention to the inclinations of judges.

Client: Are there any hard and fast guidelines as far as what kind of support she's most likely to get or does it just totally depend on . . .

Lawyer: Easy answers aren't there as often as you'd like to find them. The guidelines, of course, will look to her age, her earning ability, her needs. We can start going through the list. The length of the marriage is some factor in it, so is the standard of living that the two of you enjoyed. If she can't go out and you have the ability to support her at that level, she's got a claim that she ought to be supported at that level.

Client: Yeah.

Lawyer: We ought not to be offering too much. Precedent seems to be more generous than judges are in paying spousal support. As much as you are concerned right now about what she might be getting, the judges are really not generous at all. This is a somewhat conservative county and there's a backlash for a woman to go out and do whatever a man can. So why not? Why can't she go and take care of herself? You take care of yourself.

By invoking the judge or the court to guide settlement negotiations, lawyers reach for an external, objective standard. This standard works to reinforce their power since only they have sufficient experience to know what judges generally do or how they are likely to respond to particular claims. When judicial behavior is invoked in this way, it relieves both lawyer and client of the moral responsibility for figuring out what is fair and of communicating that in a persuasive way to the other side.[9] In these instances lawyers appeal to an image of what has been called "positivist advocacy" (Simon, 1978: 30) and reinforce the belief that divorcing spouses are, by virtue of their marital discord, unable without outside guidance to find ways of arranging their future relations.

"GETTING TO YES": PLANNING THE STRATEGY OF SETTLEMENT

While lawyers describing the settlement process frequently make reference to norms and predictions of judicial decisions, those norms and predictions do not in themselves guarantee that an agreement will be reached or that any agreement that can be reached will be advantageous. As a result, lawyer and client in divorce cases are often quite preoccupied with trying to figure out the strategy and tactics of the negotiation process. This effort involves assessing the goals, expectations, and sensitivities of the other side, devising a proper negotiating posture, and figuring out how to make the right mix of concessions and demands. As they make such assessments and efforts lawyers caution clients that the negotiation process is uncertain and volatile, that no set of strategy and tactics can insure success. As one California lawyer put it during a conversation about spousal support,

> You can't ever predict the chemistry of negotiations. I've seen people who say "I wouldn't give one more cent to that bitch if she was the last person in the world." And twenty minutes later, he's given $600 more. Why? Because he saw all of a sudden it was time to finish; it was time to end it. So that's the essence of the chemistry of negotiation. You don't know what's going to happen.

As lawyers and clients try to devise a strategy to produce an advantageous settlement, lawyers seek information about their client's spouse, his or her habits and dispositions. As we saw in Chapter 2, while they try to avoid getting involved in characterizations of the spouse's character defects or behavior during the marriage, lawyers need information and predictions about likely spousal behavior during the negotiation process. Generally, however, lawyers do not invite global characterizations. Instead they ask for assessments about spousal reactions to particular actions and events. Thus, for example, one California lawyer asks whether her client's husband will respond better to written or oral communication during the negotiation process.

> *Lawyer:* Let me ask you this, because you know him a lot better, which do you think he'd be more likely to give a good response to, something that's in writing, that he needs to respond to in writing?

Client: Yes.

Lawyer: Or something oral?

Client: No. He needs it written. He can't deal off the top of his head.

Another example of this attempt to elicit information about probable reactions to specific details of the negotiation process occurred in a Massachusetts case in which lawyer and client discussed the starting point for the division of the marital assets.

Client: I don't want to offer what I really feel is fair if it's going to have to be "I'll trade this, no this and this and this," which it may have to be.

Lawyer: Yeah. In a case like this my feeling in terms of negotiations, if you will, is to start by saying fifty-fifty. That's usually where everybody starts. How would Marg react if she heard that your lawyer was proposing a fifty-fifty split? Even if she didn't like it at that point I don't see that there's much she could do other than throw up her hands and say, "Well forget it, let's go straight to court," and I don't think she would do that based on what you've told me.

Client: You know what it could boil down into is the fact that Marg and I both really know what we want. And, depending on you, and the other lawyer, then there's actually going to be two, three conflicts going on. Her against her lawyer, because she has said well, "This seems reasonable, but my lawyer is going to ask for more than that."

Lawyer: Okay.

Client: So she's fighting her lawyer, her lawyer is fighting you and me, and there may be some sort of undercurrents between you and me.

This is a vivid picture of the complexity and fragility of power in lawyer-client relations. While the lawyer imagines the focal point of opposition to be between the divorcing spouses, her client deftly reminds her that lawyers and clients may not share interests and values, that their relations may be conflictual. He describes a process in which each articulated action may be met with an equally strong resistance.

Generally, however, clients acquiesce in their lawyers' requests for information about spouses or predictions about their responses to overtures. This brief exchange is typical:

Lawyer: And there are a lot of downfalls, a downside to holding a deed of trust.

Client: Well these people that we have, what if they foreclose on us? So I'm going to wait a little longer and see if they'll sign a quitclaim. Oh, there's another thing. This thing. Is this right?

Lawyer: He forgot to put on tenants in common. Otherwise it's fine.

Client: I am very concerned. I know as tenants in common you can sell your share of the house.

Lawyer: Nobody will ever buy it.

Client: Are you sure?

Lawyer: I'm not 100 percent sure, but who would want to buy a half interest with you?

Client: God only knows. Jim can be really funny and I'm just wondering if he couldn't set up something that could force me out of the house. Could he set up something where he could sell it to somebody with the idea of forcing me out of the house?

Lawyer: I don't know the man. I mean I really don't know.

Client: Most of the time he is a real nice guy, but every once in awhile he gets a bee in his bonnet and goes off the deep end. He's very, very easily swayed by people.

The following dialogue is also typical of clients who acquiesce to their lawyers' requests for information about spouses:

Lawyer: If you ask for a promissory note you're going to make her nervous right away. That's from what you've told me. Mind you, I've never seen her. I only know your wife through you. She seems like the type that if you come to her and say, "We're going to go to the bank and sign your name and it doesn't mean anything anyway."

Client: She won't do it.

Lawyer: She's going to balk, and all of a sudden she's going to say, well, "Why the hell did he want me to do that?"

Client: No, she's going to think, I'm getting screwed, is what she's going to think.

This last lawyer, like most others, reminds the client of her own relative ignorance concerning the spouse, and her dependence on an accurate portrayal by the client. In so doing she provides the basis for later disclaimers or explanations when particular efforts do not work out as planned. Then she and other lawyers can shift responsibility back to the client by focusing on inaccuracies or mistakes in the client's portrayal of the spouse. By emphasizing the importance of information about the spouse, and their dependence on the client for such information, lawyers are able to distance themselves from stalemates in negotiations and from negotiated outcomes that clients later come to resent.

While they are reticent to assert expertise when it comes to the other spouse, lawyers are not reluctant to advise their own clients how they must behave during the negotiation process. The message is quite clear and consistent. If agreement is to be reached, the client must put aside her emotions. The client must be rational and not give into the anger, resentment, and frustration that is so much a part of the divorce process (Griffiths, 1986).

Here again, Jane's case is illustrative. Her negotiations with Peter began by focusing on the relative importance of the emotions engaged by the legal process and the symbolic aspects of the divorce, as opposed to its financial and material dimensions. Throughout, Peter invoked the ideology of separate spheres and warned his client not to confuse the realms of emotion and finance. He instructed her that she could expect the legal process to work well only if she could exclude so-called emotional material from her deliberations.[10] As McEwen et al. observe (1994: 169),

> In divorce cases a failure to deal with nonlegal issues may prevent the attorney from getting her work accomplished. For example, angry and upset clients may be "unreasonable" and may resist settlement or demand legal tactics that, in the lawyer's view, have no chance of success . . . . Divorce attorneys thus struggle to manage emotional clients and to find ways to work through that emotion, deflecting it, suppressing it, or venting and putting it behind.

Yet what counts as a legal issue is precisely what is in play. Noting how and where lawyers try to relegate issues to the realm of emotion is important if we are to understand the way meanings are constructed and power is exercised in the divorce lawyer's office.

What becomes labeled as emotional material is rather complex and difficult for both lawyer and client to sort out. Thus Jane was, in the first instance, eager to let her lawyer know that she felt both anger and mistrust toward many participants in the legal process. This combination of feelings was clearly expressed as she talked about the restraining order against her and the manner in which it was issued:

> *Jane:* So I was a total ass. I moved out of the house and left myself vulnerable to that, which I was certainly not informed of by any attorney in the process of mediation. And I was setting myself up for that.

> *Peter:* In my view, it would have been a rather extraordinary attorney that could have advised you of that, because, in my view, that's not the law. So I'm hard pressed to see how a lawyer could have said, "Don't move out of the house or you may prejudice your situation."

> *Jane:* But obviously, some attorney did, right? We have the case of Paul Foster, who interprets the law in that fashion. Well, I'm angry about all that.

While her lawyer once again validates Jane's sense of the legal error involved in issuing the restraining order, her anger is fueled by the failure of her husband's lawyer to accept this interpretation of the law. Thus Jane continues to express her hostility, especially when the conversation turns directly to her husband's lawyer:

> The other option could have been that Norb would have gotten different legal advice from the beginning. So the thing that I'm concerned about is Foster. I'm concerned about the kind of person he is. I distrust him as thoroughly as I do Norb, and I think you have been very measured in your statements about him. I think he's a son-of-a-bitch,

and there's nothing I've seen that he's done that changed my mind about that. And I think that he has a client that can be manipulated.[11]

Jane's mistrust is not reserved exclusively for the opposition. She is, to an extent, wary of her own lawyer as well:

> This is a very vulnerable time in my life, and one of the things that has happened is a major trust relationship has ended. And then suddenly in the space of what—six weeks or something—I'm supposed to entrust somebody else, not only with the intimate details of my life, but with the responsibility for representing me. And that's not easy for me under any circumstances. I really like to speak for myself.

Given the predicament in which this client finds herself—needing to trust a stranger when trust has just been betrayed by an intimate— and, given her concerns about her husband and the lawyers involved in the case, it is not surprising that the issue of trust is paramount when she considers how to reach a negotiated agreement.

> *Jane:* One of the things I'm feeling is a tremendous discontent that some form of negotiation is going to now begin without any act from Norb that establishes trust . . . .
>
> It doesn't seem that I have a lot of options. I simply will have to accept that, and I guess I will have to live with that pain. I think it's dreadfully unfair. But it doesn't seem that I can get any satisfaction.
>
> *Peter:* That's not entirely true. You can litigate. Strongly we can litigate.
>
> *Jane:* Well, I think the only question then is whether or not an overture is even possible before litigation. I'm not sure. I have these things separated in my mind, but how can I trust this human being to do anything? I don't know if I can. I feel that pretty strongly.
>
> *Peter:* I don't blame you. I don't blame you at all.

Because she feels betrayed by her husband, Jane wants "some gesture from him" as a means of establishing the basis for negotiations. Moreover, she feels that she is already two points down vis-à-vis her husband. First, he has the house and has denied her any access to it, although her departure was an act of generosity done for the good of the marital community. Second, she "knows" that he is going to get the house and that she will at best get half its market value. She repeatedly asks Peter about gestures or concessions to even this score:

> So I wrote this as a draft to send to Norb. And obviously I'm still waffling. I don't know exactly how to give up this hearing. Part of me says, it's real clear and I ought to. But I want some gesture from him. . . .
>
> Okay. That's not going to be a problem for me. I don't think that one percentage point is going to be a problem for me. This is the problem for me. I feel that even to get to this point, I have given up a substantial amount. One thing that I've given up is the home in Pacificola. I don't give a fuck how much cash Norb gives me, I'm not going

to be able to recreate that scene, and that's just a fact of real estate in Pacificola. I want the negotiation to begin there. I want some attention to be paid to what I have already conceded to even get to this point. . . .

I just think that's a very, very big concession, and I think if I'm to take another kind of settlement, then that is the first thing that ought to be seen. Now, that's a very good faith negotiation thing for me to do, say, "Okay, Norb has this tremendous emotional investment in the house; I'm willing to let go of mine."

How does Peter respond to Jane's emotional agenda, to her efforts to define those parts of herself that are legally relevant? With respect to the problem of trust and the need for a gesture, the lawyer once says, "Ouch," once, "I don't blame you," and once he changes the subject. He does tell the client that her husband is unlikely to reestablish trust by giving up the restraining order. In addition, there is a brief exploration of whether she could buy her husband's share of the house, an alternative doomed by earlier recognition that it would involve an expensive and probably fruitless court battle. There is, moreover, a joke about taking $25,000 to forget the restraining order. Otherwise nothing is said.

Why? Lawyer and client could have discussed the kind of gestures short of unconditional surrender that might have satisfied her and been tolerable to her husband. Peter could have explored the possibility that the husband might agree to his client's occasional, scheduled visits to the property or to $5,000 more than a fifty-fifty split in recognition of giving up the house. But perhaps he feared that further exploration might complicate his efforts to have his client focus on reaching an acceptable division of property.

Peter: Okay, now, that disagreement where we weren't on the same wavelength was really more a matter of style than of end result. Right?

Jane: What part?

Peter: What you said was that you wanted me to start these negotiations by making it clear that major concessions were being made at the outset and they were being made by you.

Jane: Yes.

Peter: Okay, I understand that now. Let's come back to the end of it. What am I shooting for? I agree. That's the way it ought to be begun, and I ought to keep coming back to that. But what am I shooting for? What's the end result? Is it what I was talking about initially?

Jane: Sure. I mean, that's as much as can be expected, I believe. Am I right in that?

Peter proposes to turn the client's demand for concessions into an opening statement and implies that an equal division of assets is the only possible legal settlement. Jane resists the proposal and contends that it is dangerous to trade values with someone that you do not trust. When you do, both the chance that they will take advantage of you in making the deal and the probability that they will fail to do what they promise are increased. Her lawyer is, and can afford to be, disinterested in trust. Protection of his client does not lie in fostering good will and mutual respect between the spouses but rather in the terms of the bargain and in its enforcement powers. His duty is to see that the settlement agreement is fair to his client, whatever the motives or morals of the other side may be, and that the structure of the agreement guarantees that his client gets what she bargained for or its substitute, or at least the best approximation available.

By downplaying the question of trust her lawyer is telling Jane that the emotional self must be separated from the legal self. Gestures and symbolic acknowledgment of wrongs suffered belong to some realm other than law.[12] These demands on her lawyer typify the kind of environment in which divorce lawyers work (Kressel, 1985; McEwen et al., 1994). Moreover, the discussion of trust and its betrayal signals to her lawyer the need for an elevated watchfulness. He may, like her earlier source of protection and romance, not be fully trusted. The gesture implicitly demanded of him is an embrace of her sense of justice and of what that implies in practical terms.

Signaling the limited relevance of gestures and criticizing the display of emotion, Peter defends himself against both the transference and the test of loyalty.[13] He must find a way to be on his client's side (e.g., repeatedly acknowledging the legal error of the restraining order) and, at the same time, to keep some distance from her (e.g., responding "Ouch" to the image of the knight). Achieving this precarious balance is a peculiar, although not unique, difficulty of divorce practice (McEwen et al., 1994: 164).

To maintain this balance Peter acknowledges the difficulty of separating emotional and property issues, but continually reminds Jane of its necessity if they are going to reach what he calls a "satisfactory disposition" of the case. The need to exclude emotional issues is thus linked to a warning that emotions can jeopardize satisfactory settlements. The notion of satisfactory disposition, however, is itself problematic. Her lawyer's definition of "satisfactory" tends to exclude the part of Jane's personality that is angry or frustrated. Satisfactory dispositions are financial. The question of who is satisfied is left unasked. For the client, no definition of the case that ignores her emotions seems right; to the lawyer, this is the only definition that seems acceptable. Moreover, the responsibility for finding ways to keep emotions under control is assigned to the client. Peter offers no help in this task even as he acknowledges its relevance for this client and for the practice of divorce law. If no settlement is reached it will, at least as far as their side is concerned, be because of a failure on the part of the client. He says,

> I mean, you're angry; you're pissed off. You've said that. But are you ready to call a halt to the anger? I'm not so sure that that's humanly possible. Can your rational mind say, "Jane, there has been enough anger expended on this; it is time to get on with your life"? If you are able to do that, great. But I don't know.

The separation of emotional and economic matters may benefit the client. While it does exact an emotional toll, concentrating on the instrumental, tangible aspects of the divorce may produce a more satisfactory disposition than focusing on the emotional concerns. Jane's lawyer may be trying to explain that in the long run she is going to be more interested in the economics of the settlement than in the vindication of her immediate emotional needs. In his view, legal justice, although narrow, is justice nonetheless, and his job is to secure for her the best that can be achieved given the legal process as he knows it.

Putting emotional matters aside may also serve the interests of lawyers untrained in dealing with emotional problems and unwilling to find ways of coping with them. It allows lawyers to sidestep what is clearly one of the most difficult and least rewarding aspects of divorce practice. In so doing they are able to avoid assuming a sense of responsibility for the human consequences of being unresponsive to emotion. In Jane's case, for example, Peter suggests that the legal process works best for those who can control their emotions and concentrate on the instrumental, the calculating, the pecuniary. The client's uncertainty about the possibility of such a separation of issues is met by the lawyer's opposing certainty that it need be done.

The lawyer's certainty is not that the client can achieve the required separation, but rather that the separation is an imperative of the legal process and that without it the system cannot efficiently deliver its goods. Here a contingent ideological production is presented as a necessity. Having expressed the ideology of separate spheres as an imperative, the lawyer is thus relieved of any responsibility for helping his client come to terms with the anger and frustration that condition her feelings about property issues. Ultimately, it seems that the client gets the message. As she says, "The extraneous factors, which are every bit as important as the rest of it, are not going to be paid attention to at all."[14]

Once some assessment of the other spouse is made and the client is appropriately socialized to the negotiation process, the planning of strategy and tactics can go forward. As they discussed the negotiation process with their clients the lawyers we observed formulated several rules of thumb, each of which embodies a common-sense conception of the bargaining process. The first such rule was offer low, demand high.

It is reflected in numerous instances in which lawyers first ask their clients what they would like to end up with and then formulate a "bargaining position" higher or lower than that end goal. It is also exemplified in a conversation about child support between a Massachusetts man and his lawyer.

Client: She was saying that her attorney thought they should get $500 a month.

Lawyer: Here comes the number.

Client: I feel much better.

Lawyer: When I talked with her attorney we were sparring for numbers. Now we know where we are starting.

Client: Okay.

Lawyer: I'll say, "We don't have much money." By the time we start taking positions she's going to be coming from $500 and I'm going to be coming from $200 and we are going to find it's going to have to be somewhere in between.

Client: Uh-huh.

Lawyer: I'm not going to offer anything over $200 and I'm not going to bind you to anything without your approval.

Client: Yeah, okay.

Lawyer: I think perhaps $200 a month will make a world of difference to her.

Client: Uh-huh.

Another example of the ask-for-more-than-you-really-want principle is provided in the following brief discussion between a California woman and her lawyer:

Client: I would be perfectly happy with the house payment. I really would be.

Lawyer: Well, I would like to see you getting a minimum of $500 a month from him. That would take care of the house payment and at least the taxes.

Client: Yeah, if I could get the money to put away for the taxes.

Lawyer: I would suggest that you talk to your husband and say, "Look, I need a minimum of $500." I just think you ought to tell him $500. I'll tell him $600, then negotiate down to $500 and he'll give you $400, and if you want to settle for that, I don't think it's enough, but at least it's better than nothing.

The settlement process is interpreted as a process fraught with insincerity and bluff. Lawyers regularly refer to the negotiation process as a "game." As one put it, "It's basically not unlike two kids on Mulholland Drive in Los Angeles. It's who blinks first." In such a situation lawyers suggest it is important to take advantage of any weakness in one's opponent. In so doing, they convey an important message about the distance between law and justice, and they invite their clients to see the legal process as "a flawed instrument which must be played with skill and finesse" (Merry, 1990: 142).

> *Lawyer:* Now, this is a terrible thing to say, since his attorney hasn't been doing family law for very long, she may not be aware of the fact that you don't take off the sales costs if you keep the house. So we can at least offer . . .

> *Client:* Say that again now, say that to me.

> *Lawyer:* Okay. If you were going to keep the house, you cannot take off the 7 percent approximate selling costs because the cases say that you are keeping the house, therefore you don't have that expense. But if you were to sell the house, obviously you are going to pay a 5 percent commission and 1 percent for title insurance and costs of closing and escrow. So generally when you are dealing with another family law attorney you say, "Well, let's take off the 7 percent," and the other side says, "Are you kidding?" Sometimes in negotiations you end up doing it anyways simply in order to end it, but I'm just saying that it's a terrible thing to say, but we may have a little advantage over the other attorney because she may not realize that you don't have to take that off. So what we can do is present it as, well, "Of course, we take off the 7 percent that it would cost to sell the property."

> *Client:* Oh well, okay.

> *Lawyer:* I mean, you know, you start from there and you can always negotiate the other way. If she says, "Well, you ought to know better than that," then I would say, "Well, I just figured I'd try it."

> *Client:* Try it, you may as well. Sure.

> *Lawyer:* So if she catches us at it, fine, but if we can, you are talking about $7,000 less that you would have to come up with. Well actually it would be $3,500 because we are splitting it between the two of you. So if we can save a little bit here and little bit there. The more we can cut it down the easier it's going to be for you to be able to buy the house out from him.

The formulation of high demands, the making of low offers, or the attempt to take advantage of certain weaknesses may not be cost-free. The primary risk is that the other side will be "offended" and will shift from negotiation to "the litigation mode." Thus lawyers and clients, even as they formulate their initial positions, try to figure out how they will be received by the other side. Moreover, the anticipation of such reactions sometimes leads to revisions in those positions. As the following lawyer and client talk about how long the client would like to be able to remain in the marital home, the anticipation of the spouse's adverse response looms large:

Client: I would prefer not to even have child support. I would just prefer to have the house for a period of time.

Lawyer: Why don't we leave off the second alternative and just say let's
start with seven years? You'd like to live in the house for seven years
and you will pay all the mortgage payments and you probably should
pay the insurance; you probably should pay the taxes, okay?

Client: Yeah, he's really going to balk at seven years. It seems like an
awfully long time.

Lawyer: Okay, give me another alternative. I'm just picking arbitrary
years out.

Client: Yeah, I know.

Lawyer: He's going to want to negotiate it down.

Client: My bottom line would have to be two years. That's where I
would like to finally end up. So you can start wherever you want to.

Lawyer: All right, maybe I'll start at five years.

Client: Okay.

The concern about calculating offers and demands in such a way as
to maximize negotiating leverage without being seen as too demanding,
aggressive, or tricky is also reflected in the following story told by a California lawyer:

Client: Do you think that's going to scare her off? You have no way of
knowing, do you?

Lawyer: Well, it's the line of alienation, and what happens then. I have a
case now in which a very good lawyer, who is a friend of mine, is on the
other side, and we've been working together as we always work
together. And then one day his client gave my client a quitclaim deed
for a $1 million piece of property. My client came in and said, "What's
this?" The lawyer didn't know that his client was going to give it to my
client to give to me. And I called up and I got this guy on the phone
and said, "What's going on over there?" and he said, "I have no idea
what's happening." But immediately my defenses were up. Lawyers can
be fairly aggressive people anyway. So my sense is that, if anything, if
she [the other lawyer] doesn't think it's right down the line, she doesn't
have a lot of sense of negotiating. In other words, if it's not real close to
it, she doesn't say, "I'll just call him back and say 'I want more.'" So we
run a risk if it's too far out of line of her just saying, "Bad offer; see you
in court."

Client: Just like that.

Lawyer: Yeah, we run a risk.

A second rule of thumb is that negotiation involves a process of
exchange in which clients make "trades" at the margins. Trading is possible because divorces involve many separate issues—real and personal

property, child and spousal support, visitation, custody. Lawyers, however, generally talk about settlement as a "package" and urge clients to think about making trades to produce the best possible total settlement. Thus, in one Massachusetts case, a lawyer urged her client to make concessions on the amount of weekly child support in return for automatic cost-of-living increases:

> I'm just sort of throwing out a few things that I think should go with the package. Some of them are worth something and you should think about this with him and also react as we're talking on Friday in terms of maybe being worth trading for other things. I mean, five or ten dollars difference in the amount per week might be worth it if you're going to get the automatic cost of living. So that you're sure that at least what you're getting will keep pace.

A third rule of thumb—that it is important to hold something valuable in reserve to be able to make a concession at a strategically important moment—is exemplified in the following exchange concerning a pension plan.

> *Lawyer:* I have a hunch, though I've had no discussions about it, that she wants that money now.
>
> *Client:* Uh-huh.
>
> *Lawyer:* Okay? I don't think I'd give it to her now.
>
> *Client:* Okay, tell me about it.
>
> *Lawyer:* I'll tell you why. I think I'd hold that back and cave in on that in the end. I think you'd go after all the other goodies and then hold back on the $10,500 and cave in on that last. That's the money that's going to get her going.
>
> *Client:* What would you want, what would you suggest instead? What would your offer be?
>
> *Lawyer:* My offer would be that when the house is sold the $10,500 is worked out.
>
> *Client:* Oh.
>
> *Lawyer:* It's your case and it's your life, but I would hang tough on that real close to the end and see if you can get other things and then give up on the $10,500.
>
> *Client:* Okay.
>
> *Lawyer:* Because that's got to be the thing they want the most.

Holding out and making concessions at just the right moment potentially establishes a kind of moral leverage in negotiations that may be important in moving them along or in exacting another concession at a later point. As one lawyer put it in advising his client to waive spousal support, doing so would reap benefits later on because, "it makes you look nice." Another lawyer suggested that he would start discussions about the disposition of some jointly owned securities by "making a big deal about the fact that you're making a big concession on the house." As another Massachusetts lawyer put it in explaining what would happen if her client agreed to relinquish her claim on her husband's business, "then we'd weigh things on the scales and tell them that they have to give us what we're asking for here, this is only fair."

Ultimately, however, many lawyers warned their clients that trades and concessions might not be enough to secure an advantageous agreement and that they had to be prepared to shift from settlement to adjudication. Being tough is required when being nice fails. Threatening trial and preparing for it are said to be necessary to insure that bargaining positions appear credible. In one California case in which the male client wanted more liberal visitation than the wife was willing to allow, his lawyer urged him to demand joint physical custody, and said, "In order to make your wife believe you are really going for joint custody you have to mount the attack, okay? You have to get psychologists involved and . . . let a little bad blood."

In addition, lawyers regularly advise clients to take procedural steps, like filing motions or what in California are called "at-issue memoranda," to keep the threat of contested trials alive. Such a threat is said by many lawyers to be essential in providing the impetus for the negotiations. Finally, lawyers argue that as the prospect of a trial becomes more real, negotiations become more intense and realistic. As one Massachusetts lawyer said in explaining why he wanted to begin deposing witnesses,

> When things start getting real tough, it's been my experience that everybody's more willing to talk. Now, everything is too distant, but as we get closer to trial they'll get more realistic and they'll be willing to sit down and say okay, let's figure this thing out.

CONCLUSION

The process of constructing the meaning of settlement is a risky business from the lawyer's point of view. While most clients are generally willing to try to reach a negotiated agreement or are eventually persuaded to do so, client expectations seem to their lawyers either diffuse or "unrealistic." Clients, even when schooled in the tactics of negotiation and the need for concessions, seem to be psychologically unprepared for the disappointments that are almost inevitably part of the settlement process. Lawyers treat client goals as exaggerated and lean on the client to be "realistic" and understand that two people cannot live as well separately as they can together. As one lawyer put it, "Well, unfortunately with a dissolution, it seems like everybody loses because all of a sudden you've got double living expenses." Another lawyer told her client that a good settlement is one that "both parties can live with. Maybe you are not totally happy with it, but it will be a compromise settlement." Still another lawyer responded to his client's insistence that there be no child support included in an agreement by saying, "One of the things I find is a best way of looking at divorce is to understand that each party has to be mutually dissatisfied with the result." And a fourth lawyer said during an early conference:

> *Lawyer:* Part of my job is to help get you grounded and to be realistic as to what's possible.
>
> *Client:* I hate those words: realistic.
>
> *Lawyer:* What words do you like? Give me some words you like and we'll use those words. What I'm concerned with is that you not harbor any desires that are too far out of the realm of possibility.

Here we see a vivid and unusually explicit example of client resistance to the power that lawyers seek to exercise in the construction of legal meanings.

Despite the warnings and disclaimers, lawyers worry that clients will blame them for failing fully to attain their goals and satisfy their expectations. They are acutely aware of the fragility of their power and the vulnerability of their position. As a result, throughout the case lawyers stress that the final decision about settlement rests with the client. Lawyers play down their power and influence in constructing the meaning of settlement. Some lawyers even refuse to advise their clients about whether they should sign an agreement.

> *Lawyer:* It's really all your decision because you have to live with it the rest of your life.
>
> *Client:* I know.
>
> *Lawyer:* If I make the decision for you and later on you are unhappy about it you are going to say, "Well why did she choose this road?"

Others stress that clients must take responsibility for the decision not to go to trial. As one California lawyer put it,

> It's up to you to say let's play by a different plan. And then we get your wife in here on a deposition and we basically grill her about her employment possibilities. I ask for an order that she go to an employment counselor and be reviewed then. So you've escalated it for her. In other words, it's a cause-and-effect that she is, in fact, irritating you, therefore, you're escalating the litigation. And that has to be your decision.

Such comments put distance between the lawyer and any subsequent second thoughts that clients may experience. To listen to these lawyers, one would think that they played little or no role in any decisions during the settlement process and that they were simply neutral agents responsive to client desires.

By describing settlement as an adversarial process, lawyers also protect themselves from clients who may come to believe that they were badly served in negotiations. Settlement, like the rest of law, is characterized by conflict and driven by careful strategic considerations. Lawyers stress that even as they try to negotiate a settlement, they are representing the client's interests. They paint a picture of contention carried on through bilateral negotiations rather than combat before a judge. They describe their own role as essentially no different in negotiation than in court. As one California lawyer explained to his client, "You have hired me to represent your interests, and I do that in two fashions. One, I tell you the way I truly see the picture and then I try to advance your cause as aggressively as I can." Thus lawyers, especially in California where mediation is common and has a favorable image, often go to great lengths to stress the difference between the kind of negotiations they conduct and mediation.[15] As one lawyer put it when his client inquired about mediation,

> *Client:* Well, do you think our property division is too complex for mediation or does that have any bearing on it?
>
> *Lawyer:* I'm sorry, I misunderstood what you meant by mediation. You mean resolution of this outside of the court system?
>
> *Client:* Yeah, I guess so. There's some attorney-counselor types that promote more of a mediation; just kind of supervising a conversation on property division instead of having each side represented by their own attorney and battling it out.
>
> *Lawyer:* Well, if that's the only choice you have, it sounds like mediation would be pretty good. I don't have any direct experience with mediation. I've heard very little about it. I don't see how it can work. I don't see how it can work generally for the same reason that I can't represent both you and Barbara. It's like a used-car salesman. You say, "Shall I buy a used car or a new car?" He says, "Buy a used car, all the depreciation is gone." But he stands to make money off of it. You've come to me to represent you in this and if we send you to mediation somehow I'm going to be doing myself out. I don't really feel that way because I can fill my time with something else, I have no need to run up time and expenses on a particular case, not at all. But what do you see different in terms of what I just got through telling you about trying to encourage Barbara to work on a negotiated settlement of property as opposed to going to court and fighting about it? If we can sit down and say here's the things we have to divide up, here's the easy questions, here's the easy answers to those things, here's the tough stuff so let's see what we can reach on that. Because you both are probably going to walk away with more if you can do it that way than going to court and fighting about it. Now that's what the objective of mediation is. I don't see much difference then. The most important differ-

ence is the one that I was just pointing out, that is, you'll be advised what your rights are and she'll be advised what her rights are. I'll prepare the agreement and I'll put in about three different places there how she's been advised to get an attorney and if we do everything right it will stick. She's an adult, she will have been informed of what's going on, she will be encouraged to get her own attorney, and it will essentially be a fair agreement anyway, but if you make close calls it's not my job to advise her, it's my job to advise you.

In the end, what lawyers try to do in constructing the meaning of settlement helps to give meaning to law itself. As they encourage clients to be "realistic" in their objectives, portray settlement as cost-effective in achieving those goals, try to convince their clients that settling is not selling out and that the lawyer who negotiates a settlement is, nonetheless, still a zealous advocate for a partisan point of view, they reveal the fragility of their power and their own acute sense of vulnerability. They also speak of law in two different and contradictory ways, as both different and separate from social life and yet, at the same time, inexorably embedded in the antagonisms and conflicts of the social relations from which it arises and from which it tries to distance itself.

6

Conclusion

[L]aw is not what judges say in the reports but what lawyers say—to one another and to clients—in their offices.
—Martin Shapiro, "On the Regrettable Decline of Law French"

The fragility of power in lawyer-client interactions in divorce arises, in part, from two competing sets of assumptions. The first is that lawyers are trained, experienced professionals, operating in a domain whose language, rituals, and customs they know well. In this domain, professionalism means the ability to manipulate symbols in legally efficacious ways, to identify and interpret institutional signals, and to understand the legal meaning of divorce. The second assumption about lawyer-client relations in divorce is that lawyers are under an obligation to operate as agents of their clients, to translate client goals into effective strategy, and to respect the decisions clients make and the directions they provide.[1]

Professionalism and agency pull in opposite directions by simultaneously assigning primacy to both lawyer and client, and thus complicate the social processes through which partial interpretations and contingent meanings are universalized and reified. In this opposition, ideas of professionalism and agency that seem, in theory, well settled are in actuality quite unstable. As a result, lawyer-client relations are sites of conflict and negotiation in which the conditions of power change from moment to moment and in which both parties are as calculating and strategic in their relations with each other as they are in their dealings with their formal adversaries. These calculations and strategies play themselves out in the varied domains of meaning in which lawyers and clients must operate. In those domains power is manifest in struggles over whose view of reality should be accepted and whose partial and contingent understandings should be treated as adequate.

Associated with the tensions and struggle that render power fragile are contradictions and disarticulations in the construction of meanings that make those meanings elusive. Lawyers and clients produce for each other understandings that may be neither internally coherent nor compatible from one subject matter to another. While lawyers tell their clients that the law requires them to be reasonable and to be ready to put aside formal contest, the law that makes such demands seems to be neither reasonable nor able itself to escape an adversary posture.

In this book we have taken a close and detailed look at how divorce law is practiced and at the experience of being a client going through a divorce. We have seen how lawyers and clients struggle to define mutually acceptable rules of relevance; we have described complex processes of negotiation through which goals and objectives are defined and revised; and we have examined how understandings about the nature of the legal process inform strategy and tactics in divorce litigation. We have treated the lawyer's office as a site of meaning making in which professional power is exercised and resisted, and in which lawyer-client interaction becomes the interpretable text of law-in-action. What is available in this seldom-explored site is an understanding of the subjects that lawyers and clients discuss in their conferences, the explicit and implicit rules of relevance that limit the choice of those subjects, what lawyers and clients have to say about them, and how their perspectives and interpretations conflict, coalesce, and are transformed, over time and at different times. Since interpretations once offered and views once adopted have consequences for the understanding of power, we have traced as well the struggles in which lawyers and clients are engaged as each seeks to have her perspective accepted by the other.

Throughout, we have explored several domains of meaning: social relations, law, and the disposition of the divorce itself. In each of these domains we have described the meanings that are offered, resisted and negotiated as lawyers and clients establish the terms on which professional service will be rendered and as they work their way through the social and legal worlds of divorce. We have seen the construction of an ideology of separate spheres, where law is understood to be bounded and unresponsive to the concerns of everyday life. We have seen the construction of a picture of law that emphasizes informality and the idiosyncracies of its officials and the pervasiveness of adversariness and advantage-seeking in the legal process. In each of these constructions we have read the texts of lawyer-client dialogue for what they might reveal about the complex intersections of meaning and power.

This form of interpretive scholarship, so far only an emerging trend in sociolegal studies (see Harrington and Yngvesson, 1990), calls scholars away from the concerns that have previously dominated studies of lawyers and other legal actors and institutions.[2] These traditional studies direct attention less to the construction of meaning and more to the allocation of tangible resources, the "who gets what" of law. They are less interested in readings of law than in understanding what accounts for variation, change, and distribution in the material outcomes of the legal process. In contrast, we believe that the production of meaning in and through law is both independently significant and inseparable from the social relations in which meaning is made. "Who says what" is as important as "who gets what" in revealing law's power.

The lawyer-client interactions we have observed involve ongoing, varied, changing efforts to negotiate shared understandings of people and events, and agreement on realistic goals and expectations, a division of responsibility, legally acceptable and efficacious ways of presenting oneself and responding to others, and definitions of satisfactory resolutions of divorce. The negotiation of meaning in each of these areas is rarely neat and orderly. With clients who want clarity in advice and communication, and lawyers who want clarity in client goals and expectations, both encounter ambiguity and circularity; with clients who want direction and action, and lawyers who want rational client decision making, both encounter drift and delay. Conversations are started but often are never completed; agreements are reached, only to unwind rapidly. In this ambiguity and circularity, drift and delay, and in the accompanying negotiations of meaning, power is exercised and resisted. The subjects of these negotiations cross the boundaries between law and society and intermix the social world of the client, the legal world of divorce, and the nature of professional services.

Throughout their interactions, lawyers and clients mark conversational space as a way of defining the appropriate scope of the legal divorce. Clients often seek to expand the conversational agenda to encompass a broader picture of their lives, experiences, and needs. In so doing, they contest the ideology of separate spheres that lawyers seek to maintain. Lawyers, on the other hand, passively resist such expansion (Griffiths, 1986). They close down the aperture; they are interested only in those portions of the client's life that have tactical significance for the prospective terms of the divorce settlement or the conduct of the case. Although O'Gorman (1963: 132–34) reports that over two-thirds of the lawyers in his sample described themselves as counselors who considered it to be their "job . . . to ascertain the nature of the client's problem and then work toward a solution that is fair to both parties," the lawyers that we studied did not take a broad perspective on their professional mission. They did not act as "counselors for the situation" nor did they try to provide psychological, emotional, or moral support or guidance for their clients.[3]

If any part of the social world of the client is captured in the lawyer's office, it is usually restricted to the client's relationship with his spouse and children. The client's life at work, and with friends or parents, is largely ignored. Unless they are trying to explain or predict spousal behavior that is directly relevant to the divorce process, lawyers rarely even inquire about the client's social world. Lawyers are, however, continually confronted by clients who want to discuss the causes of marriage failure and the content of relations with their spouse during the divorce, as well as matters occurring at work or with friends. Lawyers do not ask, but they are told anyway. They appear in these dramas as sounding boards rather than principal actors.

Clients describe their spouse and the failure of their marriage in the language of blame and exculpation, in which blame belongs to their spouse and in which the clients own the exculpation. Marriage failure and divorce difficulties are attributed by clients to defects in their spouse's character and personality. Their own behavior in these struggles is spoken about as if it were almost entirely shaped by situational factors. This is a kind of philosopher's nightmare in which the self is responsive only to circumstance, while the other is seen to exercise, and abuse, free will. The sole relief from this stark and conflicted picture of marital behavior is an occasional charitable inclination toward the spouse prompted by a rare bout of guilt.

Where the issue is marriage failure, lawyers retreat in silence and, at the first opportunity, change the subject, often quite abruptly. However, where the issue is the nature of the spouse's behavior during the divorce itself, lawyers join the conversation. They typically attribute that behavior to the context of divorce or other situational factors. In this process of imagining the origins of, and motives for, things that the spouse says and does, lawyers, as the experts on divorce-related behavior as well as on divorce law and process, have the upper hand over their clients. They selectively appropriate parts of the social world while maintaining the general boundaries between the legal and the social. This effort may be resisted, but it is rarely withdrawn. Clients do not simply acquiesce, however; they persistently return to the question of who did what and why, and they repeatedly seek to broaden the range of consideration.

If lawyers adopt a restricted role in grappling with their clients' social world, they take an expansive, tutorial posture toward the world of law, constantly demonstrating that in that world they are on familiar terrain and can operate with flexibility, originality, and power. They use and communicate their knowledge of the law and their understanding of the legal process as a resource in educating clients about what is "realistic" in the legal process of divorce. They use this knowledge strategically to move clients toward positions they deem to be reasonable and appropriate. As a result, they establish links between the production of meaning that occurs in their interactions with clients and the behaviors and actions they wish to encourage.

Yet it is not the technical world of law, of sophisticated interpretation of specialized rules, that lawyers describe in their efforts to give meaning to the legally realistic. Divorce lawyers do not construct the meaning of law in terms of a world of self-executing rules. Rather, they speak in terms of a world of uncertain and competing interpretations, in which personal agendas, organizational needs, and individual personalities play central roles. They chip away at the legal facade until its "reality" is exposed, until the client realizes that she is enmeshed in a system ridden with hazards, surprises, and people who are out to do her harm. They demonstrate the presence of the everyday in the domain of law even as they assert law's autonomy.[4]

By focusing on the mistakes, irrationality, or intransigence of others, lawyers create an inventory of explanations that puts some distance between themselves and responsibility for any eventual disappointment. Yet even as they create doubts about the legal process, lawyers must give clients some reason to rely on them. An emphasis on insider status is one means of doing this. Nothing is guaranteed, lawyers acknowledge, but the best chance for success rests with those who are familiar with local practice and who have a working relationship with officials who wield local power. By stressing the importance of being an insider, lawyers are not necessarily suggesting that the system is corrupt. They are not promising that they have an extralegal way to deal with the legal system, but they are creating an environment in which clients might come to believe that they are being helped to attain a reachable goal despite being trapped in a system laced with uncertainties.

In one of the classic articles in sociolegal studies, Robert Mnookin and Lewis Kornhauser (1979) describe how private agreements in divorce and other cases are negotiated in light of known rules that are considered to be a form of bargaining endowment. The process is captured by their trenchant phrase, "bargaining in the shadow of the law." Our observations, on the other hand, suggest a more complicated process in which the lawyer's office becomes a site for the play of power and the construction of meaning as lawyers bargain with their own clients. When bargaining with the other side, lawyers are dealing with parties that are as likely to know as much about the relevant rules as they do. But when lawyers are negotiating with their own clients, they are dealing with legally naive figures and can invoke law's shadow more tactically. They construct meanings in the service of power.

Moreover, because divorce law is extremely flexible and because it expressly allows for a wide range of discretion in its application, the shadow that it casts over lawyer-client negotiations is partial and flickering. The claim to legal knowledge does not itself insure that lawyers will succeed in their efforts. In this domain, clients are as resistant in "not getting the message" as lawyers are in the domain of social relations. Though explicit conflict is rare, closure about what is reasonable and realistic is hard to produce. Goals often remain unclear and agendas unsettled. Cases drift.

To get clients to move toward what lawyers define as realism and reason, as well as to facilitate efforts at negotiated settlement, lawyers have to struggle against the resistance that comes from continuing inclinations toward contest. In divorce work this means that lawyers urge their clients to view the emotional process of dissolving an intimate relationship in instrumental terms. Lawyers try to talk their clients into a frame of mind appropriate to the "needs" of legal business. Lawyers serve the legal system by urging clients to "redefine . . . [their] situation and restructure . . . [their] perceptions" to facilitate a reconciliation between client objectives and the needs of legal institutions (Blumberg, 1967: 20). Lawyers and clients struggle over the boundaries between law and society and over what part of the client's personality is relevant to the legal process.

The discussion of whether to fight or settle is more than a conversation about the most appropriate way to dispose of the case. Contained within this discourse is what we call the "legal construction of the client," a construction in which a self that is acceptable to the legal process is the object of negotiation and conflict (Gabel, 1980; Unger, 1975). Legal professionals behave as if it were natural and inevitable that a litigant's problems be divided up and dealt with in the manner that the legal process prescribes (Unger, 1975). As a result, in most cases, they reify the boundaries of legal relevance, legitimating some parts of human experience and denying the relevance of others.

In evaluating settlement, contest and resistance is the order of the day. As divorce lawyers put it, clients are able to make adequate arrangements with their spouses only when they can contemplate their relationship unemotionally. The program lawyers present to their clients appropriates the marriage to the realm of property and defines the connection to their spouse exclusively in those terms. Lawyers advise that the legal process works best for those who can control their emotions and concentrate on the instrumental, the calculating, the pecuniary. Lawyers argue that the separation of the emotional from the practical dimensions of divorce is an imperative of the legal process without which the system cannot efficiently deliver its goods. Clients, on the other hand, talk about property issues as if they were embedded in a broader context. For many clients the property settlement seems impossible if the emotional dimensions of the relationship are declared out of bounds. They cannot become free of their spouse if they think about legal problems in material terms only. Clients speak about the separation of emotional and financial issues as being difficult to effect because it is unnatural. The market does not exhaust their realm of values, and they have difficulty assigning governing priority to it.

If lawyers and clients are in some fundamental way at odds about the role that emotions ought to play in the legal process of divorce, they do usually come to share a common view about the superiority of settlement over trial and about the fundamental nature of settlement negotiations. In the early stages of many divorce cases, lawyers must work hard to reduce their clients' expectations to what they regard as reasonable levels. The expectations that require modification not only concern outcomes, but also relate to the procedural paths that should be followed to achieve substantive goals.

When divorce lawyers talk about their practices with social scientists, they speak the language of fairness and express concern for the effect of settlement on both parties (see O'Gorman, 1963; Kressel, 1985). But this is not the rhetorical posture that they generally adopt with their clients. As they discuss negotiated settlements, lawyers construct a picture of adversariness and portray the search for advantage simply as being displaced into another arena. Settlement is described as the result of a fight carried on outside the courtroom; it is the private, two-party version of the three-party adversarial process that is trial. Lawyers go forth in settlement negotiations to do battle for their clients, to get what the client wants. Although eventually the language and logic of compromise must creep back into the conversation, lawyers are reluctant to speak a language of accommodation lest it be interpreted by their clients as a sign of disloyalty, of less than full-bodied endorsement of clients' objectives and values. They give meaning to law by highlighting the pervasiveness of adversariness and advantage-seeking rather than fairness and equity.

In addition, lawyers tout negotiations as being high on flexibility, predictability, and cost-effectiveness. They can contain the long-term effects of bitterness, hostility, and frustration. And they may constitute the first step in building a post-divorce arrangement for cooperative problem solving. Trials, on the other hand, are portrayed by lawyers in the language of danger. They are dangerous because judges are alleged to be insensitive to the nuances of particular situations, generally because they are unwilling to devote the time and patience to the details of each case that can be mobilized in settlement negotiations. Trials are also dangerous because they are scheduled at the court's convenience, often long after the parties wish to proceed to closure, and because their combined costs are a considerable, uncontrollable, even devastating drain on the marital estate.

Divorce lawyers realize that when the case for settlement is first proposed to them, many clients cannot be convinced at a single stroke to abandon trial as a mode of disposition and embrace negotiations. They must not only be persuaded that settlement is the more prudent course, they must also be emotionally prepared to engage in negotiations with the very party who has upset their life, even betrayed their marriage.

Lawyers are aware, then, that reaching a commitment to effective negotiations may require the simple passage of time and that no real attempt at settling cases ought to begin before clients have come to terms with the psychic dimensions of divorce. The pace of proceedings may also slow due to other reasons: divorce lawyers often fail to pursue their clients' cases as vigorously as the clients would like because they, like lawyers in many specialties, take on more business than they can process and thus place clients in a sort of legal limbo. Lawyers also may simply be disorganized and lose touch with the progress of clients' cases. In specific instances it is difficult to tell which process is at work—maturation of the claim, delay in the queue, or being lost in the pile.

As they construct the meanings of law and the legal divorce, lawyers and clients cover a wide range of subjects—the distribution of property, the level of support, the rights to custody, the speed with which things are done, the wisdom of the rules and the judges, the roles that lawyers are willing to play, the times at which they are available, and the fees that they charge. In each of these areas lawyers and clients have different agendas as well as different initial understandings of law and justice. As a result, lawyer-client conferences involve complicated processes of negotiation in which each party attempts to hold firm to the agenda while conceding just enough to keep their business moving. The competing perspectives of lawyer and client and the manner in which they are articulated to each other establish the cultural boundaries within which the strategy and tactics of divorce litigation develop. When divorce clients demand to know about the legal rules that will be applied, the probabilities of achieving various results, the costs they will incur, the pace at which various things will happen, and the roles that different actors will play, there are no standard answers that lawyers can give. What the lawyer can provide is not a "corpus juris" learned in law school or available in any texts, but a picture of the legal system in the community in which she is practicing.[5]

As in any negotiation, both parties begin with different information. At its simplest, clients know their histories and goals, lawyers must learn about them; lawyers know the law and legal process, clients must find out about them. But assertion and resistance is much more pervasive and complicated than can be explained by the need that both lawyer and client have to fill gaps in their own stock of information. Differences emerge over goals, tactics, responsibilities, and values. Every lawyer-client conference is thus to some extent a contest over meanings. At the same time, meanings are themselves deployed strategically and in an inconsistent and contradictory fashion: each of the participants sets out to fulfill his own agenda and concedes ground to the other uneasily and with frequent backsliding. Shifting moments of conflict and accommodation between lawyer and client shape the course of divorce litigation—when negotiations are initiated, how they are conducted, what is asked for and offered, and how closure is reached.

The dialogue between lawyers and clients reveals the sense of rights, actionable injuries, and justice that people bring to the legal process and that the process, through the words and actions of lawyers, is willing to recognize and act upon. Clients bring to their encounters with lawyers an expectation that the justice system will impartially sort the facts in dispute to provide a deductive reading of the "truth." For them, the domain of law should both accommodate the social world and, at the same time, rescue them from the turmoil that divorce brings to that world. They expect the legal process to take their problems seriously, and they usually seek vindication of the positions that they have adopted. They expect the legal process to follow its own rules, to proceed in an orderly manner, and to be fair and error-free. As Merry (1985: 68) notes, most litigants begin with a fairly strong belief in "formal justice." By the time a problem has become serious enough to warrant bringing it to a lawyer and mobilizing the legal process, "the grievant wants vindication, protection of his or her rights, an advocate to help in the battle or a third party who will uncover the 'truth' and declare the other party wrong. Observations suggest that courts rarely provide this . . . but inexperienced plaintiffs do not know this" (Merry and Silbey, 1984: 153; see also Engel, 1984).

Lawyers believe that part of their job is to bring these expectations and images of law and legal justice closer to the "reality" that they experience daily by constructing new meanings and new understandings. The legal process provides an arena where compromises are explored, settlements are reached, and, if money is at issue, assets are divided. Because lawyers' experience is so much more extensive than that of clients, lawyers attempt to "teach" their clients about the requirements of the legal process and to socialize them into the role of the client. As a result, some of the client's problems and needs will be translated into legal categories (Cain, 1979) and many more will have legal labels attached to them. Yet, in the end, the fit between the legal categories through which lawyers see the world of divorce and the social and personal meanings that divorce holds for most clients is rarely very good.

This does not mean that clients relinquish control, or that lawyers take charge. Often neither is the case. Because clients may appear to acquiesce in the meanings presented by their lawyer does not mean that they do not exercise power over their lawyer during the very process through which their acquiescence is obtained. They do so by bringing matters into the conversation beyond those that are technically relevant and with which lawyers feel comfortable, and they do so even after lawyers think that these matters have been put aside. They do so by resisting recommendations that a lawyer believes are obviously in the client's interest. They do so by pressing lawyers to explain and justify advice given, actions taken, and results produced in light of the client's sense of what is appropriate and fair. Even as they are being "managed," clients transform the agendas of lawyers as well as their preferred professional style. Thus, the meaning of professionalism and the nature of professional is challenged at the same time as it is maintained and reproduced.

In all of the domains of meaning making in which lawyer and client interact, professionalism, on the one hand, and the nature of the agency relationship, on the other, render the power that each can exercise over the other fragile and contingent. As a consequence, ideological construction of "law" and "society" in lawyer-client interactions in divorce produces meanings that are often elusive. Conferences generally do not proceed on a straight intellectual line as does the ideal examination of a witness at trial. Rather, they skip around as each participant tries to legislate particular meanings in the course of the interaction. Because meanings are developed as part of a dialogue that is shaped by client questions, expectations, and demands, their construction is neither linear nor free of contradiction. Lawyer-client interactions are contested, personalistic, and, in almost all instances, more complicated experientially than technically.

In these interactions the meanings produced are inextricably linked to the efforts of both lawyers and clients to exercise "control" over one another. But these meanings are also independently significant in revealing the power of law. As we have seen, the production of meaning proceeds in three strands in the divorce cases that we observed. First, it constructs an ideology of separate spheres, isolating emotions from other domains of human experience and disenfranchising affective life in legal affairs. Then, having distanced law from the emotional and the affective, it subordinates rule systems to personalistic inclinations and resources. And third, it produces a picture of law as inexorably adversarial and opportunistic rather than fair or just. It is in the face of tensions and ambiguity in these messages that meaning seems elusive. But, as Fish (1991: 195) reminds us, these tensions and ambiguities are "a description of strengths rather than weaknesses." Law's strength exists in its capacity to keep alive meanings that seem inconsistent, while presenting itself as universal and rational (Fish, 1991: 203).

To what extent is our view of the production of meaning and the play of power in lawyer-client interaction limited to the divorce cases from which it is derived? Divorce practice *is* different from most other areas of legal practice.[6] Divorce, more than most litigation, originates in personal failure and rejection. The number of clients in divorce who are experiencing some form of personal crisis is high, probably higher than in parallel fields such as criminal law, personal injury, worker compensation, landlord and tenant, consumer, and bankruptcy. As a consequence, the negotiation of reality may be more difficult and salient in divorce. And because divorce law is itself at one end of the rules-discretion continuum, the opportunity for creativity in interpreting the legally possible is greater than in fields in which rules narrow the scope of interim maneuvers and acceptable outcomes. Perhaps most important, the relative social status and economic power of divorce lawyers and their clients, rather than conforming to a uniform pattern, as may be the case in fields as diverse as criminal and corporate law, is more varied since the status of clients reflects that of the population at large. Thus divorce lawyers tend to encounter clients of diverse social and economic status and, as a result, are less likely to develop patterns of domination or control than lawyers whose position relative to their clients is more consistent.

On the other hand, much of the production of and struggle over meaning and many of the enactments of power between divorce lawyers and their clients occur as well in other areas of practice. Lawyers and clients must always negotiate a consistent version of events, an account of the client's situation, and interactions with the other side. They must negotiate a fit between the client's goals and expectations and the results achievable through legal process. They must negotiate about the timing of action to be taken in pursuit of the client's goals and about the division of labor between them. In each of these instances, whether the area of law be commercial or criminal, power and meaning are neither stable nor static.

Only on rare occasions then does interaction between lawyers and clients in any field resemble the straightforward provision of technical services to a generally complacent, dependent, and weak laity. That interaction is, more often, complex, shifting, frequently conflicted, and negotiated. In the relationship between lawyer and client, the professional provider, like it or not, shares power and participates in ideological production with the client. It is a relationship where the knowledge and experience of each may be challenged by the other, where the economic investment of any particular lawyer in any particular client may equal or outstrip the opposite, where lawyers have conflicts of interest that clients seek to identify and protect against, and where the humanity of each may be constantly under scrutiny by the other. Thus the nature of lawyer-client relationships beyond the context of divorce cannot be captured by simple models of professional or lay dominance or simple estimates of lawyer and client resources.

In the end, then, a relationship that from the outside appears orderly, if not cooperative, is, on closer examination, quite often competitive and confused. Far from embodying the majestic pretensions of law itself, lawyer-client interaction reflects the conflict and chaos that typifies the construction of meaning and play of power in those many mundane occasions on which people seek to create meaning and promote their own interests under conditions of stress and uncertainty. By attending to those interactions we see both the fragility of power as it is exercised and the elusiveness of meaning as it is constructed.

Notes

CHAPTER 1

1. In 1991, 2,374,000 Americans got divorced. This number has been fairly constant since 1974 (U.S. Bureau of the Census, 1993; Table 91).

2. "Divorcing people must renegotiate, almost entirely on their own, changes in family life, loyalties with in-laws, parenting responsibilities, and relationships with friends" (Hopper, 1993: 133–34).

3. Harrington and Yngvesson (1990: 140–41) argue that "interpretive sociolegal inquiry is based on an interest in questions about the way law gets separated from material life—from its own role in creating the relations of material life. This question," they contend, "draws attention to practices of law that are taken for granted, practices that make law appear to stand apart from social relations and to be of a different and separate order, rather than a continuous part of social practice."

4. "Law as ideology is not a sphere from which meanings emerge and to which meanings are carried back, and practice is not a process separable from law. Rather law is found, invented, and made in a variety of locations . . . through a variety of practices that are themselves ideological" (see Harrington and Yngvesson, 1990: 142).

5. As Bourdieu (1987: 817) puts it, meaning is created in "the confrontation between different bodies . . . moved by divergent special interests."

6. As Yngvesson (1989: 1709) asserts in describing another set of interactions between legal professionals and laypersons, "The exchange is clearly an unequal one, most apparent in the control exercised by court officials and others through their knowledge of legal and therapeutic discourse, and their authority as experts to use this knowledge to label the behavior of others."

7. In the research from which this book is derived, we developed an observational account of lawyer-client interaction in divorce cases. We chose to examine divorce because it is a serious and growing social problem in which the involvement of lawyers is particularly salient and controversial. Concern among many divorce lawyers about their role suggested that field research on lawyer-client interaction in this area would encounter less resistance than in other areas of legal practice.

8. There is, of course, the question of whether participation in the study suggests that the lawyers in our samples are in some important respects differ-

ent from the others we contacted. They did not appear so. Except as noted, they did not seem to have different kinds of clients, practices, or different orientations toward practice; to have a reputation for different ethical standards; to engage in different promotional practices; or to charge different fees. In fact, we believe that inclusion in the study was chiefly determined by the coincidence of who was able to find cooperative clients when the project was fresh in their minds.

9. As David Garland (1990: 19) notes, "Punishment is not wholly explicable in terms of its purposes because no social artefact can be explained in this way. Like architecture or diet or clothing or table manners, punishment has an instrumental purpose, but also a cultural style and historical tradition, and . . . if we are to understand such artefacts we have to think of them as social and cultural entities whose meanings can only be unravelled by careful analysis and detailed examination."

10. "[T]he power exerted by a legal regime consists less in the force that it can bring to bear against violators of its rules than in its capacity to persuade people that the world described in its images and categories is the only attainable world in which a sane person would want to live" (Gordon, 1984: 108).

11. For a discussion of law's constitutive powers at the level of "clusters of beliefs," see Gordon (1982: 287).

12. For a classic example of such an approach in the study of lawyer-client interaction, see Rosenthal (1974).

13. For an important discussion of this conception of legal rules as purposive instrumentalities, see Silbey and Bitner (1982: 399, 400). As these authors write, 'Neither the purposes nor the uses of any specific law are fully inscribed upon it. Therefore, the meaning of any specific law, and of law as a social institution, can only be understood by examining the ways it is actually used."

14. Sarat and Kearns (1993) label this the "instrumentalist" perspective in sociolegal research.

15. We need not attribute to this kind of work any particular view about the "mechanisms" by which law affects social life—among others, these might include force, the threat or fear of force, or, very differently, the creation of new legal statuses. However it does its work, law's job is to regulate effectively the behaviors of legal subjects, the things they do or abstain from doing. The effectiveness of legal regulation may be directly observable in behavior (e.g., driving faster on the interstate after speed limits were raised from 55 to 65 mph) or it might be only indirectly detectible (e.g., the increased confidence in banks following the creation of the FDIC) by inferring actions from beliefs. The point is that scholars interested only in behavior and the material outcomes of law need not share any particular view about the kinds of intervening mechanisms deployed by law to shape or sustain various social arrangements.

16. The key to this understanding of law is the belief that there is a fairly firm division between the legal and the social, with law being an important influence on society, but standing outside of it. As Gordon (1984: 60) has observed, writers in this tradition

> divide the world into two spheres, one social and one legal. Society is the primary realm of social experience. It is "real life": What's immediately and truly important to people . . . goes on there . . . . "Law" or "the legal system," on the other hand, is a distinctly secondary body of

phenomena. It is a specialized realm of state and professional activity that is called into being by the primary social world in order to serve that world's needs. Law is auxiliary—an excrescence on social life, even if sometimes a useful excrescence.

So conceived, legal scholarship begins with legal rules and processes and ends in an examination of their effectiveness in regulating or changing everyday life; in other words, in a study of the extent to which this law has, or has failed to have, *the intended role* in shaping the domain of activity in question.

Instrumentalists speak about the success or failure of law, and measure success by the ways legal rules are used and resisted (see Sarat, 1985; Abel, 1973). Sometimes, it appears, this view rather narrowly links the operations of law to coercion and constraint and so purports to measure legal effectiveness by looking for "conforming conduct."

> The "instrumental theory" integrates notions of action and law. Once created by human beings, laws and legal institutions appear as objective constraints on behavior. Citizens perceive the legal system as a constraint and orient their behavior accordingly. Therefore, if the law is effective, the actual behavior of citizens will correspond to the behavior prescribed by legal doctrine. (Trubek and Esser, 1989: 15)

As a consequence, this perspective fails to take into account that law is already an integral part of that which it regulates.

For a contrasting view, namely that law mirrors society and that changes in law tend to follow social changes and are often intended to do no more than to make those changes permanent, see Friedman (1975). Grant Gilmore (1977: 110–11) argues, "Law reflects but in no sense determines the moral wisdom of a society. The values of a reasonably just society will reflect themselves in a reasonably just law . . . . The values of an unjust society will reflect themselves in an unjust law."

17. Indeed, what Hunt (1985: 16–17) says about ideology in general, namely that "ideology is a social process that is realized in and through social relations," could equally be said about law as a kind of ideology.

18. In *Local Knowledge,* Clifford Geertz (1983: 218, 230) suggests that

> law, rather than a mere technical add-on to a morally (or immorally) finished society, is, along of course with a whole range of other cultural realities, . . . an active part of it . . . . Law . . . is, in a word, constructive; in another constitutive; in a third, formational . . . . Law, with its power to place particular things that happen . . . in a general frame in such a way that rules for the principled management of them seem to arise naturally from the essentials of their character, is rather more than a reflection of received wisdom or a technology of dispute-settlement.

Geertz's remarks help one understand why instrumentalists are naturally inclined to think of legal systems as "struggling to retain what seems like a tenuous grasp on the social order . . ." (Silbey, 1990: 20). But for someone like Geertz, the apparent frailty of law's hold on social life derives from the mistaken assumption that individuals are "autonomous and self-constituting" (Trubek and Esser, 1989: 17), when what seems more plausible is that "the values, knowledge, and evaluative criteria embodied in the subjectivity of actors are not individually held units of meaning but rather are the threads or traces of a collectively held fabric of social relations" *Id.* The standard critique of instrumentalism also rejects the "radical distinction between ideas and behavior" and the conception of "action as responding to external sanctions, legal or otherwise" *Id.*

19. Gordon (1984: 109) suggests that "Lawmaking and law-interpreting institutions have been among the primary sources of the pictures of order and disorder, virtue and vice, reasonableness and craziness, realism and visionary naiveté and some of the most commonplace aspects of social reality that ordinary people carry around with them and use in ordering their lives."

20. However pervasive the consciousness-setting capacity of social practices, at the level of conventional social arrangements the constitutive nature of law is perhaps most clearly seen in the case of subordinated groups such as women, people of color, and the handicapped (see Gordon, 1984: 103–4). A generation ago handicapped people, for instance, were immobilized by a world that made no concessions to their difficulties in transport or access to basic needs beyond their homes. Without any special legal protections, such as those since created in the federal Americans with Disabilities Act of 1990, they were routinely *assumed* to be underskilled, unreliable, and virtually unemployable. Imagine, then, the effect that a legal regime that had turned its back on such people had on their self-definition and self-respect and how they were viewed and treated by their families and other intimates and by public officials. Imagine as well the changes that have been produced in these attitudes and behaviors by laws that have required society to spend hundreds of millions of dollars simply to assure that handicapped people can move about the world with reasonable ease and now insist that they are entitled to the same guarantees about employment as the traditionally protected classes (see Engel, 1993).

21. See also Blumberg (1967: 32), who finds criminal defense lawyers to be "agent-mediators who help the accused redefine his situation and restructure his perceptions concomitant with a plea of guilty."

22. For a somewhat different reading of Macaulay's argument, see Trubek (1984: 619–20).

23. The distinction between effectiveness and effects might initially seem suspect since it is impossible to determine law's effectiveness without knowing its effects, or some of them. But the qualification, "or some of them," makes all the difference. To the extent that law is viewed as a machine and, more specifically, as a machine for promoting previously identified ends, policies, or purposes, then the relevant effects are just those that advance or imperil these intended outcomes (see Dewey, 1939; Fuller, 1964). These are the only effects that matter. Only these effects determine a law's effectiveness and so its instrumental value (Feeley, 1976; Casper and Brereton, 1984). As Gordon (1984: 70) puts it, this view "almost unconsciously reserves even what it believes to be the very marginal opportunities for legal influence on the direction of social change to an elite of policymakers."

Historically, sociolegal scholars like Macaulay not only have begun their inquiry from the perspective of legal materials, but have favored some legal materials (namely, rules) over others, focusing on the way these particular carriers of legal direction are used, violated, or ignored. Rules tend to compartmentalize social phenomena and to operate on those aspects of social life that are most amenable to this kind of all-or-nothing normative ordering. The effect is to make a law's immediate consequences more apparent. On the other hand, law and society scholarship that centers on rules is all the more likely to absorb their "logic" and, like the rules themselves, detach the regulated activities from their full social setting.

The history of social research on law is closely tied to the search for the conditions under which law is effective, to efforts to understand when legislation or judicial decisions can reliably be counted on to guide behavior or produce social changes in expected or desired ways. "Legal effectiveness research" (Sarat, 1985) begins by identifying the goals of legal policy and moves to assess its success or failure by comparing those goals with the results produced. Where, as is almost invariably the case, the results do not match the goals, attention typically shifts to the factors that might explain the "gap" between law on the books and law in action. By understanding the causes of observed discrepancies, hope is kept alive of reducing or eliminating such gaps in the future and thus increasing law's effectiveness. Gap research has been important in generating key insights in the study of legal phenomena and continues to represent a dominant mode of scholarship (Black, 1989).

24. This cultural domination is reflected in what Merry calls "legal consciousness," that is, "the way people conceive of the 'natural' and normal way of doing things, their habitual patterns of talk and action, and their commonsense understandings of the world" (1990: 5).

25. When "court staff reshaped 'vicious' actions as 'normal' behavior" (1988: 433), Yngvesson provides a strong indication that the clerk's transformation is not always accepted. In the case of the "Bad Neighborhood," the clerk rejected the indigenous myths of a poor and disorganized community and asserted conventional middle-class beliefs in their stead. What was the reaction? "The wife of the Polish complainant left the courtroom, spitting on the floor and screaming her frustration at the clerk" (1988: 439).

26. "Reinforced" seems to introduce the notion of effect, the notion that these ideas already existed in the community and were in this instance supported by the actions of the legal officials so that they had greater standing or stature or power or stability than before the officials acted. Yngvesson (1988) does not discuss this issue of effect explicitly, but many of the abstractions from her data sound as though she is talking about more than what words mean, that she is talking about the consequence of those meanings. For instance:

1. The courthouse is transformed into an arena "for *constituting* what the local community is" (420).
2. The way that the issues were defined by the clerk "*required a transformation* in the world of each [disputant]" (426).
3. The clerk's "participation actively involved the courthouse in what Bourdieu (1987: 834) has called 'the practical activity of *worldmaking*'" (426).
4. The clerk uses "the complaint procedure for *maintaining* a moral order" (443).

27. Merry's statement of the localized version of the constitutive power of law is powerful, elegant, and immediately intelligible. However, most of the cases she analyzes, including those that she claims "illustrate the arguments of the book as a whole" (1990: 150), suggest that law is weak, ineffective, unpersuasive, and operates most frequently by *retreat* rather than *conversion*.

The key to the constitutive power of law is found in citizen reaction to court redefinition of their problems. If the people who apply to the court for legal relief and see their problems in legal terms come to view their problems in the moral or therapeutic terms favored by the court, then law in these instances has played the transformative role claimed for it by Merry. If they do not, then it has not.

The data, and Merry's own characterizations of it, suggest that this transformation rarely occurs. "Plaintiffs resist this [the court's] cultural domination by asserting their own understanding of the problem, usually by insisting on talking about it in legal discourse" (1990: 147).

We have reviewed all of the cases that Merry discusses in the book. Some are passing references, some are analyzed at length. If the constitutive effect resides in the transformative power of court officials, of their ability to get the litigants to see the problems underlying the cases as they do, to approach these problems in the discourse that the officials prefer, then the effect is quite weak. Merry discusses twenty-five cases, or sets of cases. (The numbers in the text add up to more than twenty-five because some cases were coded in more than one category.) In eleven of the cases there is not sufficient information to evaluate the effect of legal intervention. In twelve of the cases the court officials are unsuccessful in getting the litigants to reinterpret their experience in the terms preferred by the officials. In only six instances is there any evidence of a transformation in perspective and in three of those the only indication is that the litigants accepted a mediation settlement. In other words, in only three cases in the entire book can we say with confidence that court officials were able to persuade litigants to switch from a legal to a moral or therapeutic discourse.

28. "When an individual or social group manages to block a field of relations of power, to render them impassive and invariable and to prevent all reversibility of movement . . . we are facing what can be called a state of domination" (see Foucault in Bernauer and Rasmussen, 1988: 3).

29. "'[T]he rhetoric of motives' here, and in other domains of social life, is all about getting one plausible vocabulary rather than another accepted as real" (Hopper, 1993b: 811).

30. For an interesting case study of this process, see Rosen (1984).

31. As Foucault (see Bernauer and Rasmussen, 1988: 11) puts it, "I hardly ever use the word 'power' and if I do sometimes, it is always a short cut to the expression I always use: the relationships of power . . . . I mean that in human relations, whatever they are—whether it be a question of communicating verbally, as we are doing right now, or a question of a love relationship, an institutional or economic relationship—power is always present."

32. Moreover, as Yngvesson (1988: 445) notes, professionals are constrained by the very resources that seem to empower them. "Fundamental to this tension is an ambiguity in the meaning and implications of 'knowledge' as both empowering and subjecting. The one who 'knows' has 'a practical understanding of or experience with' and is thus more powerful, but 'to know' is also 'to be subject to' and thus in a sense 'controlled by.'"

33. Our view of power differs significantly from the view that prevails in most of the literature on the legal profession. Heinz (1983: 891), for example, believes that the crucial distinction in the lawyer-client relationship is whether lawyers have the power to modify their clients' goals, and that lawyer control over tactics and techniques is both assumed and irrelevant.

34. On the idea of client as consumer, see Nader (1976: 247) and Carlson (1976: 287). Griffiths (1986: 155) notes that "clients make a fairly passive impression, asking few questions, showing little interest in the procedural and legal aspects of their divorce, and manifesting little inclination to use legal strategies in their conflict with their spouse."

35. Macaulay's (1979) analysis of the range of transformative effects that lawyers have on clients' goals contrasts with the picture presented by Cain. It is not clear whether the difference reflects differences in American and British practice or differences in the sensitivity of legally trained and lay observers. The low frequency of clients exhibiting "inappropriate" behavior in Cain's data suggests that the cases she observed were considerably more straightforward than those generally encountered by American lawyers.

36. Rueschemeyer (1973: 112) believes that American lawyers are more closely in tune with their clients' orientations than are continental lawyers, whose roles are explicitly defined and whose personal contact with clients is less frequent.

37. In a similar vein, Olson (1984: 131–35) summarizes the studies in several countries that find client participation to vary directly with socioeconomic status; see Handler (1978: 25), O'Gorman (1963: 58–59), Buckle and Buckle (1977: 25), Blumberg (1967: 28–38), Baldwin and McConville (1977: 295–96), Felstiner (1979: 321), and Tomasic (1978: 99). But also see Katz (1979: 447), Sorauf (1976: 155), and Carlin (1966: 166) for the argument that lawyers with low-status clients are subject to more client pressures to violate ethical norms.

38. Two things should be noted about the conventional views of power in the lawyer-client relationship. First, those views are basically structural: they suggest that power varies by status, economic resources, field of law, or the vagaries of particular clients. Second, they treat power as a resource that one or another of the parties to a lawyer-client relationship possesses.

39. For an interesting exploration of this spatial metaphor, see Dumm (1990: 29, 34).

40. "A tactic insinuates itself into the other's place, fragmentarily, without taking it over in its entirety, without being able to keep it at a distance. It has at its disposal no base where it can capitalize on its advantages, prepare its expansions, and secure independence with respect to circumstances" (de Certeau, 1984: xix).

41. As de Certeau argues, "The latter is devious, it is dispersed, but it insinuates itself everywhere, silently and almost invisibly . . . through its ways of *using* products" (1984: xii–xiii).

42. What lawyers tell their clients about such behavior validates or denies preconceptions and beliefs, and structures, at least in part, the way clients "experience and perceive their relations with others" (Hunt, 1985: 15).

43. This interpretation of law by divorce lawyers is "private." It is hidden from public accountability. It is accomplished by lawyers for clients through talk that does not occur in a public forum and is not otherwise "publicized." Like changes in the post–World War II divorce law itself, which Jacob (1988) has termed a "silent revolution," this construction of law's operation is also silent. It is not self-evident even to its practitioners, although they generally do not deny its validity when it is called to their attention. Because it is not part of any public experience, it must be learned anew by each client in the unfolding relationship with the lawyer in divorce.

CHAPTER 2

1. Hopper (1993b: 805) argues that while the breakup of marriage is often filled with ambivalence and complexity for both parties, "Once divorce begins, people usually identify themselves as either the one who wants the divorce or as the partner who does not want the divorce. . . . [M]ost divorcing people describe their divorces as non-mutual and . . . they have no difficulty specifying who decided on a divorce and who did not." Contrary to our findings, Hopper argues that at the same time "nearly all divorcing people accepted mutual blame for the ultimate dissolution" (1993a: 143).

2. Such accounts are, of course, not legally irrelevant. In Massachusetts they remain legally relevant under the fault option as well as in terms of the state's equitable distribution scheme for dividing marital property. Moreover, in both Massachusetts and California the conduct of the spouse may play an important part in custody disputes. Yet we observed that the culture of no-fault seems to be widespread among lawyers. Even in custody and property disputes, lawyers tend to avoid participating in their clients' narratives of blame and fault.

3. A similar tendency has been noted by Griffiths (1986: 152). Griffiths says that "Clients often want to unburden themselves of the emotional and social side of their divorce and most lawyers listen patiently to this . . . they emphasize their role as lawyer not so much by cutting off the flow of legally irrelevant communication as by reacting to it with little more than social platitudes."

4. "A motive," Kenneth Burke argued (1954: 25), "is not some fixed thing . . . which one can go and look at. It is a term of interpretation, and being such it will naturally take its place within the framework of our *Weltanschauung* as a whole . . . ."

5. While Mills called attention to the strong connection between interpretive activities and social structure, he tended to ignore the processes of interaction through which vocabularies of motive emerge. Thus his perspective seems somewhat mechanistic and deterministic. The interpretation of action implicit in the use of vocabularies of motive is itself one part of the activity of building, maintaining, or changing social relations. In this sense it might be said that employing particular vocabularies of motive makes possible the construction of particular social institutions or that social institutions can be formed only where common vocabularies of motive exist or where there is sufficient sharing of culture that such vocabularies can be quickly constructed. Others, however, have focused on the ways in which meanings emerge in social life. See, for example, Berger and Luckmann (1966); Goffman (1959); Scheff (1966). Most often those who study that process describe it as one of negotiation.

They treat social interactions as a process of exchange in which participants create shared understandings and interpretations through a series of proposals and counterproposals, sometimes explicit but most often implicit in their interaction. Thus the vocabulary of motive that a group legitimates is itself the result of a group process. Furthermore, the idea of negotiating reality suggests that social interaction requires agreement and closure. Those who use that idea argue that while social interaction may be conflictual and associated with inequalities of power, it generally proceeds until a shared agreement is reached (see Scheff, 1966; Sudnow, 1965).

6. Investigation of the way lawyers and clients use vocabularies of motive requires attention to the norms and orientations of ordinary citizens and legal

professionals. Clients bring to their interactions with lawyers what Schutz (1962) called a "natural attitude" or an "attitude of everyday life." In this attitude the way the world appears is accepted as the way the world really is. The self is perceived to be at the center of society and events are interpreted in terms of their impact on the self. Lawyers, on the other hand, might be expected to think of motives and actions in what Habermas (1970: 65) called "rational-purposive" terms; terms in which technical rules and a problem-solving orientation are more important than emotional reactions and justifications of self. In the combination and confrontation of these views, law is given social meaning and, in turn, it provides new perspectives on social relations and social behavior.

7. This tendency of lawyers to ignore their clients' central concerns limits the extent to which lawyers can act as important agents of transformation. See Felstiner, Abel, and Sarat (1980–81).

8. The construction and interpretation of motives within these narratives generally proceeds at two levels, one "geographic" and the other evaluative. Lawyer and client generally try to locate particular action or events in some social space; that is, they try to identify the source of those actions and events. Their attribution of motivation involves arguments concerning the causes of behavior and decisions about whether it originates from within the personality and character of the actor or is a response to external circumstances.

This inside/outside way of describing interpretations and explanations of the actions of others is suggested by the attribution theory of social psychology (see Heider, 1958; Nisbett and Ross, 1980; Kelly and Michela, 1980). Attribution theorists argue that in the construction of vocabularies of motive the first task is causal judgment:

> [here] the observer seeks to identify the cause . . . to which some particular effect may most reasonably be attributed. The second task is social inference: the observer of an episode forms inferences about the attributes of relevant entities, that is, either the dispositions of actors or the properties of situations to which those actors have responded. (Ross, 1977: 175)

But the efforts of lawyers and clients to understand the geography of motivation requires further inquiry into two aspects of the conduct under scrutiny. First, there is the question of whether the conduct is distinctive; that is, whether it is directed solely at a particular person and limited to a particular instance, or whether the action recurs in different circumstances and is, therefore, consistent. Second, there is the question of whether the behavior in question is widely shared or typical of the way most people behave (attribution theorists call this the dimension of consensus). Where an action, behavior or event is common in the behavioral repertoire of an actor but is believed to be relatively uncommon in the population, people generally attribute that behavior to the personal disposition or character of the actor; on the other hand, where it is unusual for an actor to behave in a particular way and where most people do not act that way most of the time, people generally locate the source of the action outside the actor in circumstances or context (see Coates and Penrod, 1980–81). Thus the geographic dimension of the vocabularies of motive found in lawyer-client interaction theoretically involves an intricate judgmental process in which lawyers and clients behave as "intuitive psychologists" (Ross, 1977). However, the stability of lawyer and client attributions in divorce and the instrumental origins that we report here suggest a less complicated psychological process.

The second dimension of the vocabularies of motive that we find in lawyer-client conversations is evaluative. The question is whether, from the perspective of the interpreting agent, the behavior produced by a person or circumstance is socially desirable. The two dimensions are, however, not completely independent; internal attributions are generally associated with blame while explanations of behavior in situational terms tend to be exculpatory.

9. Reports of interpretive research generally stay close to the data on which they are based. Thus this book contains extensive quotations from the lawyer-client conferences we observed and the interviews we conducted. The quotations are based on the tape recordings we made of those conferences and interviews. We have edited these materials in the following ways (for the model on which our scheme is based, see O'Barr and Conley, 1992: 10): (1) we deleted fragmentary utterances and false starts; (2) we corrected grammatical errors that made the quotations hard to understand; (3) we illuminated unclear antecedents; (4) we occasionally changed a word or phrase when the speaker's intent appeared clear to us from the context, but was not incorporated in the actual words the speaker used.

10. Weitzman (1985: 25) reports that "many men and women were dismayed to learn that [under a no-fault system] no one cared about who was 'responsible' for the divorce." What this means is that attorneys are often in the difficult position of having to educate their clients about the new legal norms. However, she reports that while many lawyers point out that questions of fault are not relevant in court, many "'still allow clients to discuss these matters because it is a safety valve . . . .'"

11. Similar inconsistencies have been noted in other contexts by Finchman (1985); Jones and Davis (1965); and Kelly (1967).

12. After a long time spent figuring out how to have the papers served in the least upsetting way, the divorce petition was filed.

13. Harris and Shultz (1993) criticize law schools for banning emotions from the classroom, while Nussbaum (1993) faults judges for acting as if there were a polar opposition between emotion and reason.

14. This characterization somewhat overstates our American data. Nevertheless, clients frequently want more social support and less legal emphasis than lawyers provide.

15. This analysis of the vocabulary of motive also points out the contradictions built into the ideological structure of no-fault divorce. In a fault system the personalities and behavior of the spouses are always a major concern in the case. The lawyer gathers information concerning these issues, primarily from his client. As any other lawyer preparing a case, he must check and test the information his client provides by cross-examining the client. He cannot uncritically accept the social world of the client or ignore his client's characterizations of the behavior of the spouse. Such cross-examination may or may not alter or defuse inflamed or exaggerated characterizations (see O'Gorman, 1963: chap. 6), but it at least avoids implicit acceptance or approval of the client's faultfinding. By making tests of client characterizations an important part of the lawyer's role in divorce, fault, paradoxically, may have facilitated negotiations. In the no-fault world, settlements may be complicated precisely because the lawyer has no

incentive or need to challenge client imputations of motive and their associated faultfinding (Erlanger et al., 1987). The no-fault client may enter negotiations never having had anyone challenge her characterizations of the culpability of the spouse and may end up being asked to make a deal, or reach a compromise, with someone who is portrayed, throughout the legal process, as hostile or greedy or unreliable. For no-fault divorce to work at a psychological level, the client ultimately must be persuaded that a fifty-fifty property split is emotionally fair, or she will resent the outcome. If a client's evaluation of her spouse is negative and untested, she will have difficulty achieving this perspective, and the more the lawyer ignores the client's characterization, the less likely the client will reconcile herself to the justice of the inevitable outcome.

In other words, lawyer acquiescence in the separation of the emotional and legal divorce is encouraged by no-fault. Lawyers avoid coming to terms with client constructions of the social world and limit their own commentary to those aspects of the divorce that are definitely part of the legal process. Because lawyers generally have little expertise in helping clients to examine or reframe their experience critically, or in helping them to understand, perhaps even empathize with, their spouse's perspective, they capitalize on the opportunity to put that world beyond their professional responsibilities. In so doing, in confining themselves to the vocabulary of motives seemingly appropriate to the world of no-fault divorce, the legal construction of social relations tends to undermine its psychosocial foundations. No-fault has not stripped the divorce situation of allegations of spousal inequity and, like it or not, it has not removed lawyers from the battle over morality in marriage.

The full rhetorical effect of a switch from fault to no-fault divorce is even more complicated. In a fault system, the lawyer's first task was to identify the positive and negative dimensions of the behavior of both spouses. Although lawyers were concerned with the reality value of client characterizations of their own and their spouse's behavior and inclined to take action to get a dispassionate fix on such recitals, they also had the tactical objective of learning to paint the spouse's behavior in as poor a light as possible. Whether the end result of that process was more or less consistent with reasonable negotiations than the situation in no-fault, where lawyers neither restrain their clients' hostility nor feel obligated to manufacture a dismal picture of the opposing side, is problematic.

CHAPTER 3

1. Lawyers frequently exert considerable pressure on their own clients to be reasonable. When possible, they cooperate with the lawyer for the other party in seeking to get their respective clients to agree to a reasonable settlement. They use all sorts of ad hoc tactics to try to bring about a "reasonable divorce." But the key to their role is a common strategy from which they seldom diverge: the maintenance of a stance of relative neutrality (Griffiths, 1986: 166).

2. For a discussion of the rationales for imputing goals to clients who do not, or cannot, articulate them, see Luban (1981).

3. Some lawyers may be so committed to a particular political perspective on divorce that they do not easily recognize clients who are uneasy about or reluctant to endorse such a program. Alfieri (1991a: 2123–24) calls this phenomenon "pre-understanding." "Pre-understanding is a method of social con-

struction that operates by applying a standard narrative reading to a client's story."

4. For a discussion of the techniques of sifting, see Binder, Bergman, and Price 1991: 104–23.

5. Lawyers rarely present something as their own opinion. Their rationalizations for steering the discussion and persuading clients are largely presented in terms of the formal and practical margins set by the legal system, by the law, and more particularly by the decisions that can be expected from the local court. What is contingent is presented as if it were necessary.

6. For a discussion of various roles that lawyers play in divorce, see O'Gorman (1963: chap. 6).

7. Other work emphasizes the way client stories are silenced in lawyer-client interaction (see Cunningham, 1989; White, 1990; Alfieri, 1991a). Our observations suggest that clients resist the definitions of reality their lawyers provide through persistent and recurring assertion.

8. This is, of course, subject to the norms of informed consent (see Spiegel, 1979).

9. For an illustration in another area of law, see Durkin, Dingwall, and Felstiner (1991).

10. This is, of course, predictably the case where the client is not paying the bill, as in the legal services context. We were surprised that it was also true in the fee-for-service context.

11. Power, as is now widely recognized, is exercised in the refusal to act just as surely as it is involved in assertion (see Lukes, 1974; Bachrach and Baratz, 1970: 43–46).

12. As Griffiths puts it (1986: 166), "Lawyers' control over the legal procedure makes available various techniques for cooling off conflict. Simple delay is often used to this end."

13. Client procrastination may relate to major as well as minor matters. We observed a client decline to tell his spouse that he intended to seek a divorce after he assured his lawyer that he would; another client refused, without explanation, to authorize service of a divorce petition on the spouse from whom she repeatedly claimed she wished to be divorced; and a third client successfully evaded her lawyer's entreaties to agree to a medical examination to determine whether she was fit to hold a job.

14. For an argument about how lawyers should respond, see Luban (1981: 491).

15. Nick and Durr attended part of the first lawyer-client conference that we observed.

16. At the time we entered the case Kathy was clearly still trying to hold onto the marriage. She was psychologically unwilling or unable to accept the idea of being rejected. For a superb picture of the psychological dynamics of separation, see Vaughan (1986).

17. At another point in this conference we observe the first hint of how the lawyer tries to keep the conversation focused on financial matters: when the client starts to talk about her struggle to help her "kid through his drug problem," the lawyer successfully changes the subject to the house and car payments. That part of the client's social world relating to her child's problems is not to be part of the "reality" of this case.

18. Given Wendy's previously demonstrated tendency to extrapolate from her experiences with other cases to the reality of Kathy's case, Wendy may assume she does not need to ask in order to know what her client wants. Assuming rather than asking is, in this instance, an exercise of power by indirection. This power consists in what is not being said, with the burden then shifted to the client, contrary to the picture of lawyer-client relations in which lawyers are portrayed as agents of their clients.

19. On the power of silence as a strategy of power and resistance, see Scott (1990: 17–18).

20. For a discussion of the impact of divorce on the economic status of women, see Weitzman (1985: 323–56).

21. It is as if we were being given access to the kind of "hidden transcript" that Scott (1990: 4–5) argues is constructed to resist dominant power.

22. "I do" is also an eerie reminder of the marriage vow: "Do you take . . . ?" "I do."

23. This is the exact dialogue:

Wendy: I can't see that we can come up with enough to offset your equity in the house unless he's willing to take a note or something to that effect. Have you discussed this with him at all?

Kathy: At one time he said that he might be willing to go along, but this was about two months ago.

Wendy: I think you have to give him a note for $24,000.

Kathy: That's a tremendous amount.

Wendy: Maybe we can get him to keep on making the house payments?

Kathy: I doubt it very much. I think he's really sick of it.

Wendy: You've had a long marriage and you should be entitled to some support because he does make a lot more money than you do. So that's something we have to consider. You could sell the house and get a condominium or buy a mobile home.

Kathy: I would prefer to keep my house if I could.

Wendy: The only way we can get this part resolved is by getting that little loose end tied up, the value of some sculptures. We have all the figures on everything else. I can write her [Nick's lawyer] a comprehensive letter saying I think we should do it this way. I don't think your husband is going to agree to it, but I think at least we will get things moving again.

24. Wendy interrupts Kathy's attempt to explain how she is going to kick her youngest child out of the house with a question about the sculptures. This interchange repeats a sequence in the first conference and reflects Wendy's unwillingness to give her client's nonfinancial personal problems a place on the agenda. Although those problems have no legal standing, they are not explicitly ruled out of order; rather, they are shunted aside by a change in subject.

25. The difficulty faced by Kathy in relating a coherent program to her husband is reflected in the disorganization of Wendy's suggestions.

1. The nice thing would be if you could buy him out and then, eventually, if you sell it you'll have the rollover by yourself.

2. Another alternative would be taking spousal support of whatever your house payment is, $400 something a month, and saying, okay, I'll give you a note for $20,000 and what you do is [just give it back to him].

3. Now you might also work out some kind of agreement with him that you will owe him $20,000 from the house that you will pay him when you sell the house or die, which ever comes first.

4. Do we divide it up then [at the time of sale] and figure out your [husband's] equity based on what the actual price of the house is or do you take your chances with me and hope it goes up in value, or if it goes down in value, you get less money?

5. What we can do is put something to the effect that you'll keep the house, the house will be sold no later than or listed for sale no later than such-and-such a date, that upon the close of the house, that within sixty days thereafter, either one of you may put on a cap under the issue of support for the court to determine what your needs are at that time.

6. [You could waive support in exchange for his interest in the house.] I really think that you would be giving up far more than you would be getting in a case like that because you are talking about $400 a month, which is $4,800 a year, and in four years he would have paid you $20,000. If in that four-year period of time you were to get injured and could not work, you may need to have the support continued. If you waive it for now and forever more, then if you get sick in two years, you may end up having to sell the house and live off that and go on welfare eventually because you have no recourse to have him help you. So it's one of those things you have to decide.

7. Another possibility is the two of you refinance the house and he gets his $20,000 out that way, and then you have a bigger house payment and guess who is going to help with that, too?

8. Of course, we talked about the possibility of using the renter to pay off the $20,000.

9. Also you could arrange with your husband for interest only, payable at the end of five years or something and negotiable, renegotiable at that time.

10. Maybe he'd also work out something where he'll only have to pay half the support and he'll waive, he'll give you the house. I mean, that's another thing to look at. Say "Look, I'll agree to take only $200 a month support in exchange and even make it nonmodifiable or something."

26. Throughout the case Wendy has been inconsistent, inattentive, and too late in her efforts at a joint construction of the social and legal world. In the defining enactment of power, Wendy gave Kathy more responsibility than Kathy could carry, and she did this despite her misgivings about Kathy's ability to imagine the future realistically and confront its difficulties.

27. At this point in the case the client asked that we stop observing conferences and not interview her further. She did not give a reason for withdrawing from the study. Her withdrawal paralleled the way clients react to the accumulation of unstated dissatisfaction with lawyers. The exit without explanation marked the limits of her tolerance for the social science strategy in which everything becomes a subject of inquiry. It was both a gesture of resistance and an assertion that no more questions would be answered, not even that of why she

was withdrawing. In a domain where clients become subjects, it was a striking enactment of her power in relation to us.

CHAPTER 4

1. Survey research suggests that exposure to a wide variety of legal actors and institutions, including lawyers, plays a powerful role in shaping perceptions of, and attitudes toward, law. Citizens tend to revise views held prior to such contact and to generalize from contacts with particular parts of the legal system in making judgments about the whole (see Merry, 1985: 68–69; Sarat, 1977: 441).

2. The American Bar Association's Canons of Professional Ethics, Model Code of Professional Responsibility, and Model Rules of Professional Conduct each contain language suggesting that lawyers should help organize and maintain public support for and confidence in the legal system. Canon 1 of the 1908 Canons of Professional Ethics stated that "[i]t is the duty of the lawyer to maintain towards the Courts a respectful attitude, not for the sake of the temporary incumbent of the judicial office, but for the maintenance of its supreme importance." The 1981 Model Code of Professional Responsibility notes that "while a lawyer as a citizen has a right to criticize [adjudicatory officials] publicly, he should be certain of the merit of his complaint, use appropriate language, and avoid petty criticisms, for unrestrained and intemperate statements tend to lessen public confidence in our legal system" (footnotes omitted). The 1983 Model Rules of Professional Conduct is less direct in asserting the professional obligation of lawyers to speak and act so as to maintain public confidence in the legal system, but the Preamble reminds lawyers that they "should demonstrate respect for the legal system and for those who serve it, including judges, other lawyers and public officials." The Model Rules contains provisions restricting attorney speech that "will have a substantial likelihood of materially prejudicing an adjudicative proceeding, "Rule 3.6 (1983), and that the lawyer "knows to be false" in regard to a judge or other "public legal officer." Rule 8.2 (see Morgan and Rotunda, 1985).

3. See Annotation, Attorney's Criticism of Judicial Acts as Grounds of Disciplinary Action, 12 A.L.R. 3d 1408 (1967). In the past, the clearest restriction on attorney remarks involved public statements made in the course of ongoing litigation; such statements could result in contempt of court. See cases cited in Annotation, at 1418–27. However, the bar disciplinary apparatus has also been mobilized to sanction lawyers for unfavorable characterizations made in the press (see State v. Nelson, 210 Kan. 637, 504 P.2d 211 (1972); Justices of the Appellate Div. v. Erdmann, 39 A.D. 2d 233, 333 N.Y.S. 2d 863 (1972), ret'd, 301 N.E.2d 426, 33 N.Y. 2d 559, 347 N.Y.S.2d 441 (1973)); in the course of campaigns for judicial or other public offices (see, e.g., Nebraska State Bar Ass'n v. Michaelis, 210 Neb. 545, 316 N.W.2d 46 (1982)); in pleadings and briefs (in papers filed in a federal district court, the defendant's attorney stated: "the state trial judge avoided the performance of his sworn duty. To repeat a timeworn phrase—you cannot get justice in a state court where the judge is a product of the prosecutorial system which aided dramatically in elevating him to the bench. A product of that system who works close *(sic)* with the Sheriffs and who must depend on political support and re-election to the bench is not going to do justice." His reprimand was upheld, by a county court, in *In re* Shimek, 284 So. 2d 686 (Fla. 1973)); and even

in private correspondence between lawyers and judges (see *In re* Chapak, 66 F. Supp. 265 (E.D.N.Y. 1946)). In 1985, the U.S. Supreme Court overturned a disciplinary sanction that had been imposed on the basis of remarks and criticisms contained in a letter written by an attorney to the secretary of a district court judge (see *In re* Snyder, 472 U.S. 634 (1985)).

Courts asked to enforce or review such disciplinary efforts have recognized, in dicta, the potential conflict between First Amendment guarantees and bar disciplinary codes (*In re* Sawyer, 360 U.S. 622 (1959)). Partly as a result of this conflict, courts have reached widely divergent results in trying to decide whether to impose sanctions where attorneys have made public criticisms of judges. For cases where sanctions were imposed or upheld, see Eisenberg v. Boardman, 302 F. Supp. 1360 (W.D. Wis. 1969) (attorney circulated statement designed to humiliate judge); *In re* Lacy, 283 N.W.2d 250, 251 (S.D. 1979) (attorney quoted in press as saying "state courts were incompetent and sometimes downright crooked"); *In re* Raggio, 87 Nev. 369, 487 P.2d 499 (1970) (attorney wrote magazine article criticizing judges in intemperate terms); see also *In re* Friedland, 268 Ind. 536, 376 N.E.2d 1126 (1978) (attorney suspended for referring to paternity hearing as "ordeal," "travesty," and "the biggest farce I've ever seen"); *In re* Paulsrude, 311 Minn. 303, 248 N.W.2d 747 (1979) (attorney disbarred for in-court remarks, which included calling judge a "horse's ass" after an adverse ruling and labeling the proceedings a "kangaroo court"). For cases not disciplining attorneys for criticizing judges see, for example, State v. Nelson, 210 Kan. 637, 504 P.2d 211 (1972) (no discipline imposed where attorney made only general accusations and was speaking as losing party in litigation); Justices of Appellate Div. v. Erdmann, 33 N.Y.2d 559, 301 N.E.2d 426, 347 N.Y.S.2d 441 (1973) (attorney not subject to discipline even though he called appellate judges "whores who become madams," and claimed that the only way to become a judge was "to be in politics or to buy it"); State Bar v. Semann, 508 S.W.2d 429 (Tex. Civ. App. 1974) (no discipline imposed against attorney who wrote letters to newspapers critical of judge's qualifications to hold office).

4. Gordon (1984a: 110) argues that "when a lawyer helps a client arrange a transaction so as to take maximum advantage of the current legal framework, he or she becomes one of the army of agents who confirm that framework by reinforcement."

5. From this perspective, law is a rule system: rules determine how law operates, how legal procedures work, and how legal decisions are made. Rules also insure that the legal process will be orderly, regular, and predictable, and that legal decisions will be made impartially, fairly, and in a nonarbitrary fashion. In short, rules determine the ability of law to regulate the social order. Reflecting these assumptions, formalist discourse portrays individual legal actors as highly constrained by a regimen of clearly articulated rules; rules matter, people do not. Discretion is, in this discourse, minimal and inconsequential. As Dicey argued (1915: 202), rules insure "the absolute supremacy or predominance of regular law as opposed to the influence of arbitrary power, and exclude the existence of arbitrariness, or prerogative, or even of wide discretionary authority." The idea that rules can and should constrain the choices made by legal decision makers is seen in many different theories of judicial decision making (see, e.g., Dworkin, 1977; Hart, 1961).

6. Yet critical scholarship has, for the most part, failed to examine carefully

the actual behavior of lawyers. For an exception, see Gordon (1984b). Like most legal academics, critics concentrate on interpreting legal doctrine to expose "legal formalism" as an empty legitimating myth and to indict judges as purveyors of that myth (see Dalton, 1985; see also Kelman, 1981; Kennedy, 1976). They assume that lawyers play a similar role. While they seek to uncover complexity and contradiction in doctrine, critics act as if the legitimating messages communicated at different locations and by different actors within the legal system were consistent.

7. Peter graduated from one of the country's top-ranked law schools. He was forty years old at the time of the conference and had practiced for fourteen years. His father was a prominent physician in a neighboring city. Peter had spent four years as a public defender after law school and had been in private practice for ten years. He considers himself a trial lawyer and states that he was drawn to divorce work because of the opportunity it provides for trial work.

8. The view that courts honor and protect long-term continuing relations between legal actors and that a key service provided by lawyers is entry to that network has been best developed with respect to criminal courts (see Eisenstein and Jacob, 1977; Feeley, 1979; Heumann, 1977).

9. Merry (1990: 179) also notes that for most citizens who have not had experience with lawyers or courts, "[t]he law serves as a source of secular moral authority, defining everyday social relationships and promising protection . . . . [They] see law as a source of authority in a society organized by rules, not by violence . . . . Their consciousness of legal entitlement conforms to fundamental categories of law itself . . . ." Like us, Merry (1990: 142) finds that when these people deal with the legal system, "With experience, . . . [it] gradually ceases to be a place for awe and fear . . . . It seems like a flawed instrument which must be played with skill and finesse." Citizens discover "that their legal consciousness differs in subtle ways from that of the clerks, prosecutors, and mediators they meet there" (Merry, 1990: 179).

10. As we saw in Chapter 2, tendencies toward self-exculpation and blaming are quite common in divorce, although the use of the language of justice toward such ends is not.

11. There is not much doubt from the transcript that Jane has come to accept the legal ideology presented by her lawyer. During the course of the conference, she describes a legal system that requires trust from people who have been badly betrayed, threatens judicial abuse, leaves human rights unprotected, fails to provide true justice, is staffed in part by amateurs issuing sloppy orders, and is contaminated by hard lawyers manipulating weak clients. On the other hand, it is possible that clients do not project from their experience to the legal order generally, as in the case of Indian litigants who considered themselves victimized by the legal levels they have experienced yet continued to have faith in the next higher tier in the system (see Kidder, 1973).

12. Such explanations are almost always provided in the first conference and are quite formulaic. In Massachusetts, the perfunctory run-through of the statutory parameters of the legal process of divorce is usually the preface to a discussion of whether the divorce will be filed, or counterfiled, on fault or no-fault grounds.

13. While this is generally true even when clients ask what the law is in relation to some particular topic, there are rare exceptions. In one Massachusetts

case, for example, the client asked whether it mattered that the marital home was in her husband's name. Her lawyer answered by saying:

> There's a real neat case . . . I don't know if it's real neat . . . some divorce lawyers are really horrified by Rice v. Rice which says . . . equitable . . . first one that made it clear that it didn't matter whose name . . . .

A similarly unusual reference occurred in a California case where a client asked whether she would be able to stay in the marital home after the divorce. To this her lawyer noted:

> There is a famous case called the Duke case. You don't need to know all the details now, but the Duke case—that's why we have a phrase in law called "they duked it out"—the Duke case basically said that Mrs. Duke, who was in very bad economic shape, . . . It dealt with her ability to stay in the house. And so, we now know that a judge has the discretion literally to say to your husband, "I understand that you own half the house, but I'm not going to order this lady out . . . ."

In two specific contexts, the presence of rules tends to be made explicit on a more regular basis. The first is the rules concerning community property in California. In these discussions community property is not defined in any precise terms but seems to have become a folk term. It is used in the same way that "visitation" or "custody" is used. The second area in which explicit reference to rules is common is in conversations about the tax consequences of divorce, property division, and alimony or child support. Client questions about what such events will mean to the Internal Revenue Service are often met with an explicit reference to some rule or provision of the tax code.

14. Our research included frequent observations of lawyer-to-lawyer talk in the hallways and conference rooms of courts as well as observations of such talk in more informal settings. For similar conclusions about lawyer-to-lawyer talk, see Feeley (1979: chap. 6) and Mather (1979: chap. 6).

As insiders, lawyers are interested in the way rules are manipulated by the people they deal with every day. Their code, their standard way of thinking about the legal process, would be unintelligible without rules; it is, however, a code in which rules operate in the background, so that in practice, calculations and decisions are made without explicit rule references. When they talk with their clients, lawyers begin, in a way, in the middle.

15. Lawyers do not explain the special concern for guiding lay juries that accounts for particular rules of evidence. As a result, they do not suggest that judicial "flexibility" is appropriate or understandable.

16. The thoughtful client may realize that lawyers, in what they choose to say about rules and judges, also exercise immense discretionary power.

17. There is, of course, another message that might be discerned if one were to focus on the frequency with which lawyers implicitly make reference to rules. In those instances, lawyers seldom speak about the efficacy of law or rules. Nevertheless, the way they talk suggests that this silence is a function not of cynicism about rules but of the pervasive way that rules are interwoven into lawyers' thinking about divorce. However, given the ambiguity that arises from the gap between the way lawyers take rules for granted in their thinking and their

explicit critique of particular rules in talking to clients, clients are likely to come away with a view about the relevance of rules in the divorce process that is very different from their lawyer's actual perspective.

18. It is not surprising that divorce lawyers de-emphasize rules. The rules in divorce typically invite a high level of discretion, and issues often become matters of individual equity rather than formalized rules (see Davis, 1969: 43).

19. These are the very characterizations of judges that, were they to be made public, might provoke disciplinary action. See Kentucky Bar Ass'n v. Heleringer, 602 S.W.2d 165 (Ky. 1980), cert. denied, 449 U.S. 1101 (1981) (judge's decisions called "highly unethical and grossly unfair"); *In re* Estes, 355 Mich. 411, 94 N.W.2d 916, cert. denied, 361 U.S. 829 (1959) (trial court said to have "violated every rule in the books"); Nebraska State Bar v. Rhodes, 177 Neb. 650, 131 N.W.2d 118 (1964) (court described as a "kangaroo court"); *In re* Hinds, 90 N.J. 604, 449 A.2d 483 (1982) (lawyer characterized judge as racially biased); State Bar v. Seman, 508 S.W.2d 429 (Tex. Ct. App. 1974) (judge called a "midget among giants").

20. This message provides a rhetorical justification for lawyer paternalism (see Wasserstrom, 1975). It also provides justification for lawyers who withhold access to legal knowledge and, in so doing, it reinforces the tendency of professionals to treat their expertise as a private possession (see Katz, 1984).

21. A similar phenomenon is described in a study of the way members of Congress describe that body to their constituents (Fenno, 1978: 166–67).

22. This is not a problem limited to divorce (see Mather and Yngvesson, 1980–81).

23. This emphasis on connection and reputation as the key service provided by lawyers is not unusual where a lawyer's practice tends to be confined to a single geographic area (see Carlin, 1962; Landon, 1985; Nelson, 1986).

24. A public suggestion of judicial favoritism or an alleged pattern of undue influence has frequently subjected lawyers to disciplinary proceedings. Compare the quoted material with the statement by defendant attorney Nelson that, "The courts are . . . much more concerned with who appears before them than with what the facts are and what the law is." State v. Nelson, 210 Kan. 637, 504 P.2d 211 (1972); see also Ramirez v. State Bar of California, 28 Cal. 3d 402, 619 P.2d 399, 169 Cal. Rptr. 206 (1980).

25. Given the absence of research similar to our own, it is difficult to say whether the discourse of the lawyers we observed is characteristic of other settings or areas of legal practice. However, some similar themes have been reported elsewhere. We know, for example, that an emphasis on personal contacts, local knowledge, and reputation is often part of the transaction between lawyers and clients in criminal cases (see Blumberg, 1967; Mather, 1979). In that context, lawyers stress their connections to, and reputation with, local prosecutors as they try to "sell" plea bargains to their clients. In contexts other than divorce or criminal prosecution, where law is more rule-intensive, it may be that lawyers talk to their clients about the discretion that an oversupply of rules makes available to legal officials. The "availability of law" has been documented by Silbey and Bitner (1982), but their description does not extend to the way that the consequences of that phenomenon are explained to laypeople. Moreover, in any context where clients are sophisticated users of legal services, have frequent dealings with legal officials, or operate in bureaucratic

environments, such cynical interpretations may have less impact than they have on divorce clients.

If mass legal consciousness has, in fact, taken a turn toward cynical instrumentalism, the pattern of practice that we observed in the divorce context may be a contributing factor. On the other hand, if the American public is mystified by the pretenses of legal formalism and is, as a result, allegiant, it remains so in spite of the law talk of the divorce lawyer's office.

26. Critical scholars would not, however, be content with the way in which the unmasking of law is used to maintain client dependency and reinforce professional power (see Simon, 1984).

CHAPTER 5

1. As McEwen et al. (1994: 157) argue, "[T]he result of this dilemma is a pattern of negotiations between lawyers that is adversarial and stylized."

2. As we saw in our discussion of the case of the unsupported wife in Chapter 3, there are obvious and important exceptions to this generalization.

3. For a similar observation in another context, see Alexander (1992).

4. The lawyer's expressed preference for trial work means that this tilt toward negotiations may be at the cost of some professional fulfillment.

5. References to therapists were as rare in our Massachusetts cases as they were common in the California sample.

6. The settlement preference of no-fault divorce corresponds to the movement in family therapy toward the "constructive divorce." It could well be that various professionals dealing with divorce have simultaneously registered and reinforced the emergence of new cultural mores concerning marriage and its dissolution.

7. Erlanger et al. (1987: 593) report similar findings in their study of divorce cases in Wisconsin. As they put it, "The lawyers in particular describe a widespread professional belief that divorce litigation is traumatic and that good lawyers keep their clients out of court . . . . Most of the lawyers we interviewed say they feel responsible for encouraging informal settlement." See also Ingleby (1988).

8. If the meaning that lawyers construct for clients about negotiations is that the good settlement is advantageous rather than fair, how can the effort be successful on both sides of contested negotiations? How can lawyers on both sides convince their clients that they have achieved a better than equitable outcome through negotiations?

Having observed only one side of these cases, we do not have direct evidence. But the answer may lie in the lawyers' propensity for reference to an external standard. As we argue in the next section, lawyers trying to persuade their clients to settle frequently tell them what a court would do if forced to decide an issue. Since the client has no independent evidence of judicial propensities, by varying what they say about those propensities, lawyers on both sides in the same case can convince their clients that they are getting more than is fair in settlement negotiations.

9. Judges are said to be both irrelevant and powerful. They will be kept from direct interference with negotiated settlements, but the terms of those

agreements will be influenced by decisions judges would make. These imagined decisions reflect both settled law and individual judicial propensities.

10. Although most lawyers we studied tried to avoid discussion of their clients' emotional problems, this conference is not characteristic of the sample in two respects. First, there is more explicit talk about emotions than one would typically find. For this client, the discussion of her emotions seems to satisfy a need in and of itself. Second, some lawyers clearly encourage clients to link their feelings to the divorce process, primarily when the lawyer feels that the client may otherwise be willing to surrender too much too quickly or when the lawyer seeks to use the client's "agitated state" as a bargaining ploy.

11. This attitude toward the other lawyer is dangerous if a settlement is to be reached. A client's concern about, even anger toward, the spouse's lawyer is a frequent theme in the conferences we have observed. Lawyer responses are, in most cases, ambivalent. Blaming the intransigence or incompetence of the other lawyer is frequently used to explain problems or disappointments in the progress of the case. However, this tactic often is balanced by the proposition that it is nevertheless possible for the opposing lawyers to work together to iron out the disputes in the case. Rarely does a lawyer refuse to concede that the other lawyer is, on a global level, somehow "reasonable."

12. He is, in addition, defending himself against a kind of emotional transference. Much of the emotional talk in this conference involves the lawyer himself, directly or indirectly. In the discussion of trust the client makes the lawyer into a kind of husband substitute ("a major trust relationship has ended. And then . . . I'm supposed to entrust somebody else . . . "). The client described him as her "knight in shining armor," an image of protection and romance; she acknowledges having sexual fantasies about him ("So the way I phrased it to Irene was, instead of sitting around mind-fucking my situation with Norb all the time, I began to have wonderful sexual fantasies about my attorney"); and she speaks of her expectation that he will protect her from "judicial abuse."

13. We are unable to say whether transference by clients and protective measures by lawyers are common in other configurations of lawyer and client gender.

14. A similar need to "forget your emotional feelings" is stressed by a Massachusetts lawyer counseling his client about child support.

> Well, it's all a matter of mathematics. If you forget your emotional feelings you figure out how much the deduction will help you. If you need help here, I'll help you figure it out. It's just a matter of basic figures.

Clients who cannot or will not follow such advice are said by their lawyers to be vulnerable and likely either to ask for too much or to be too eager to reach a negotiated agreement. Thus, as one California lawyer said,

> *Lawyer:* I don't know what I'm going to do with you.
>
> *Client:* I know.
>
> *Lawyer:* What you do then is call me and say, he wants such and such and then I'll say, "What do you think about that? Well, what do you think? You are the one that has to live with it." But, the main thing is that I don't want you to get upset or unhappy or ecstatic or morose or any emotion at all and agree to something that later on you have to live with that's not in your best interest. And that's my main concern.

Client: No. I know. And that's my main concern too.

Lawyer: Because after awhile you get to thinking, well, it will end it if I say okay.

Client: I know. I thought that the other night. I thought, oh, I just want to get this over with.

15. For an interesting discussion of the way divorce lawyers regard mediation, see McEwen et al., 1994.

CHAPTER 6

1. The client's right to decide and direct is affirmed in the ethical strictures of the legal profession (see Rule 1.2 (a), Model Rules of Professional Conduct; Morgan and Rotunda, 1985: 76) and in the rhetoric through which lawyers legitimate their roles and activities (see Simon, 1978, 1984).

For a somewhat different view, see Kronman (1993) and Luban (1988). Kronman (1993: 132, 133) argues that "the lawyer's job is not merely to supply whatever means are needed to achieve the client's goals but also to deliberate with the client and on his behalf about these goals . . . . In many cases, it is only through a process of joint deliberation, in which the lawyer imaginatively assumes his client's position and with sympathetic detachment begins to examine the alternatives for himself, that the necessary understandings emerge."

2. In the context of divorce, these concerns are focused on the varying approaches, styles, and practices of lawyers and how they differentially affect men and women clients, active and passive clients, middle-class and working-class clients, under- and overeducated clients, and clients who had been through divorce before and those who had not. They sponsor intercase comparisons of results across issues such as child and spousal support, property divisions, and custody arrangements. For example, O'Gorman's (1963) classic study of divorce lawyers and clients is devoted to these inquiries. Indeed, O'Gorman produces an elegant causal model of divorce practice in which lawyers' social, educational, and professional characteristics first are associated with orientations toward people and finances and then with role definitions in divorce cases (counselor or advocate) that, in turn, are associated with different behaviors with respect to clients (1963: chap.5, 6).

3. This definition of the professional task was as consistent in Massachusetts, where the lawyer was generally the only professional consulted by the client during the divorce, as it was in California, where a significant portion of clients either had received or were receiving some form of psychological counseling from another professional.

4. This double gesture is discussed, in another context, by Fish (1991).

5. "[L]egal culture not only differs in different contexts, but law is 'invented,' negotiated, or 'made' in local settings" (Yngvesson, 1989: 1690).

6. For a discussion of the nature of those differences, see O'Gorman 1963: 61–64).

References

Abbott, Anthony (1989). *The System of the Professions*. Chicago: University of Chicago Press.

Abel, Richard (1973). "Law Books and Books about Law," *Stanford Law Review* 26:175–228.

———(1989). *American Lawyers*. New York: Oxford University Press.

Ackerman, Bruce (1984). *Reconstructing American Law*. Cambridge, MA: Harvard University Press.

Alexander, Janet (1992). "Do the Merits Matter? A Study of Settlements in Securities Class Actions," *Stanford Law Review* 43:497–598.

Alfieri, Anthony (1990). "The Politics of Clinical Knowledge," *New York Law School Law Review* 35:7–27.

———(1991a). "Reconciling Poverty Law Practice: Learning Lessons of Client Narrative," *Yale Law Journal* 100:2107–47.

———(1991b). "Speaking Out of Turn: The Story of Josephine V.," *Georgetown Journal of Legal Ethics* 4:619–53.

Bachrach, Peter and Morton Baratz (1970). *Power and Poverty: Theory and Practice*. New York: Oxford University Press.

Baldwin, John and Michael McConville (1977). *Negotiated Justice: Pressures to Plead Guilty*. London: Martin Robertson.

Bankowski, Zenon and Geoff Mungham (1976). *Images of Law*. Boston: Routledge & Kegan Paul.

Becker, Howard (1970). "The Nature of a Profession." In *Sociological Work*, ed. Howard Becker. Chicago: Aldine Publishing Company.

Bennett, W. Lance and Martha Feldman (1981). *Reconstructing Reality in the Courtroom*. New Brunswick, NJ: Rutgers University Press.

Berger, Peter and Thomas Luckmann (1966). *The Social Construction of Reality: A Treatise in the Sociology of Knowledge*. Garden City, NY: Doubleday.

Bernauer, James and David Rasmussen (1988). *The Final Foucault*. Cambridge, MA: MIT Press.

Binder, David, Paul Bergman, and Susan Price (1991). *Lawyers As Counselors: A Client-Centered Approach*. St Paul, MN: West Publishing.

Black, Donald (1989). *Sociological Justice*. New York: Oxford University Press.

Blumberg, Abraham (1967). "The Practice of Law as a Confidence Game," *Law and Society Review* 1:15–39.

Bourdieu, Pierre (1977). *Outline of a Theory of Practice*. Cambridge: Cambridge University Press.

————(1987). "The Force of Law," *Hastings Law Journal* 38:805–53.

Bottoms, A. E. and J. D. McClean (1976). *Defendants in the Criminal Process*. Boston: Routledge & Kegan Paul.

Brandeis, Louis (1933). "The Opportunity in Law." In *Business—A Profession* Boston: Hale, Cushman and Flint.

Buckle, Suzann R. Thomas and Leonard Buckle (1977). *Bargaining for Justice: Case Disposition and Reform in Criminal Courts*. New York: Praeger.

Burke, Kenneth (1950). *A Rhetoric of Motives*. Englewood Cliffs, NJ: Prentice Hall.

————(1954). *Permanence and Change*. 3d ed. Berkeley: University of California Press.

Cain, Maureen (1979). "The General Practice Lawyer and Client," *International Journal of the Sociology of Law* 7:331–54.

Carlin, Jerome (1962). *Lawyers on Their Own: A Study of Individual Practitioners in Chicago*. New Brunswick, NJ: Rutgers University Press.

————(1966). *Lawyers' Ethics: A Survey of the New York City Bar*. New York: Russell Sage Foundation.

Carlson, Robert (1976). "Measuring the Quality of Legal Services: An Idea Whose Time Has Not Come, "*Law and Society Review* 11:287–318.

Carr-Saunders, A. M. and P. A. Wilson (1933). *The Professions*. Oxford: Clarendon.

Casper, Jonathan (1972). *Lawyers before the Warren Court: Civil Liberties and Civil Rights, 1957–1966*. Urbana: University of Illinois Press.

Casper, Jonathan and David Brereton (1984). "Evaluating Criminal Justice Reforms," *Law and Society Review* 18:121–44.

Coates, Dan and Steven Penrod (1980–81). "Social Psychology and the Emergence of Disputes," *Law and Society Review* 15:664–80.

Comaroff, Jean (1985). *Body of Power, Spirit of Resistance: The Culture and History of a South African People*. Chicago: University of Chicago Press.

Cunningham, Clark (1989). "A Tale of Two Clients: Thinking About Law as Language," *Michigan Law Review* 97:2459–996.

————(1992). "The Lawyer as Translator: Representation as Text: Towards an Ethnography of Legal Discourse," *Cornell Law Review* 77:1298–1387.

Dalton, Claire (1985). "An Essay in the Deconstruction of Contract Doctrine," *Yale Law Journal* 94:997–1114.

Danet, Brenda, Kenneth Hoffman, and Nicole Kermish (1980). "Obstacles to the Study of Lawyer-Client Interaction: The Biography of a Failure," *Law and Society Review* 14:905–22.

Davis, Kenneth Culp (1969). *Discretionary Justice: A Preliminary Inquiry*. Baton Rouge, LA: LSU Press.

de Certeau, Michel (1984). *The Practice of Everyday Life*. Berkeley: University of California Press.

Derber, Charles, William Schwartz, and Yale Magrass (1990). *Power in the Highest Degree: Professionals and the Rise of a New Mandarin Order*. New York: Oxford University Press.

Dewey, John (1939). *A Theory of Valuation*. Chicago: University of Chicago Press.

Dicey, A.V. (1915). *Introduction to the Study of the Law of the Constitution*. London: Macmillan.

Doane, Jeri and Emory Cowen (1981). "Interpersonal Help-Giving of Family Practice Lawyers," *American Journal of Community Psychology* 9:547–58.

Dumm, Thomas (1990). "Fear of Law," *Studies in Law, Politics and Society* 10: 29–60.

Durkin, Tom, Robert Dingwall and William L. F. Felstiner (1991). *Plaited Cunning: Manipulating Time in Asbestos Litigation.* American Bar Foundation Working Paper No. 9004.

Dworkin, Ronald (1977). *Taking Rights Seriously.* Cambridge, MA: Harvard University Press.

Eckhoff, Torstein (1966). "The Mediator, the Judge and the Administrator in Conflict Resolution," *Acta Sociological* 10:148–72.

Eisenstein, James and Herbert Jacob (1977). *Felony Justice: An Organizational Analysis of Criminal Courts.* Boston: Little, Brown.

Engel, David (1984). "The Oven Bird's Song: Insiders, Outsiders and Personal Injuries in an American Community," *Law and Society Review* 18:551–82.

———(1993). "Law in the Domains of Everyday Life: The Construction of Community and Difference." In *Law in Everyday Life,* eds. Ausin Sarat and Thomas R. Kearns. Ann Arbor: University of Michigan Press.

Erlanger, Howard, Elizabeth Chambliss, and Marygold Melli (1987). "Participation and Flexibility in Informal Processes: Cautions From the Divorce Context," *Law and Society Review* 21:593–604.

Feeley, Malcolm (1976). "The Concept of Law in Social Science: A Critique and Notes on an Expanded View," *Law and Society Review* 10:497–523.

———(1979). *The Process Is the Punishment.* New York: Russell Sage Foundation.

Felstiner, William (1979). "Plea Contracts in West Germany," *Law and Society Review* 13:309–26.

Felstiner, William, Richard Abel, and Austin Sarat (1980–81). "The Emergence and Transformation of Disputes: Naming, Blaming and Claiming," *Law and Society Review* 15:631–54.

Fenno, Richard (1978). *Home Style: House Members in Their Districts.* Boston: Little, Brown.

Finchman, Frank (1985). "Attributions in Close Relationships." In *Attribution,* eds. John Harvey and Gifford Weary. Orlando, FL: Academic Press.

Fish, Stanley (1991). "The Law Wishes to Have a Formal Existence." In *The Fate of Law,* eds. Austin Sarat and Thomas R. Kearns. Ann Arbor: University of Michigan Press.

Flood, John (1987). "Anatomy of Lawyering: An Ethnography of a Corporate Law Firm." Ph.D. diss. Northwestern University.

Foucault, Michel (1979). *Discipline and Punish: The Birth of the Prison.* Translated by Alan Sheridan. New York: Vintage Books.

Frank, Jerome (1949). *Courts on Trial: Myth and Reality in American Justice.* Princeton, NJ: Princeton University Press.

Friedman, Lawrence (1975). *The Legal System: A Social Science Perspective.* New York: Russell Sage Foundation.

Fuller, Lon (1964). *The Morality of Law.* New Haven, CT: Yale University Press.

Gabel, Peter (1980). "Reification in Legal Reasoning," *Research in Law and Sociology* 3:25–50.

Gabel, Peter and Paul Harris (1982–83). "Building Power and Breaking Images: Critical Legal Theory and the Practice of Law," *NYU Review of Law and Social Change* 11:369–411.

Galanter, Marc (1974). "Why the 'Haves' Come Out Ahead: Speculations on the Limits of Legal Change," *Law and Society Review* 9:95–160.

———(1984). "Worlds of Deals: Using Negotiation to Teach About Legal Process," *Journal of Legal Education* 34:268–76.

————(1987). "Adjudication, Litigation and Related Phenomena." In *Law and the Social Sciences,* eds. Leon Lipson and Stanton Wheeler. New York: Russell Sage Foundation.

Garland, David (1990). *Punishment and Modern Society: A Study in Social Theory.* Chicago: University of Chicago Press.

Genn, Hazel (1987). *Hard Bargaining.* London: Oxford University Press.

Geertz, Clifford (1983). *Local Knowledge: Further Essays in Interpretive Anthropology.* New York: Basic Books.

Giddens, Anthony (1979). *Central Problems in Social Theory: Action, Structure and Contradiction in Social Analysis.* Berkeley: University of California Press.

Gilkerson, Christopher (1992). "Poverty Law Narratives: The Critical Practice and Theory of Receiving and Translating Client Stories," *Hastings Law Journal* 43:870–945.

Gilmore, Grant (1977). *The Ages of American Law.* New Haven, CT: Yale University Press.

Glendon, Mary Ann (1991). *Rights Talk: The Impoverishment of Political Discourse.* New York: The Free Press.

Goffman, Erving (1956). "The Nature of Deference and Demeanor," *American Anthropologist* 50:473–502.

————(1959). *The Presentation of Self in Everyday Life.* Garden City, NY: Doubleday.

Goode, William (1956). *After Divorce.* Glencoe, IL: The Free Press.

Gordon, Robert (1982). "New Developments in Legal Theory." In *The Politics of Law,* ed. David Kairys. New York: Pantheon.

————(1984a). "Critical Legal Histories," *Stanford Law Review* 36:57–126.

————(1984b). "Legal Thought and Legal Practice in the Age of American Enterprise 1870–1920." In *Professions and Professional Ideologies in America,* ed. G. Geison. Chapel Hill: University of North Carolina Press.

Gordon, Robert and William Simon (1992). "The Redemption of Professionalism?" In *Lawyers' Ideals/Lawyers' Practices: Transformations in the American Legal Profession,* eds. Robert Nelson, David Trubek, and Rayman Solomon. Ithaca, NY: Cornell University Press.

Greenhouse, Carol (1986). *Praying for Justice: Faith, Order, and Community in an American Town.* Ithaca, NY: Cornell University Press.

Greenhouse, Carol, Barbara Yngvesson, and David Engel (1994). *Law and Community in Three American Towns.* Ithaca, NY: Cornell University Press.

Griffiths, John (1986). "What Do Dutch Lawyers Actually Do in Divorce Cases?" *Law and Society Review* 20:135–75.

Grossman, Joel, Herbert Kritzer, Kristin Bumiller, and Stephen McDougal (1981). "Measuring the Pace of Civil Litigation in Federal and State Courts," *Judicature* 65:86–113.

Habermas, Jurgen (1970). *Toward a Rational Society.* Translated by J. Shapiro. Boston: Beacon Press.

Halem, Lynne (1980). *Divorce Reform: Changing Legal and Social Perspectives.* New York: The Free Press.

Handler, Joel (1978). *Social Movements and the Legal System: A Theory of Law Reform and Social Change.* New York: Academic Press.

Harrington, Christine and Barbara Yngvesson (1990). "Interpretive Sociolegal Research," *Law and Social Inquiry* 15:135–48.

Harris, Angela and Marjorie Shultz (1993). "A(nother) Critique of Pure Reason:

Toward Civic Virtue in Legal Education," *Stanford Law Review* 45:1773–1805.

Hart, H.L.A. (1961). *The Concept of Law.* Oxford: Clarendon Press.

Heider, Fritz (1958). *The Psychology of Interpersonal Relations.* New York: John Wiley & Sons.

Heinz, John (1983). "The Power of Lawyers," *Georgia Law Review* 17:891–911.

Heinz, John and Edward Laumann (1982). *Chicago Lawyers: The Social Structure of the Bar.* New York: Russell Sage Foundation.

Herrman, Margaret, Patrick McKenry, and Ruth Weber (1979). "Attorneys' Perceptions of Their Role in Divorce," *Journal of Divorce* 2:313–22.

Heumann, Milton (1977). *Plea Bargaining.* Chicago: University of Chicago Press.

Hirschman, Albert (1970). *Exit, Voice and Loyalty.* Cambridge, MA: Harvard University Press.

Hopper, Joseph (1993a). "Oppositional Identities and Rhetoric in Divorce," *Qualitative Sociology* 16:133–56.

———(1993b). "The Rhetoric of Motives in Divorce," *Journal of Marriage and the Family* 55:801–13.

Hosticka, Carl (1979). "We Don't Care What Happened, We Only Care About What Is Going to Happen," *Social Problems* 26:599–610.

Huebner, Daniel (1977). "Scapegoating the Attorney, a Displacement of Marital Anguish," *Journal of Contemporary Psychotherapy* 9:112–15.

Hunt, Alan (1985). "The Ideology of Law: Advances and Problems in Recent Applications of the Concept of Ideology in the Analysis of Law," *Law and Society Review* 19:11–38.

Hunting, Robert and Gloria Neuwirth (1962). *Who Sues in New York City? A Study of Automobile Accident Claims.* New York: Columbia University Press.

Illich, Ivan, Irving Zola, John McKnight, Jonathan Caplan, and Harley Shaiken (1978). *Disabling Professions.* London: Marion Boyers.

Ingleby, Richard (1988). "The Solicitor as Intermediary." In *Divorce Mediation and the Legal Process,* eds. Robert Dingwall and John Eckelaar. London: Oxford University Press.

Jacob, Herbert (1988). *Silent Revolution: The Transformation of Divorce Law in the United States.* Chicago: University of Chicago Press.

Johnson, Earl (1980–81). "Lawyers' Choice: A Theoretical Appraisal of Litigation Investment Decisions," *Law and Society Review* 15:567–610.

Johnson, Terrance (1972). *Professions and Power.* London: Macmillan.

Johnston, Janet and Linda Campbell (1988). *Impasses of Divorce: The Dynamics and Resolution of Family Conflict.* New York: Free Press.

Jones, Edward and Keith Davis (1965). "From Acts to Dispositions." In *Advances in Experimental Social Psychology,* vol. 2, eds. Leonard Berkowitz. New York: Academic Press.

Kagan, Robert and Robert Rosen (1985). "On the Social Significance of Large Law Firm Practice," *Stanford Law Review* 37:399–443.

Katz, Jack (1979). "Legality and Equality: Plea Bargaining in the Prosecution of White Collar and Common Crimes," *Law and Society Review* 13:431–60.

Katz, Jay (1984). *The Silent World of Doctor and Patient.* New York: Free Press.

Kelly, Harold (1967). "Attribution Theory in Social Psychology," In *Nebraska Symposium on Motivation,* vol. 15, David Levine. Lincoln: University of Nebraska Press.

Kelly, Harold and John Michela (1980). "Attribution Theory and Research." In *Annual Review of Psychology,* vol. 31, eds. M. R. Rosenzweig and L. W. Porter. Palo Alto: Annual Reviews.

Kelman, Mark (1981). "Interpretive Construction in the Substantive Criminal Law," *Stanford Law Review* 33:591–673.

———(1987). *Critical Legal Studies.* Cambridge, MA: Harvard University Press.

Kennedy, Duncan (1976). "Form and Substance in Private Law Adjudication," *Harvard Law Review* 89:1685–1778.

Kidder, Robert (1973). "Courts and Conflict in an Indian City: A Study in Legal Impact," *Journal of Commonwealth Political Studies* 11:121–37.

Klare, Karl (1978). "Judicial Deradicalization of the Wagner Act and the Origins of Modern Legal Consciousness, 1937–1941," *Minnesota Law Review* 62:265–339.

Kressel, Kenneth (1985). *The Process of Divorce.* New York: Basic Books.

Kressel, Kenneth, Martin Lopez-Morillas, Janet Weinglass, and Morton Deutsch (1978). "Professional Intervention in Divorce: The Views of Lawyers, Psychotherapists, and Clergy," *Journal of Divorce* 2:119–55.

Kressel, Kenneth, Allan Hochberg, and Theodore Meth (1983). "A Provisional Typology of Lawyer Attitudes Towards Divorce Practice," *Law and Human Behavior* 7:31–49.

Kritzer, Herbert (1990). *The Justice Broker: Lawyers and Ordinary Litigation.* New York: Oxford University Press.

———(1991). *Let's Make a Deal: Understanding the Negotiation Process in Ordinary Litigation.* Madison: University of Wisconsin Press.

Kronman, Anthony (1993). *The Lost Lawyer: Failing Ideals of the Legal Profession.* Cambridge, MA: Harvard University Press.

Landon, Donald (1985). "Clients, Colleagues and Community," *American Bar Foundation Research Journal* 1985:81–111.

Lasswell, Harold (1936). *Politics: Who Gets What, When, How.* New York: McGraw Hill.

Leff, Arthur (1970). "Ignorance, Injury and Spite," *Yale Law Journal* 80:1–46.

Lévi-Strauss, Claude (1967). *Structural Anthropology.* Translated by Claire Jacobson and Brook Schoepf. Garden City, NY: Anchor Books.

Levinger, George (1979). "A Social Psychological Perspective on Marital Dissolution." In *Divorce and Separation,* eds. George Levinger and O. C. Moles. New York: Basic Books.

Lopez, Gerald (1992). *Rebellious Lawyering: One Chicano's Vision of Progressive Law Practice.* Boulder, CO: Westview Press.

Luban, David (1981). "Paternalism and the Legal Professional," *Wisconsin Law Review* 1981:454–93.

———(1988). *Lawyers and Justice: An Ethical Study.* Princeton, NJ: Princeton University Press.

Lukes, Stephen (1974). *Power: A Radical View.* London: Macmillan.

Lyman, Stanford and Marvin Scott (1975). *The Drama of Social Reality.* New York: Oxford University Press.

Macaulay, Stewart (1963). "Non-Contractual Relations in Business," *American Sociological Review* 28:55–67.

———(1979). "Lawyers and Consumer Protection Laws," *Law and Society Review* 14:115–71.

MacDougall, Donald (1984). "Negotiated Settlement of Family Disputes." In *The*

Resolution of Family Conflict, eds. John Eekelaar and Sanford N. Katz. Toronto: Butterworths.

Mann, Kenneth (1985). *Defending White Collar Criminals.* New Haven, CT: Yale University Press.

Margulies, Peter (1990). "'Who Are You to Tell Me That?': Attorney-Client Deliberation Regarding Nonlegal Issues and the Interests of Nonclients," *North Carolina Law Review* 68:213–52.

Mather, Lynn (1979). *Plea Bargaining or Trial?* Lexington, KY: Lexington Books.

Mather, Lynn and Barbara Yngvesson (1980–81). "Language, Audience and the Transformation of Disputes," *Law and Society Review* 15:775–822.

McEwen, Craig, Lynn Mather, and Richard Maiman (1994). "Lawyers, Mediation, and the Management of Divorce Practice," *Law and Society Review* 28:149–86.

Melli, Marygold, Howard Erlanger, and Elizabeth Chambliss (1988). "The Process of Negotiation: An Exploratory Investigation in the Context of No-Fault Divorce," *Rutgers Law Review* 40:1133–72.

Merry, Sally (1985). "Concepts of Law and Justice Among Working Class Americans: Ideology as Culture," *Legal Studies Forum* 9:59–70.

——— (1990). *Getting Justice and Getting Even: Legal Consciousness Among Working-Class Americans.* Chicago: University of Chicago Press.

Merry, Sally and Susan Silbey (1984). "What Do Plaintiffs Want?" *Justice System Journal* 9:151–78.

Mills, C. Wright (1940). "Situated Action and Vocabularies of Motive," *American Sociological Review* 5:904–13.

Mishler, Elliot (1985). *The Discourse of Medicine.* Norwood, NJ: Ablex Publications.

Mnookin, Robert (1984). "Divorce Bargaining: The Limits of Private Ordering." In *The Resolution of Family Conflict,* eds. John Eekelaar and Sanford N. Katz. Toronto: Butterworths.

Mnookin, Robert and Lewis Kornhauser (1979). "Bargaining in the Shadow of the Law," *Yale Law Journal* 85:950–97.

Moore, Wilbert (1970). *The Professions: Roles and Rules.* New York: Russell Sage Foundation.

Moore, Wilbert and Melvin Tumin (1949). "Some Social Functions of Ignorance," *American Sociological Review* 14:787–95.

Morgan, Thomas and Ronald Rotunda (1985). *Selected Standards on Professional Responsibility.* Mineola, NY: Foundation Press.

Nader, Ralph (1976). "Consumerism and Legal Services: The Merging of Movements," *Law and Society Review* 11:247–256.

Nardulli, Peter (1978). *The Courtroom Elite.* Cambridge, MA: Ballinger.

Nelson, Robert (1986). "Reconsidering the Obvious: Lawyers and the Structure of Influence in Washington." Unpublished manuscript.

——— (1988). *Partners with Power: The Social Transformation of the Large Law Firm.* Berkeley: University of California Press.

Nisbett, Richard and Lee Ross (1980). *Human Inference: Strategies and Shortcomings of Social Judgment.* Englewood Cliffs, NJ: Prentice Hall.

Nussbaum, Martha (1993). "Use and Abuse of Philosophy in Legal Education," *Stanford Law Review* 45:1627–45.

O'Barr, William and John Conley (1992). *Fortune and Folly: The Wealth and Power of Institutional Investing.* Homewood, IL: Business One Irwin.

O'Gorman, Hubert (1963). *Lawyers in Matrimonial Cases.* Glencoe, IL: Free Press.

Olson, Susan (1984). *Clients and Lawyers: Securing the Rights of Disabled Persons.* Westport, CT: Greenwood Press.

Parsons, Talcott (1954). *Essays in Sociological Theory,* Glencoe, IL: Free Press.

Priest, George and Benjamin Klein (1984). "The Selection of Disputes for Litigation," *Journal of Legal Studies* 13:1–55.

Posner, Richard (1973). "An Economic Approach to Legal Procedure and Judicial Administration," *Journal of Legal Studies* 2:399–458.

Radcliffe-Brown, Alfred (1940). "Presidential Address: On Social Structure," *Journal of the Royal Anthropological Institute,* 70:1–12.

Reed, John (1969). "Lawyer and Client: A Managed Relationship?" *Academy of Management Journal* 12:67–80.

Riessman, Catherine (1990). *Divorce Talk: Women and Men Make Sense of Personal Relationships.* New Brunswick, NJ: Rutgers University Press.

Rosen, Lawrence (1984). *Bargaining for Reality: The Construction of Social Relations in a Muslim Community.* Chicago: University of Chicago Press.

Rosenthal, Douglas (1974). *Lawyer and Client: Who's in Charge?* New York: Russell Sage Foundation.

Ross, H. Laurence (1970). *Settled Out of Court.* Chicago: Aldine.

Ross, Lee (1977). "The Intuitive Psychologist and His Shortcomings." In *Advances in Experimental Social Psychology,* vol. 10, ed. Leonard Berkowitz. New York: Academic Press.

Rossit, Ino, ed. (1974). *The Unconscious in Culture: The Structuralism of Claude Lévi-Strauss in Perspective.* New York: Dutton.

Rowe, Thomas (1984). "Predicting the Effects of Attorney Fee Shifting," *Law and Contemporary Problems* 47:139–71.

Rueschemeyer, Dietrich (1973). *Lawyers and Their Society.* Cambridge, MA: Harvard University Press.

Sabalis, Robert and George Ayers (1977). "Emotional Aspects of Divorce and Their Effects on the Legal Process," *The Family Coordinator* 26:391–94.

Sarat, Austin (1977). "Studying American Legal Culture," *Law and Society Review* 11:427–88.

———(1985). "Legal Effectiveness and Social Studies of Law: On the Unfortunate Persistence of a Research Tradition," *Legal Studies Forum* 9:23–32.

Sarat, Austin and Thomas R. Kearns (1993). "Beyond the Great Divide: Forms of Legal Scholarship and Everyday Life". In *Law in Everyday Life,* eds. Austin Sarat and Thomas R. Kearns. Ann Arbor: University of Michigan Press.

Sarat, Austin and Susan Silbey (1988). "The Pull of the Policy Audience," *Law and Policy* 10:97–166.

Scheff, Thomas (1966). *Being Mentally Ill.* Chicago: Aldine Publishing.

———(1968). "Negotiating Reality: Notes on Power in the Assessment of Responsibility," *Social Problems* 16: (1968), 3–17.

Scheingold, Stuart (1974). *The Politics of Rights: Lawyers, Public Policy, and Political Change.* New Haven, CT: Yale University Press.

Scheppele, Kim (1989). "Foreword: Legal Storytelling," *Michigan Law Review* 87:2073–98.

Schutz, Alfred (1962). *Collected Papers, I. The Problem of Social Reality.* The Hague: Martinus Nijhoff.

Scott, James (1990). *Domination and the Arts of Resistance: Hidden Transcripts.* New Haven, CT: Yale University Press.

Scott, Marvin and Stanford Lyman (1968). "Accounts," *American Sociological Review* 33:46–62.

Shapiro, Martin (1981). "On the Regrettable Decline of Law French: Or, Shapiro Jette le Brickbat," *Yale Law Journal* 90:1198–1204.

Silbey, Susan (1990). "Law and the Order of Our Life Together: A Sociological Interpretation of the Relationship Between Law and Society." In *Law and the Order of Our Life Together,* ed. Richard Neuhaus. Grand Rapids, MI: William Eerdmans Publishing.

Silbey, Susan and Egon Bitner (1982). "The Availability of Law, " *Law and Policy Quarterly* 4:399–434.

Simon, William (1978). "The Ideology of Advocacy," *Wisconsin Law Review* 1978:30–144.

———(1980). "Homo Psychologicus: Notes on a New Legal Formalism," *Stanford Law Review* 32:487–560.

———(1984). "Visions of Practice in Legal Thought," *Stanford Law Review* 36:469–508.

———(1991). "Lawyer's Advice and Client Autonomy: Mrs. Jones's Case," *Maryland Law Review* 50:213–26.

Singer, William (1984). "The Player and the Cards: Nihilism and Legal Theory," *Yale Law Journal* 94:1–70.

Sorauf, Frank (1976), *The Wall of Separation: The Constitutional Policies of Church and State.* Princeton, NJ: Princeton University Press.

Spangler, Eve (1986). *Lawyers for Hire.* New Haven, CT: Yale University Press.

Spiegel, Mark (1979). "Lawyering and Client Decisionmaking: Informed Consent and the Legal Profession," *University of Pennsylvania Law Review* 128:41–140.

Sudnow, David (1965). "Normal Crimes: Sociological Features of the Penal Code in a Public Defender's Office," *Social Problems* 12:255–76.

Tomasic, Roman (1978). *Lawyers and the Community.* Sydney: Allen and Unwin.

Trubek, David (1984). "Where the Action Is: Critical Legal Studies and Empiricism," *Stanford Law Review* 36:575–622.

Trubek, David and John Esser (1989). "Critical Empiricism in American Legal Studies: Paradox, Program or Pandora's Box?" *Law and Social Inquiry* 14:3–52.

Turner, Eric (1980). "The Role of the Lawyer in Matrimonial Cases," *Villanova Law Review* 25:696–716.

Unger, Roberto (1975). *Knowledge and Politics.* New York: Free Press.

U.S. Bureau of the Census (1993). Statistical Abstract of the United States, 113th ed. Washington, DC.

Utz, Pamela (1978). *Settling the Facts: Discretion and Negotiation in Criminal Courts.* Lexington, KY: Lexington Books.

Vaughan, Diane (1986). *Uncoupling.* New York: Oxford University Press.

Wallerstein, Judith and Joan Kelly (1980). *Surviving the Breakup: How Children and Parents Cope with Divorce.* New York: Basic Books.

Wasserstrom, Richard (1975). "Lawyers As Professionals: Some Moral Issues," *Human Rights* 5:1–24.

Weber, Max (1947). *The Theory of Social and Economic Organization.* Translated by Talcott Parsons and A. M. Henderson. Glencoe, IL: Free Press.

Weitzman, Lenore (1984). "No Fault Divorce and the Transformation of Marriage." Paper presented at the annual meeting of the Law and Society Association, Boston, June.

———(1985). *The Divorce Revolution.* New York: Free Press.

White, James Boyd (1985). "Law as Rhetoric, Rhetoric as Law: The Arts of Cultural and Communal Life," *University of Chicago Law Review* 52:684–702.

White, Lucie (1990). "Subordination, Rhetorical Survival Skills, and Sunday Shoes: Notes on the Hearing of Mrs. G.," *Buffalo Law Review* 38:1–58.

———(1992). "Seeking . . . 'The Faces of Otherness . . .': A Response to Professors Sarat, Felstiner, and Cahn," *Cornell Law Review,* 77:1499–1511.

Wilkins, David (1990). "Legal Realism for Lawyers," *Harvard Law Review* 104:468–524.

Williams, Gerald (1983). *Legal Negotiation and Settlement.* St. Paul, MN: West Publishing.

Williams, Raymond (1977). *Marxism and Literature.* Oxford: Oxford University Press.

Wolff, Robert Paul (1965). *Critique of Pure Tolerance.* Boston: Beacon Press.

Yngvesson, Barbara (1985). "Re-Examining Continuing Relations and the Law," *Wisconsin Law Review* 1985:623–46.

———(1988). "Making Law at the Doorway: The Clerk, the Court, and the Construction of Community in a New England Town," *Law and Society Review* 22:409–48.

———(1989). "Inventing Law in Local Settings: Rethinking Popular Legal Culture," *Yale Law Journal* 98:1689–1709.

———(1993). *Virtuous Citizens, Disruptive Subjects: Order and Complaint in a New England Court.* New York: Routledge.

Index